LITERATURE IN PSYCHOANALYSIS

Related titles from Palgrave Macmillan

Ruth Parkin-Gounelas, *Literature and Psychoanalysis: Intertextual Readings*

Shelley Saguaro (ed.), *Psychoanalysis and Woman: A Reader*

Kylie Valentine, *Psychoanalysis, Psychiatry and Modernist Literature*

LITERATURE IN PSYCHOANALYSIS

A Reader

Edited by Steve Vine

First published 2005 by
PALGRAVE MACMILLAN
Houndmills, Basingstoke, Hampshire RG21 6XS and
175 Fifth Avenue, New York, N. Y. 10010
Companies and representatives throughout the world

PALGRAVE MACMILLAN is the global academic imprint of the Palgrave
Macmillan division of St. Martin's Press, LLC and of Palgrave Macmillan Ltd.
Macmillan® is a registered trademark in the United States, United Kingdom
and other countries. Palgrave is a registered trademark in the European
Union and other countries.

ISBN-13: 978- 0–333–79174–5 hardback
ISBN-10: 0–333–79174–6   hardback
ISBN-13: 978–0–333–79175–2 paperback
ISBN-10: 0–333–79175–4   paperback

This book is printed on paper suitable for recycling and
made from fully managed and sustained forest sources.

A catalogue record for this book is available
from the British Library.

A catalog record for this book is available
from the Library of Congress.

10   9   8   7   6   5   4   3   2   1
14   13   12   11   10   09   08   07   06   05

Printed in China

The Child is father of the Man

For Tom and Sam,
who showed me how to read Wordsworth differently

Contents

Acknowledgements   ix

Introduction: Literature in Psychoanalysis   1

PART I   Shakespeare, *Hamlet*
Introductory Note: *Hamlet* in Psychoanalysis   18

  1. Dismember Me: Shakespeare, Paranoia and the Logic
     of Mass Culture   25
     LINDA CHARNES

  2. *Hamlet*'s Flesh: Lacan and the Desire of the Mother   36
     JULIA REINHARD LUPTON and KENNETH REINHARD

  3. Family Romance or Family History? Psychoanalysis
     and Dramatic Invention in Nicolas Abraham's
     "The Phantom of Hamlet"   47
     NICHOLAS RAND

**PART II   E.T.A. Hoffmann, "The Sandman"; Sigmund Freud,
"The 'Uncanny'"**
Introductory Note: Uncanny Literature – Freud and
the 'Uncanny'   60

  4. The Double is / and the Devil: The Uncanniness of
     "The Sandman"   68
     SARAH KOFMAN

  5. Fiction and its Phantoms: A Reading of Freud's
     "Das Unheimliche" (The "uncanny")   84
     HÉLÈNE CIXOUS

6 "The Sandman": The Uncanny as Problem of
Reading   97
   LIS MØLLER

PART III Sigmund Freud, *The "Wolf Man"*
Introductory Note: Constructing and Deconstructing the
"Wolf Man"   112

7 Fictions of the Wolf Man: Freud and Narrative
Understanding   122
   PETER BROOKS

8 The Wolf Man's Magic Word   136
   NICOLAS ABRAHAM and MARIA TOROK

9 *Fors*: The Anglish Words of Nicolas Abraham and
Maria Torok   160
   JACQUES DERRIDA

PART IV Hélène Cixous, *Portrait of Dora*;
Sigmund Freud, *Dora*
Introductory Note: *Dora* in Freud and Feminism   180

10 The Untenable   187
    CATHERINE CLÉMENT and HÉLÈNE CIXOUS

11 The Lake of Seduction: Body, Acting, and Voice in
Hélène Cixous's *Portrait de Dora*   196
    ERELLA BROWN

12 "You Freud, Me Jane"   211
    ELISABETH BRONFEN

Bibliography   220

Index   230

Acknowledgements

The editor and publishers wish to thank the following for permission to use copyright material:

Nicholas Abraham and Maria Torok, for material from *The Wolf Man's Magic Word* by Nicholas Abraham and Maria Torok, trans. Nicholas Rand (1986) pp. lxx–lxxii, 3–26. Original French language copyright © 1976 by Editions Aubier Flammarion, Paris. English translation copyright © 1986 by the University of Minnesota, by permission of University Minnesota Press;

Elizabeth Bronfen, for material from *The Knotted Subject: Hysteria and its Discontents* (1998) pp. 332–77. Copyright © 1998 Princeton University Press, by permission of Princeton University Press;

Peter Brooks, for material from *Reading for the Plot: Design and Intention in Narrative* (1984) pp. 264–85. Copyright © 1984 Peter Brooks, by permission of Alfred A. Knopf, a division of Random House, Inc;

Erella Brown, for material from "The Lake of Seduction: Body, Acting, and Voice in Hélène Cixous's *Portrait de Dora*", *Modern Drama*, 39: 4 (1996) pp. 626–49, by permission of Modern Drama;

Linda Charnes, for material from "Dismember Me: Shakespeare, Paranoia, and the Logic of Mass Culture", *Shakespeare Quarterly*, 48: 1 (1997) pp. 1–16. Copyright © Folger Shakespeare Library, by permission of The Johns Hopkins University Press;

Hélène Cixous, for material from "Fiction and its Phantoms: A Reading of Freud's *Das Unheimliche*", *New Literary History*, 7: 3 (1976) pp. 526–48, by permission of the author;

Hélène Cixous and Catherine Clément, for material from *The Newly Born Woman*, trans. Betsy Wing (1986) pp. 147–160. Original French language copyright © 1975 by Union Generale d'Editions, Paris. English translation copyright © 1986 by the University of Minnesota, by permission of University of Minnesota Press and I.B. Tauris & Co;

Jacques Derrida, for material from "*Fors*: The Anglish Words of Nicholas Abraham and Maria Torok", *The Georgia Review*, 31 (1977), by permission of The Georgia Review;

Sarah Kofman, for material from *Freud and Fiction*, trans. S. Wykes (1991) pp. 121–162, by permission of Polity Press and Northeastern University Press;

Julia R. Lupton and Keith Reinhard, for material from *After Oedipus: Shakespeare in Psychoanalysis* (1993) pp. 66–76. Copyright © 1993 by Cornell University, by permission of Cornell University Press;

Lis Møller, for material from *The Freudian Reading: Analytical and Fictional Constructions* (1991) pp. 111–39, by permission of University of Pennsylvania Press;

Nicholas Rand, for material from "Family Romance or Family History? Psychoanalysis and Dramatic Invention in Nicholas Abraham's 'The Phantom of Hamlet'", *Diacritics*, 18: 4 (1988) pp. 20–30. Copyright © The Johns Hopkins University Press, by permission of The Johns Hopkins University Press.

Every effort has been made to trace the copyright holders but if any have been inadvertently overlooked the publishers will be pleased to make the necessary arrangement at the first opportunity.

Introduction

LITERATURE IN PSYCHOANALYSIS

"It was while listening to hysterics that [Freud] *read* that there was an unconscious ... something he could only construct, and in which he himself was implicated".

Jacques Lacan's comment on Freud's and Breuer's *Studies on Hysteria* of 1895 proposes that psychoanalysis begins as a scene of 'reading' in which interpreter and interpreted, analyst and analysand, are 'implicated' with one another. Freud, Lacan says, "noticed he could not avoid participating in what the hysteric was telling him, and that he was affected by it" (cited in Felman, *Literature and Psychoanalysis* 118). Freud "constructs" the hysteric's story by reading it, but also finds himself affected by the force of the very thing he is interpreting, the truant and ruseful effects of the unconscious in the analytic dialogue.

The same could be said of the relationship between literature and psychoanalysis.

On the occasion of his 70th birthday, Freud was greeted by a well-wisher as the "discoverer of the unconscious", but insisted "The poets and philosophers before me discovered the unconscious" (cited in Trilling, "Freud and Literature" 276). Literature was there before; indeed, as Maud Ellmann suggests, psychoanalysis could be said to be "in love with literature" ("Blanche" 99), for Freud's science is fascinated by literature's seductive games, artful ruses and knowing secrets, its tantalizing hints that there is 'more' to be understood, 'more' to be found in what it says than is made explicit. Literature is a tease, literature tantalizes; and psychoanalysis falls in love with what it seems both to offer and

1

withhold. It is as if literature already knew what psychoanalysis was after, as if they had been made for each other: involved, "implicated", sharing something to which psychoanalysis finally gives its own name.

"[C]reative writers are valuable allies and their evidence is to be prized highly, for they are apt to know a whole host of things between heaven and earth of which our philosophy has not yet let us dream", says Freud. "In their knowledge of the mind they are far in advance of us everyday people, for they draw upon sources which we have not yet opened up for science" (*PF* 14: 34). Fittingly, Freud draws this insight about literature *from* literature; namely, from Hamlet's remark to Horatio that "There are more things in heaven and earth ... /Than are dreamt of in your philosophy" (*Hamlet* I.v.166–7). Psychoanalysis, it seems, just can't get over literature; perpetually in pursuit of literature's wisdom, "science" at the same time finds literature "in advance" of its insights, forging ahead, slipping away, speeding on, leaving science to play catch-up, in pursuit of the "more" that literature seems to offer. Psychoanalysis may be in love with literature, as Ellmann suggests, but it seems that literature will never entirely give itself up, will never entirely surrender itself to the advances or blandishments of science. "Before the problem of the creative artist", Freud says ruefully of Dostoevsky, "analysis must, alas, lay down its arms" (*PF* 14: 441).

Commenting in 1982 on psychoanalysis's inability to master literature – and at the same time on its fascination with literature – Shoshana Felman draws on Lacan's notion of "implication" to rethink the literature-and-psychoanalysis conjunction. Displacing the traditional model of the "application" ("To Open the Question" 8) of psychoanalytic theory to literature, Felman conceives the relationship between literature and psychoanalysis as, in Peter Brooks's words, "an encounter that doesn't privilege either term, but rather sets them in a dialogue that both exemplifies and questions how we read" (*Psychoanalysis and Storytelling* 23). Psychoanalysis and literature are involved with one another rather than the one, psychoanalysis, lording it over the other as scientific master. As a marker of this, Felman notes influentially that "The key concepts of psychoanalysis are references to literature, using literary '*proper*' names – names of fictional characters (Oedipus complex, Narcissism) or of historical authors (masochism, sadism) ... Literature ... is the language which psychoanalysis uses in order to *speak of itself*". She adds: "Literature is therefore not simply *outside* psychoanalysis, since it motivates and *inhabits* the very names of its concepts" ("To Open the Question" 9). Literature is "in" psycho-analysis by *articulating* as well as exemplifying psychoanalysis's in-sights; and Felman calls for a mode of reading that attends to this implication of the two forms of discourse in a scene of mutual illu-mination and mutual questioning, a dialogue that forgoes the tradi-tional model in which psychoanalysis "explains" literature through its theoretical supremacy.

Literature in Psychoanalysis: the title of this collection hints that if literature and psychoanalysis should not be seen in a relationship of discursive mastery and servitude, literature is "in" psycho-analysis in a double sense. It is "in" psychoanalysis as a patient is in analysis, but also "in" analysis by inhabiting and illuminating the procedures of psychoanalytic discourse itself. That double sense of mutual involvement between the two enterprises informs this book throughout; for, by presenting psychoanalytic readings of literary texts and literary readings of psychoanalytic texts, the collection demonstrates in a series of practical case studies the mutually in-structive and mutually challenging relationship between the two modes of discourse.

"[P]sychoanalytic ('scientific') writings, most famously Freud's case studies of Dora or the Wolf Man, have become the object of 'literary' scrutiny, with focus on features such as narrative strategy, symbolic patterns or repressed subtexts" (*Literature and Psycho-analysis: Intertextual* x), writes Ruth Parkin-Gounelas. While Parts III and IV of this book demonstrate Parkin-Gounelas's point by focusing on these case studies, it is nevertheless the case that literary construction is not imported *in* to psychoanalysis by liter-ary critics; it is already there. Freud himself says of his speculative text *Leonardo Da Vinci and a Memory of His Childhood* (1910) that "even ... friends of psychoanalysis" might argue he has "merely written a psychoanalytic novel". Freud replies, however, by saying that he is "far from overestimating the certainty of [his] results" (*PF* 14: 227–8). In this sense, it is Freud's *own* open-ness to sceptical questioning about his "results" that, arguably, opens psychoanalysis up to literature, for Freud's "construction" of stories about the unconscious is, he acknowledges, a necessarily perilous, provisional and vulnerable one, an activity perpetu-ally open to re-construction: to a process, in his own image, of re-*novelization*.

The fact that the stories Freud tells about texts or about his patients are acts of construction or making – and we might recall here the root of the word *fiction* in the Latin *fingere*, meaning to "fashion" or "form" – does not mean that psychoanalysis is false, but that in dealing with the repressed or the unconscious psychoanalysis is forced to *construct* what is not obvious, to *present* what is not presented and to *articulate* what is unspoken. The very material with which psychoanalysis deals imposes on it a burden of construction and active interpretation: a burden, one might say, of *telling stories*. Freud acknowledges this in *Studies on Hysteria* in the case of "Elisabeth von R.", when he writes: "I have not always been a psychotherapist ... I was trained to employ local diagnoses and electro-prognosis, and it still strikes me myself as strange that the case histories I write should read like short stories and that, as one might say, they lack the serious stamp of science. I must console myself with the fact that the *nature of the subject* is evidently responsible for this, rather than any preference of my own" (*PF* 3: 231 – my emphasis). What Freud registers here is the fact that the stories his patients told him impelled *him* to tell stories, too, to produce narrative constructions of repressed, buried or forgotten psychic events. As Lacan puts it, the psychoanalyst's task is to read "what can be read; what can be read beyond what the subject has been incited to say" (cited in Felman, *Jacques Lacan* 21). Psychoanalysis is inescapably a discourse on the repressed, the silent, the unseen.

Freud's most spectacular act of theoretical *construction* of the psychically fugitive comes in the *Wolf Man* case (1914; see Part III) – in his fashioning of a buried "primal scene" (*FR* 419; *PF* 9: 285) for the Wolf Man's life which, Freud believes, is determining and yet inaccessible to the patient. But Freud was never certain about the historical reality of the primal scene that he invented for the Wolf Man (of parental coitus *a tergo*), and this indeterminacy proved remarkably productive in Nicolas Abraham's and Maria Torok's revisiting of the Wolf Man's story in *The Wolf Man's Magic Word* (1976) – excerpted in Essay 8 and commented on by Jacques Derrida in Essay 9. Abraham and Torok propose a different primal scene for the Wolf Man's life from Freud's scenario of parental coitus – this time a scene of paternal seduction or abuse – yet they *preserve* the indeterminacy of the event to the extent that, like Freud, they locate its status *between* fantasy and reality, fiction and truth. Nicholas Rand, the translator of Abraham's and Torok's book, says that this paternal seduction scene (of the sister by the father, allegedly observed by the Wolf Man) is one in relation to which "the Wolf Man cannot state whether the event or the action he witnessed was real or imagined". This means that the Wolf Man's history is one dedicated to "liv[ing] without having to say yes or no to reality or fiction while continuing to refer to both". Neither "reality" nor "fiction" is cancelled out in Abraham's and Torok's reading of the Wolf Man's repressed history; instead his story, says Rand, "suspends" the simple decidability of these alternatives but keeps the *question* of "truth and falsehood" in play as a dilemma that generates both the Wolf Man's symptoms and his meaning (*WMMW* lviii). This suspension of decidability between truth and fiction also characterized Freud's struggle to read hysteria in the 1890s: the dilemma of knowing, that is, whether the stories of trauma that emerged during his patients' analyses were the result of real memories or the products of unconscious fantasy. As Freud commented in a letter to Wilhelm Fliess in 1897, "there are no indications of reality in the unconscious, so that one cannot distinguish between the truth and fiction that is cathected with affect [i.e. charged with feeling]" (*FR* 112). In a comparable way, Freud's and Abraham's and Torok's "primal scenes" for the Wolf Man belong undecidably to reality and invention, to (scientific) psychoanalysis and (imaginative) story; they are provisional and indeterminable attempts at the narrativization of conflictual unconscious processes. They are attempts at producing what Lacan – speaking of the analytic stories composed by psychoanalysis, including the theoretical story of the "Oedipus complex" – calls a "truthful fictitious structure" (cited in Felman, *Jacques Lacan* 151).

Psychoanalysis is, in the end, arguably *about* storytelling – that is to say, about telling a workable or successful story of the self. In *Dora*, Freud says suggestively that his hysterical patients show an "inability to give an ordered history of their life in so far as it coincides with the history of their illness" (*PF* 8: 46); and Steven Marcus argues that for psychoanalysis illness amounts "at least in part to suffering from an incoherent story or an inadequate narrative account of oneself" ("Freud and Dora" 71). Freud says of his hysterics: "the patients are incapable of giving [smooth and precise histories] about themselves. They can ... give the physician plenty of coherent information about this or that period of their lives; but it is sure to be followed by another ... leaving gaps unfilled, and riddles unanswered; and then again will come yet another period which will remain totally obscure and unilluminated by even a single piece of serviceable information" (*PF* 8: 46). The patient suffers from narrational breakdown, and the reason for this is that, unwittingly, the hysteric is being interrupted by *another* mental scene – by psychical contents that have gone into repression, into the unconscious, but which now insistently and disruptively re-assert themselves in symptomatic collapses of mental functioning. The narrative continuities and coherences of the self's narration of itself are, therefore, discomposed by an *unconscious* story that frac-tures the "smooth and precise" utterance of the patient. The patient's speech wanders, loses itself, forgets itself, falls silent, doesn't make sense – becomes hysterical.

This view of psychical illness as being symptomatically embroiled with faulty narrative emerges for the first time in *Studies on Hysteria* – insofar as, in this work, Freud and Breuer note that their patients, alongside bodily symptoms,[1] are afflicted by *gaps* in their memory and the ability to be uninterruptedly conscious of their lives and actions. Most famously, one of these patients (called "Anna O." in *Studies on Hysteria*) suffered from what Breuer called "*absences*": moments in which she appeared quite literally to be taken over by another "self", another personality, the story of somebody else, and in which she was harried by hallucinations, behaving violently and "naughtily" (*PF* 3: 76, 77) as a result. Anna O.'s moments of "absence" are read by Freud and Breuer as irruptions of unconscious trauma in the patient's waking life – as blank signifiers of a forgotten story that inhabits her like a "foreign body" (*PF* 3: 57), but has been dissevered from utterance. Strangely, Anna O. – like so many of Freud's hysterical patients – suffers from traumatically repressed memories that live and repeat themselves within her but have been removed from language, narra-tive and speech, surviving only in their inscription on the body in the form of symptoms. Remembrance is forgotten, but the repressed reinsists itself in illness and in interruptions of consciousness and speech. "*Hysterics suffer mainly from reminiscences*" (*PF* 3: 58), write Freud and Breuer in *Studies on Hysteria*; and the therapeutic labour of psychoanalysis from this text onwards is to enable the patient to reconvert silent (unconscious) suffering into vocal (con-scious) speech, transmuting illness into language, lifting symptom into utterance. In Maud Ellmann's words, "the purpose of analysis is to restore to consciousness the reminiscences displaced onto the flesh" (*Psychoanalytic Literary Criticism* 76), that is, to bring about the patient's movement from suffering back into discourse. Anna O. herself gave a name to this new psychoanalytic process: she called it the "talking cure" (*PF* 3: 83), and her celebrated description grasps eloquently the sense in which psychoanalysis is about the curative power of articulation itself, the therapeutic effects of constructing or telling a "story" about the self.

But the "talking cure" in psychoanalysis is not, of course, something that the patient brings about on his or her own. Rather, it is performed in the dynamics of the analytic session itself; and it is the outcome of the transformative exchange of dialogue between the analyst and analysand, doctor and patient. As Lis Møller puts it, "[t]he successful analytic process is the interchange or interaction of two voices or two discourses. It is the production, in the fictive space of analysis, of a story that belongs, strictly speaking, neither to the analyst nor to the analysand, but to both" (*The Freudian Reading* 21). The patient, that is to say, reconfigures his or her own story *in the transferential exchange of speech* between himself or herself and the analyst; the analytic dialogue, then, is an arena in which the patient is enabled to retranscribe his or her traumatic past in the name of a curative and restored future. Instead of obsessively or compulsively *repeating* the repressed past in the shape of symptom, illness and pathology, Freud's patients, says Maud Ellmann, "*re-enact* the conflicts of their early history, 'transferring' their forgotten feelings towards their parents or their siblings onto the neutral figure of the analyst. Thus the analyst is forced to play a part, and play it badly, so that the patient may be freed from the compulsion to repeat the script of childhood" (*Psychoanalytic Literary Criticism* 8: my emphasis). What happens in the analytic scene, then, is that in the process Freud calls "transference" the patient *replays* or re-enacts his or her scenes of suffering and does so by transferring past conflicts and catastrophes on to the figure of the analyst: and this performative transference enables a curative *analysis* (rather than repetition) of the past. Thus the analytic scene functions as a *drama of symbolic re-enactment* in which "literal" suffering is replaced by "figural" or rhetorical re-creation: in the place of suffering the patient accedes to utterance, in the place of sickness the patient embraces speech, in the place of illness the patient learns articulation. Psychoanalysis is a therapeutic venture of giving speech and symbols to suffering: a "talking cure". As Lacan insists, "psychoanalysis has only a single medium: the patient's speech" (*Écrits* 40).

As a space of representational restaging, psychoanalysis is there-fore *already* a symbolic or rhetorical activity even before it turns its gaze upon literature: the tropological and figural dimension of liter-ature is arguably "in" psychoanalysis from the start. If the analytic scene comprises a symbolic and transformative revisiting of past conflicts, the arena of analysis resembles a *dramatic stage* upon which psychical raw material is reworked and reconfigured in the name of a future that is *not* the simple repetition of the past. Freud, of course, makes the structural and symbolic parallels between psy-choanalysis and dramatic action explicit in *The Interpretation of Dreams* (1900), when he says of the revelation of Oedipus's parri-cide and incest in Sophocles's *Oedipus Rex*: "The action of the play consists in nothing other than the process of revealing, with cunning delays and ever-mounting excitement – a process that can be likened to the work of a psycho-analysis – that Oedipus himself is the murderer of Laius ... the son of the murdered man and of Jocasta" (*PF* 4: 363).[2] Here drama and analysis are presented as works of revelation or disclosure (the unearthing of a repressed or forgotten story), and this is indeed the point to which Oedipus is brought at the end of Sophocles's drama: to the full and unbearable discovery of his crimes. Lacan, however, argues that "Oedipus's psychoanalysis ends only at Colonus" (cited in Ellmann, *Psychoanalytic Literary Criticism* 84) – that is, in Sophocles's second "Oedipus" drama, *Oedipus at Colonus*. In the first drama, Oedipus is faced with the recognition of his past, but in the second drama, says Lacan, he discovers the symbolic meaning of his future (the meaning of his death), and comes to an understanding of his destiny through the medium of speech. Oedipus's "talking cure" may end in death, but his assumption of his destiny leads him from suffering to a new story or narrative – to a symbolic future "beyond" the traumatically repressed past.[3]

Conducted through the medium of speech, psychoanalytic treat-ment is, Peter Brooks says, a "re-formation of the patient's life story" that occurs in the "transferential space *between* analysand and analyst" (*Psychoanalysis and Storytelling* 52: my emphasis). Transference becomes, that is, a theatrical or performative space within which the patient's past history may be both revisited and rewritten – in the name of the future and in the name of cure. This revisiting and rewriting happens *dialogically*: belonging neither to doctor nor patient singly, it is a multiform crucible of psychic and symbolic remaking in which, replaying the script of the past between them, analyst and analysand reinvent this script for the future. Symptomatic repetition becomes symbolic restitution. Speaking in *Dora* of the ways in which the patient's transferences occur in analysis, Freud describes transferences as "new editions or facsimiles" of past impulses and fantasies; in them, unconscious material is transformatively "revived" through the encounter with the analyst. These transferences may simply be "new impressions or reprints" of old impulses, or else "revised editions" (*FR* 234–5; *PF* 8: 157–8) of past materials remade for the present – but in each case they offer a space for analysis and symbolic reconfiguration. Brooks remarks that psychoanalytic transference is "a special 'artificial' space for the reworking of the past in symbolic form"; it is "textual" (*Psychoanalysis and Storytelling* 53) in the sense that it allows a new story to be told and a new story to be lived for the future.

As we will see in Part IV, *Dora* is the case that both gives Freud the most insight into the workings of the transference *and* the case that fails because of the transference – because of Freud's failure to grasp in time (for some feminist critics at all) the *symbolics* of Dora's transference. Brooks comments: "In the case of 'Dora', [Freud] appears to gain his costly 'victory' by too much imposing his construction of the text; while Dora makes the ultimate riposte available to the storyteller, that of refusing to tell further, breaking off before the end" (*Psychoanalysis and Storytelling* 57). Dora, as we will see, escapes from Freud with her story intact, unspoken. She refuses to collude with Freud in the essentially *phallocentric* story of desire that he is telling about her (namely, that she loves a family friend, Herr K., who has made sexual advances to her) – and, in her transferential relationship to Freud, she *repeats* her rejection of Herr K. in the rejection of Freud. In *Dora*, Freud fails to read (or to construct) the *other* story of his patient's desire – that is, her unconscious homosexual love for Frau K. Freud fails to use the symbolic crucible of Dora's transference to write for – and with – her a revised narrative of the past and a curative narrative for the future. For Brooks, the lesson of *Dora*, and of Freud's theoretical reflections on analysis late in his career in "Constructions in Analysis" and "Analysis Terminable and Interminable" (both 1937), is that "the analyst must learn to eschew ... imposed solutions, that the collaboration and competition of the transference ultimately must put into question the privilege of the analyst". He adds: "As with reader and text, there is no clear mastery, no assurance ... that the analyst and analysand won't trade places, at least provisionally, and perhaps frequently".

Brooks's remark about "reader and text" is part of his suggestive argument that a "transferential" model of reading can be said to operate in the case of literary interpretation as well as analysis; this is because "[t]he model of the transference ... complicates any conception of interpretation as working from outside the text – as not implicated in its production" (*Psychoanalysis and Storytelling* 58). Just as literature and psychoanalysis are "implicated" with one another (in Felman's argument), or Freud and his patients are implicated with one another in the transference, so literary text and reader inhabit one another in a dialogic encounter in which neither has simple priority – instead, meaning is generated in the exchange between the two. This is how Felman puts it: "It could be argued that people who choose to analyze literature as a profession do so because they are unwilling or unable to choose between the role of the psychoanalyst (he or she who analyzes) and the role of the patient (that which is being analyzed). Literature enables them not to choose because of the following paradox: 1) the work of literary analysis resembles the work of the psychoanalyst; 2) the status of what is analyzed – the text – is ... not that of a patient, but rather that of a master ... the ... place where meaning, and *knowledge* of meaning, reside" ("To Open the Question" 7). If neither reader nor text is a *straightforward* "master" of textual meaning, then, the transferential relationship between them means that literary interpretation is an "unstable dynamic" (*Psychoanalysis and Storytelling* 58) in which positions of mastery and lack of mastery, knowledge and lack of knowledge, are assumed and dissolved in an inconclusive and interminable dialogue of symbolic production.

Though psychoanalytic interpretations of literature, including Freud's, have generally seen literature as a body of language "to *be interpreted*" – with literature being "submitted ... to the prestige of psychoanalysis" (Felman, "To Open the Question" 5) – the other story about their involvement, as we have seen, is that literature is privileged by Freud as a source of insight about unconscious processes. Thus André Green, referring to the place of *Oedipus Rex* and *Hamlet* in psychoanalytic theory, says of Freud's love of drama: "Sophocles and Shakespeare are in a class of their own, especially Shakespeare; Freud recognized in him a master whose texts he analyzes as if they were the discoveries of some illustrious precursor". Green contends that "[t]here is a mysterious bond between psycho-analysis and the theatre" (*The Tragic Effect* 1) because in the theatre – as in the dream or the symptom – what is witnessed comes with no ready-made or deliverable meaning accompanying it. Instead, the spectator is left (like the "child … [in] the daily domestic drama") to construct the meaning of the dramatic action for him or herself: "[I]t is up to him to find it and interpret it". Green adds: "Every theatrical work, like every work of art, is an enigma, but an enigma expressed in speech: articulated, spoken and heard, without any alien medium filling in its gaps" (2). According to Green, this means that the space of the stage may come to embody the "other scene" (1) of the unconscious itself: that is to say, that scene of withheld or unspoken significance whose import can only be conjured or constructed by the spectator in a belated act of interpretation.[4] Ellmann says of Green's account of the theatre: "the images that pass before the audience correspond to those which surface in our dreams: the fleeting figures of a knowledge both debarred and inescapable" (*Psychoanalytic Literary Criticism* 40).[5]

Green's contention that the theatre works like the unconscious – is even structured *like* the unconscious – resonates with Lacan's well-known dictum that "*the unconscious is structured like a language*" (*The Four Fundamental Concepts* 20). Lacan's "return" to a linguistically based Freud, focused on the tropology of the unconscious, has engendered a school of poststructuralist psychoanalytic criticism that forgoes the traditional psychobiography of authors in favour of a (psycho)analysis of textual and rhetorical processes, considering textual strategy over psychical content. This style of criticism is well-represented in PART II in Kofman's, Cixous's and Møller's readings of Hoffmann's "The Sandman" and Freud's "The 'Uncanny'", and in Brooks's reading of the *Wolf Man* in Essay 7. Lacan's related aphorism that "*the unconscious is the discourse of the Other*" (*The Four Fundamental Concepts* 131) insists that psychoanalysis involves not just an encounter with language and discourse, but with otherness – with what remains "Other" to the discourse of the patient, the literary text, and even the analyst. John Lechte argues that "specific to the analytic project" is an "engagement with otherness […] not its control or elimination" (*Writing and Psychoanalysis* 11); and Elizabeth Wright similarly finds an attention to alterity to be a defining feature of both literature and psychoanalysis. She writes: "An acknowledgement of the permanent presence of radical otherness … becomes the central recommendation of psychoanalysis and literature alike, for both their narratives have precisely this feature, that an easy assumption is exposed to subversion by the incalculable" (*Speaking Desires* 4). The discourse of the unconscious as radically Other therefore involves a necessary openness to the effects of the "incalculable".

This has consequences not just for how we see literature but how we see psychoanalysis: it suggests that in order to be true to its founding insight, the agency of the unconscious, psychoanalysis must remain open to what it cannot conclusively master, the operation of the "Other". Psychoanalysis must remain open to otherness, and this includes the possibility – the other – of its own error. Paradoxically, in order to be true to itself, psychoanalysis has to open itself up to challenge and displacement, to the perpetual challenge of the alterity that it theorizes. As an essentially *sceptical* enterprise, psychoanalysis thus creates the conditions for its own interrogation rather than rests secure in the unapproachable light of scientific truth. Imbued with a sense of its own discursive fragility, psychoanalysis is necessarily (to adapt a formulation of Kristeva's) a language "in process/on trial" (*The Kristeva Reader* 91) – a theoretical *practice*, we might say, rather than an immutable theory.

In a self-reflexive turn, then, psychoanalytic interpretation modulates into the interpretation *of* psychoanalysis; and a number of essays in this book (such as Hélène Cixous's on Freud and Hoffmann [Essay 5], or Elisabeth Bronfen's on *Dora* [Essay 12]) demonstrate the extraordinary fruitfulness of psychoanalysis's revelation, almost against itself, of the blindnesses and errors that inhabit its own insights. Yet this self-critical turn does not come from outside psychoanalysis, but from within; and the *Wolf Man* and *Dora* are both remarkable instances of that. In fact, historically, Freud's practice as a theoretical scientist is one of restless self-revision and self-transformation. Both within and beyond Freud, psychoanalysis is an enterprise of self-questioning, a discipline of self-examination grounded in the exigencies of theoretical and therapeutic practice.

It was Freud's sense that, as Lacan says, he was "implicated" in the discourse of his hysterical patients that – in a turn towards self-analysis – led to his discovery of what he called the *"royal road to a knowledge of the unconscious activities of the mind"* (PF 4: 769): the interpretation of dreams. For Freud's groundbreaking interpretation of dreams *begins* in an act of self-analysis; in the "Preface to the Second Edition" (1908) of *The Interpretation of Dreams* (1900) he describes the book as "a portion of my own self-analysis, my reaction to my father's death" (*FR* 130; *PF* 4: 47). Freudian dream-analysis is inaugurated in a project of self-scrutiny. In Chapter II of *The Interpretation of Dreams*, the dream of "Irma's injection", Freud reads *himself* in an attempt to track the wayward paths of unconscious desire and fantasy, as well as to formulate the theory of dream-interpretation itself; namely, that "*[w]hen the work of interpretation has been completed, we perceive that a dream is the fulfilment of a wish*" (*FR* 142; *PF* 4: 198–99). In the course of his showcase analysis of the "Irma" dream, however, Freud discovers that to read the dream and the unconscious is at the same time to be *read by* them, to be grasped and comprehended by the very thing one is attempting to interpret. In the course of his reading Freud, therefore, meets a *knot* or spot of resistance to his interpretation, a blind-spot that, in a fugitive footnote, he describes as the "navel" of the dream. He says: "There is at least one spot in every dream at which it is unplummable – a navel, as it were, that is its point of contact with the unknown" (*FR* 134; *PF* 4: 186).[6] Later in *The Interpretation of Dreams* he expands on this enigmatic figure of resistance to interpretation:

> There is often a passage in even the most thoroughly interpreted dream which has to be left obscure; this is because we become aware during the work of interpretation that at that point there is a tangle of dream-thoughts which cannot be unravelled ... This is the dream's navel, the spot where it reaches down into the unknown. The dream-thoughts to which we are led by interpretation cannot, from the nature of things, have any definite endings; they are bound to branch out in every direction into the intricate network of our world of thought.   (*PF* 4: 671–2)

If Freud's reading here – his progress on the "royal road to ... the unconscious" – is halted, and he finds himself unable to advance further along the way, this point of blockage is at the same time a point of *branching-out* or divergence: a point from which, says Freud, the thoughts of the dream discandy and disperse unreachably "in every direction into the intricate network of our world of thought". An instant of stoppage, the navel is also a point of unmasterable dissemination: a way-station from which further directions of interpretation may, yet cannot, be taken. The dream "navel", then, potentially opens up intricate and infinite avenues of further interpretation, but debars them at the same time; it structurally breaks open Freud's analysis of the dream beyond the meaning (here, the "wish-fulfilment") that he ascribes to it, but does not allow him any purchase on the possibilities that are opaquely and prohibitively inscribed there. The "navel" of the dream thus marks the *unconscious* of Freud's dream-interpretation, opening up new directions for the analysis of the dream-text while at the same time cutting them – and Freud – out of the interpretive play.[7]

Paradoxically, then, if Freudian interpretation is both positioned and questioned by the operation of the thing (the unconscious, the Other) that it reads, the condition of its insight is at the same time the condition of its error. This play between blindness and insight means that psychoanalysis is neither a straightforward discourse of truth (science) nor of falsehood (fiction); instead, psychoanalysis unsettles the binary opposition of truth and fiction, finding that each strangely inhabits the other. The fact that psychoanalysis occupies this troubling hinterland between reality and fantasy, truth and invention (just as the symptoms it studies belong straightforwardly neither to the psyche nor the body, but inhabit the hybrid space of the *psychosomatic*) means that psychoanalysis challenges the divisions by which we habitually think. As a discourse it demands that we open the familiar categories of our understanding to the "Other", the repressed, the strange, the unconscious. In continual renewal itself, psychoanalysis requires that we, too, perpetually renew our symbolic constructions of language, culture and the mind.

According to Peter Brooks psychoanalysis – as an encounter with psychic and symbolic otherness, and the unconscious – constitutes itself as "inherently dialogic" (Essay 7), a field of open and perpetually opening debate. Psychoanalytic interpretation, literary or otherwise, can never come to rest in any final truth or final cure; it preserves what Elizabeth Wright calls the "incalculable". As a discourse of theory and of therapy, psychoanalysis is concerned with the continual reconfiguration of the boundaries between knowledge and invention, the presentation and the production of meaning; and it is to the challenge of this reconfiguration that *Literature in Psychoanalysis* is dedicated.

NOTES

1. These are, Freud and Breuer insist, bodily symptoms with *mental* causes. Freud's theoretical term for this is "conversion" hysteria –

which he defines as "the transformation of psychical excitation into chronic somatic symptoms" (*PF3*: 146), the conversion of mental trauma into physical affliction.

2.   For a stunning reading of the strange echoes between Sophocles's *Oedipus Rex* and Freud's psychoanalytic interpretation of it, see Cynthia Chase, "Oedipal Textuality: Reading Freud's Reading of *Oedipus*" (Ellmann, *Psychoanalytic Literary Criticism* 56–75).

3.   Shoshana Felman gives a brilliant and suggestive analysis of Lacan's account of *Oedipus at Colonus* in "Beyond Oedipus: The Specimen Story of Psychoanalysis" (*Jacques Lacan and the Adventure of Insight* 98–159). A shorter version of this chapter appears in Ellmann, *Psychoanalytic Literary Criticism* 76–102.

4.   Green writes: "[Freud] seems to have had a special affection for the theatre ... Why is this? Is it not that the theatre is the best embodiment of that 'other scene', the unconscious? It is that other scene; it is also a stage whose 'edge' materially presents the break, the line of separation, the frontier at which conjunction and disjunction can carry out their tasks between auditorium and stage in the service of representation – in the same way as the cessation of motility is a precondition for the deployment of the dream" (*The Tragic Effect* 1–2).

5.   Ellmann includes a shorter version of the first chapter of Green's *The Tragic Effect*, "Prologue: The psycho-analytic reading of tragedy", in *Psychoanalytic Literary Criticism* 39–55.

6.   Shoshana Felman gives a stunning feminist reading of the "navel" of the "Irma" dream – and the sexual politics of Freud's reading of it – in *What Does a Woman Want?* (68–120).

7.   For readings of the figure of the dream "navel" in Freud that explore its dispersive effects, see Weber (*The Legend of Freud* 75–82), Chase ("Oedipal Textuality" 69–73) and Bronfen (*The Knotted Subject* 76–87).

Part I
Shakespeare, *Hamlet*

Introductory Note

HAMLET IN PSYCHOANALYSIS

"In an analysis ... a thing which has not been understood inevitably reappears; like an unlaid ghost, it cannot rest until the mystery has been solved and the spell broken" (*PF* 8: 280). So writes Freud in his case history of "Little Hans".

It might have been said of *Hamlet* and the psychoanalytic reading of *Hamlet*; for Shakespeare's play is haunted by a ghost (that of Hamlet's father), and the psychoanalytic reading of the play by the ghosts of its unsolved enigmas.

Yet Freud would have it otherwise. In a letter written to Wilhelm Fliess in 1897 (a text which also marks the birth of the idea of the "Oedipus complex" in psychoanalysis), Freud proposes a solution to the "mystery" of *Hamlet* – as if to exorcise its phantoms. He says: "I have found, in my own case too, falling in love with the mother and jealousy of the father, and I now regard it as a universal event of early childhood" – and, after a brief reference to *Oedipus Rex* as the dramatic fulfilment of this unconscious fantasy, adds, "A fleeting idea passed through my head of whether the same thing may not lie at the bottom of *Hamlet* as well" (*FR* 116). Three years later this fleeting idea becomes fully-fledged theory in *The Interpretation of Dreams* (1900), and Freud says: "What is it ... that inhibits [Hamlet] in fulfilling the task set him by his father's ghost? The answer ... is ... Hamlet is able to do anything – except take vengeance on the man who did away with his father and took that father's place with his mother, the man who shows him the repressed wishes of his own childhood realized. Thus the loathing which should drive him on to revenge is re-

18

placed in him by self-reproaches, by scruples of conscience, which remind him that he himself is literally no better than the sinner whom he is to punish" (*PF* 4: 367). As the letter to Fliess puts it, "[Hamlet's] conscience is his unconscious sense of guilt" (*FR* 116); Hamlet, for Freud, is an Oedipus, delayed and disabled by incestuous and parricidal desire and guilt. The ghost of Hamlet's father is thus the voice of *Hamlet's* (as well as Claudius's) repressed criminality.

Freud is proud of this. While *Oedipus Rex*, he says, displays incestuous and parricidal fantasy openly, that fantasy is repressed or concealed in *Hamlet* – with the result that the play's audiences remain "in the dark" about the hero's motives (*PF* 4: 366–67). A few years later Freud comments: "the conflict in *Hamlet* is so effectively concealed that it was left to me to unearth it" (*PF* 14: 126). After this "unearthing", Freud's British disciple Ernest Jones expanded and established his master's interpretation in essays of 1910, 1923 and 1949, and from being a Romantic self-tormenter afflicted by excess of consciousness, Hamlet was transposed in psychoanalytic theory into an "hysteric" (*FR* 116; *PF* 4: 367) harried by unconscious trauma and repressed sexual guilt. For Freud, Hamlet suffers under a paternally instituted "Oedipal" law that debars incestuous attachment to the mother's body, and installs paternity as the embodiment of the libidinal prohibition that keeps culture and the desiring subject in place – and keeps Hamlet from his revenge.

Jacques Lacan points out, however, that though it is the father's function in Freud to "sustain[...] the structure of desire with the structure of the law", in Shakespeare's *Hamlet* "this too ideal father is constantly being *doubted*". Lacan asks: "Where does Hamlet's ghost emerge from, if not from the place from which he denounces his brother for surprising him and cutting him off in the full flower of his *sins*?" (*The Four Fundamental Concepts* 34, 35). Lacan argues that in *Hamlet* the father is a figure of "sin", not of law – and that his paternal law is, in effect, in dissolution. All the essays in this section elaborate in one way or another on Lacan's suggestion, for they show how in *Hamlet* the Oedipal father is toppled from his position as the embodiment of law and is reinscribed as a figure of sin, desire and crime. In different ways, each of these readings revises Freud's and Jones's Oedipal emphases, revealing how the category of the Oedipal father is in disarray in *Hamlet*. There is a "ghost", we might say, of *paternal guilt* in *Hamlet*: a ghost Freud is unable to exorcise because he is wedded to the Oedipal idea of the father as the avatar of morality and law.

According to Lacan, the father in *Hamlet* is an embodiment of the "phallus" – the phallus, for him, being that delusive signifier of presence, power and plenitude which, in a phantom effect or "phallacy",[1] gives its name to what the subject lacks. Yet *Hamlet*, as Lacan puts it, discloses the fact that "the phallus, even the real phallus, is a *ghost*". While the phallus, says Lacan, is the "signifier of power, of potency", the "manifestation" ("Desire and the Interpretation of Desire in *Hamlet*" 50, 51) of this signifier in *Hamlet* points not to its presence or plenitude, but to its nothingness. As Hamlet insists in the play, "The king is a thing … Of nothing" (III. II. 27–29); and Maud Ellmann points out that one cannot be certain whether Hamlet's statement here refers to "the king that's dead or to the king of shreds and patches who has seized his throne, because [Hamlet] knows that both are nothing, spectre and impostor" ("The Ghosts of *Ulysses*" 194). In a certain way, Hamlet is involved in a drama of inexhaustible and impossible mourning for the (dead) authority of a missing father; indeed, the play is arguably about the ghostliness or "nothingness" of paternal law itself as the guarantor of symbolic fixity and stability.

Linda Charnes (Essay 1) examines this nothingness of the father's "law" in *Hamlet* by reading the play through the work of the Slovenian Lacanian thinker, Slavoj Žižek. Applying Žižek's work on detective fiction to the structure of Shakespeare's *drama* of detection, *Hamlet*, Charnes shows how the crisis of symbolic authority that haunts Shakespeare's play can be said to anticipate the "*noir*" universe of "hardboiled" 20th century detective fiction. In the *noir* world, symbolic figures of authority lose their position as embodiments of the law and are shown to be irreparably compromised or flawed. In Lacanian terms this highlights the fact, says Charnes, that there is a "lack in the Other" (*The Sublime* 195), that is to say, in the "big Other" of the Symbolic Order that is supposed to hold culture's meanings in place, including the meaning of the law. "In patriarchal culture", she writes, "the place of the big Other may be occupied by God, King, Pope, Lord, Father"; but in the *noir* world the place in which the law is manifested (the detective and the logic of deduction) is also the very place where it is dissolved. Charnes sees this double structure already operative in *Hamlet* in the shape of the two "fathers" of the play, old Hamlet and Claudius; for while the play (and Hamlet) works to separate these figures by idealizing one and debasing the other it also, as Lacan indicates, implicates them by making the ideal father speak from a place of rankly unexpiated "sin". According to Žižekian logic, this means that the ideal Oedipal father of the Freudian reading is structurally shadowed by the "obscene" father of bodily enjoyment, a father who is the idealized father's double and repressed. For Hamlet himself, this obscene father is Claudius; yet Charnes's Žižekian approach suggests that Claudius's rankness only *masks* from Hamlet's view the inadmissible truth that the father of the law *is also the father of sin*, the father of obscenity. Charnes argues that Franco Zeffirelli's 1990 film version of *Hamlet* colludes with the "Oedipal" logic implicit in Shakespeare's play by maximizing the differences between old Hamlet and Claudius, but that in so doing the film elides *Hamlet*'s troubled and ambivalent unsettling of paternal authority: an unsettling that disrupts the "authority of the paternal metaphor".

Julia Reinhard Lupton and Kenneth Reinhard (Essay 2) similarly challenge the authority of the Oedipal, Freudian reading of the play, but they do so by extrapolating Lacan's claim that Hamlet – and *Hamlet* – is grasped by the "desire of the mother". Moreover, they resurrect a "melancholic" Hamlet who is tied to the body of the mother in opposition to the "Oedipal" Hamlet enthralled to the law of the father. In psychoanalysis, the melancholic is the one who is *unable to replace with another object* the thing he/she has lost; instead, the melancholic remains *wedded* to the lost object. As Freud hauntingly puts it in his essay "Mourning and Melancholia" (1917), "the shadow of the object [falls] upon the ego" (*PF* 11: 258) in melancholy. The melancholic cannot substitute another object for the lost object, and in effect – as Lacan proposes of Shakespeare's Hamlet – becomes unable to desire. This is why Lacan sees *Hamlet* as a "tragedy of desire" ("Desire and the Interpretation of Desire in *Hamlet*" 11), for it is a tragedy in which the protagonist is blocked in his access to his desire and is held in the illimitable mourning of melancholy. Hamlet, Lacan implies, is unable either to mourn his father with sufficient funeral rites, or to disengage himself sufficiently from the desiring body of his mother, the body from which the Oedipal father's interdiction *should* debar him but to which he remains tied in a pre-Oedipal libidinal immersion – albeit his immersion in disgust. In the abject melancholy of his disgust, Hamlet remains possessed by the mother's body and unable to disengage himself from it or its desire: in Elizabeth

Wright's words, Hamlet is "caught in the desire of the mother" (*Speaking Desires* 78). Hamlet is Oedipally unable to "mourn" the loss of his mother's body by substituting for it another object, Ophelia: instead, obsessed by the mother's body – in her "incest" with Claudius – he miserably identifies himself with it in a disgust with which he floods himself, Gertrude and the world. Hamlet is a melancholy pre-Oedipal subject who is unable to mourn his loss of the mother's body, but snarls it up in a disgust that prevents him from acceding to his desire. His father's spirit and his mother's body possess him as insistent ghost on the one hand and obtrusive flesh on the other.

Lacan says "from one end of *Hamlet* to the other, all anyone talks about is mourning" ("Desire and the Interpretation of Desire in *Hamlet*" 39); and Reinhard Lupton and Reinhard, noting that Freud's "Mourning and Melancholia" is itself haunted by the figure of Hamlet (who they call Shakespeare's "philosopher of melancholy"), point out that "*Hamlet* [is] the tragedy around which mourning is theorized in psychoanalysis" (*After Oedipus* 26). Nicolas Abraham's remarkable "Sixth Act" to *Hamlet* (discussed in Essay 3) is a fictional addition to Shakespeare's drama that brings Hamlet back on stage to confront the ghost of his father again in an encounter mediated by Fortinbras. In this audacious supplement, Abraham proves himself, say Reinhard Lupton and Reinhard, to be "the most rich and strange post-Freudian theorist of mourning" (*After Oedipus* 12); for Abraham takes *literally* the idea that there is something unexplained in *Hamlet*, something unresolved. Abraham, that is, takes up the idea that in *Hamlet* there is a ghost or phantom that has *not* been laid to rest, that has not been sufficiently symbolized or "mourned" – if mourning is understood as that process whereby the dead are internalized at the level of memory and meaning in the mind. For Abraham, something is dead in *Hamlet*, and this dead thing *escapes* the play's regime of symbolization: it is, he argues, a dead event (or ghost of an event) that eludes the play's symbolizations, yet walks through it as a phantom, secret, the symptom of something interred by the language of the play. For Abraham, as Nicholas Rand comprehensively shows (Essay 3), this phantom is the "ghost" of the father's unspoken crimes.

For T.S. Eliot, *Hamlet* is an "artistic failure" because it is "full of some stuff that the writer could not drag to light, contemplate, or manipulate into art". Arguing that the play lacks an "objective correlative" ("Hamlet" 47, 48) – or adequate symbol – for its protagonist's emotions, Eliot unknowingly hints that *Hamlet* encrypts something *unconscious* in its order of representation. Eliot's strictures paradoxically open the way for a *psychoanalytic* consideration of the play's silences, for it is in *Hamlet*'s very failures of representation that its psychoanalytic interest lies. Arguably, Abraham's "Sixth Act" dramatizes the paradox that *Hamlet* imposes on all its readers through its "ghostly" reserves: the paradox that the play's enigmas must be read, but that any reading must remain a perilous and provisional *construction*, a hazardous disclosure of what the play refuses to utter, what it keeps secret, what it cannot "drag to light", in Eliot's words. Arguably, psychoanalysis is that form of discourse that pays most respect to the reserve or secrecy that, for J. Hillis Miller, structures the literary itself: "Literature eternally keeps its secrets, and the secret is an essential feature of literature", says Miller, but the secret of literature is one that is not "in principle discoverable" ("Derrida's Topographies" 16, 17). And though Abraham *appears* to reveal or resolve *Hamlet*'s enigmas, what the "Sixth Act" implies is that all readings of *Hamlet* are necessarily acts of invention or conjuring – even though most readings of the play might seek to repress that recognition, and lay its ghosts to rest.

In the end, the play's phantoms and ghosts *remain* phantoms. Ghosts, indeed, whether of meaning or of being, cannot be "killed" or given up because they are already dead; and they obdurately haunt their spectators with their enigmatic half-life. And perhaps *that* is the way the "meaning" of *Hamlet* itself works – like a "ghost".[2] And perhaps that is the way the most unmasterable and enigmatic phantom of all – William Shakespeare – works and walks as well: like the ghost of Hamlet's father. For, as Marjorie Garber muses, "We know that Shakespeare played the part of the Ghost in *Hamlet*. What could not be foreseen ... was that he would *become* that Ghost. 'Remember me!' the Ghost cries. 'Do not forget.' And, indeed, we do not yet seem quite able to give up that ghost" (*Shakespeare's Ghost Writers* 176).

NOTES

1. The pun is Shoshana Felman's in her essay, "Woman and Madness: the Critical Phallacy" (1989).

2. For a remarkable reflection on *Hamlet*'s ghost and the "spectrality" of meaning in history, with specific reference to Marxism, see Jacques Derrida, *Specters of Marx*, 3–48.

1

Dismember Me: Shakespeare, Paranoia, and the Logic of Mass Culture

LINDA CHARNES

> Whatever we may be, for better or for worse, we are thus initially and "naturally" "idiots of the family."
>
> Peter Sloterdijk (73)

> Be thy intents wicked or charitable,
> Thou com'st in such a questionable shape
> That I will speak to thee.
> *Hamlet*, 1.4.21–23[1]

In *Enjoy Your Symptom! Jacques Lacan in Hollywood and Out*, Slavoj Žižek makes an intriguing link between a change that occurs in modern detective fiction and the emergence of film *noir*. In a chapter entitled "Why Are There Always Two *Fathers*?" Žižek defines the difference between the "classical (logic-and-deduction) detective novel" and the "hard-boiled novel" largely as a change in the subjective universe of the detective:

> ... the logic-and-deduction novel still relies on the consistent big Other: the moment, at the novel's end, when the flow of events is integrated into the symbolic universe, narrativized, told in the form of a linear story (the last pages of the novel when, upon identifying the murderer, the detective reconstructs the true course of events), brings about an effect of pacification, order and consistency are reinstated, whereas the *noir* universe is characterized by a radical split, a kind of

25

> structural imbalance, as to the possibility of narrativization: the
> integration of the subject's position into the field of the big Other,
> the narrativization of his fate, becomes possible only when the
> subject is in a sense already dead, although still alive, when "the
> game is already over," in short: when the subject finds himself at
> the place baptized by Lacan "the in-between-two-deaths" (*l'entre-
> deux-morts*). (151)

This big Other, as Lacan defines it in his second *Seminar*, is that
fantasmatic (non) Entity that doesn't "*ex-sist*" separately from the
subject but nevertheless calls the subject into "the being of the
other," into identification within the symbolic order (*The Ego*, 155,
172). It is that hypostatized phantom to whom we all address the
constitutive question: "*Che vuoi?*" or "What is it that you want of
me?" (Copjec 28) Purely structural – that is to say, devoid of any
particular content – the big Other is effective only when mis-
recognized as an essential "being" that guarantees the existence of
subjective and social formations. In patriarchal culture the place of
the big Other may be occupied by God, King, Pope, Lord, Father –
placeholders who quilt a paternal allegory over a fundamentally
antagonistic social formation and call things to order and account
within it.[2] Such interpellations, however, can operate successfully
only if the paternal metaphor remains neutral, or "in the background", as Žižek puts it. By holding itself in reserve, the big Other
allows the subject to fantasize a site – always elsewhere – of absolute knowledge, authority, and control which organizes the subject's narrative integration into the social order, assigning him or
her, as it were, a place in the story.

   Against this "neutral" structuring paradigm, Žižek aligns the
emergence of the *noir* universe with a disturbance in the field of the
big Other, one that makes the mandates of identification ambiguous. This disturbance is brought about by the revelation of another
father, a figure who emerges as "the obscene, uncanny, shadowy
double of the Name of the Father":

> ... instead of the traditional father – guarantor of the rule of Law,
> i.e., the father who exerts his power as fundamentally *absent*, whose
> fundamental feature is not an open display of power but the threat of
> potential power – we obtain an excessively *present* father who, as such,
> cannot be reduced to the bearer of a symbolic function. (*Enjoy* 158)

Whereas the classic (logic-and-deduction) detective may be worldly-
wise and even cynical (Raymond Chandler's Philip Marlowe, for

example), he still sustains belief in the abstraction called "Law", and therefore can sustain *our* identification with *his* identification with the "paternal metaphor". The hard-boiled detective, however (represented by a figure such as Dashiell Hammett's Ned Beaumont), is a kind of blank page, offering the reader no stable point of affective entry because his universe is organized according to a different logic: the logic of *noir*. At the origin of *noir*, Žižek points out, is the "humiliated father," "the paranoic Other," a figure who has sustained irreparable damage to his integrity and can no longer function as the guarantor of the symbolic and, consequently, of all the juridical, ethical, filial, and sexual organizations that derive from it.[3] The nature of this "mutation in the paternal figure" is one of prurient pleasure, the obscene enjoyment that Lacan would claim always underwrites paternal Law. This second father – the "obscene father" – is first and foremost a *"father who knows"*, and whose knowledge specifically is of the libidinal enjoyment that Law must disavow in order to maintain its unquestionable shape.[4]

The bifurcation of detective fiction into two genres – classic and *noir* – forces the reader/audience to choose between contradictory relationships to symbolic authority and Law. The former offers a pragmatic or rationalist ethos, in which what matters most is *the fact* that a crime has been committed and a law breached, a condition of social anomaly which requires only detection and punishment to set things right. The latter offers a paranoiac ethos, in which the fact of a particular crime is insufficient to explain what's really gone wrong and draws attention to a more pervasive social problem precisely by virtue of its lack of criminological "critical mass".

Although Žižek suggests that the elements of classic and *noir* detective fictions are mutually incompatible (presumably because, like oil and water, their foundational structures cannot bind), both forms, I wish to argue, descend from a single, even earlier genre: the revenge tragedy, a form of drama in which a revenger/detective discovers that a crime has been committed (usually but not always against a father figure), uncovers the details, and sets out to bring the offender to justice. The nature of that justice may be harsh – the Law of the Father to which the classical revenger subscribes doesn't yet have to efface its foundational violence in Enlightenment notions of disinterestedness. But in revenge tragedy (as in classic detective fiction) the authority of the paternal metaphor remains

intact regardless of the violence loosed in its name, for it is underwritten by the patriarchal power encoded in every aspect of ancient
and early modern life and therefore is not (overtly at least) called
into question. The classical revenge play – whether Greek or
Roman revenge tragedy, Heywood's translations of Senecan tragedy, or early modern translations of the *Oresteia* – tends to offer a
logic-and-deduction rationale that, no matter how violent or passionate, ultimately seeks to restore an ethical system based on structural checks and balances. And Renaissance revengers, despite the
contradictions and incursions of Christian philosophy, are expected
in the last instance to cease whining and get the job done.

The play that has for centuries most famously represented the
revenge-tragedy "tradition" is, of course, Shakespeare's *Hamlet*,
which, in terms of its popular or mass-cultural reception, has long
been regarded as *the classic* Renaissance revenge play. The play
clearly inherits, deploys, and satirizes certain elements of Senecan
and classical tragedy. At the same time, *Hamlet* has been read
through centuries of critical reception as breaking with that tradition – indeed, as breaking with an already-established tradition of
specifically *English* revenge tragedy. Since among extant English
plays that precede *Hamlet* (not including *Gorboduc*) there is only
one – Kyd's *Spanish Tragedy* – that fits into the subgenre we call
revenge tragedy, we are presented with an intriguing paradox. Did
Shakespeare mean the play to depart from a logic-and-deduction
formula that he presumed already existed for his audience? Or was
he attempting something more radical: namely, to launch and simultaneously critique a logic-and-deduction tradition precisely by
staging an epistemological break with it?[5] What we *can* see is that,
while there are few logic-and-deduction revengers running around
on the Renaissance stage before Shakespeare's *Hamlet* appears, the
play *acts as if there are*, constructs the subjectivity of its protagonist
as if there are, and constitutes an audience – ingenuously or disin-
genuously – that must consent (to paraphrase Frank Kermode) to
"the sense of a tradition" in order to identify with the anguish of
the protagonist.

Given the impossibility of determining exactly what the nature
of audience expectation would be with regard to an already-existing
revenge ethos, it would be more accurate to say that the play delib-
erately generates a *tradition effect* by counterposing Hamlet against
other revengers *within* the play (Fortinbras; Laertes; and, in The
Mousetrap, Lucianus) who do conform to a logic-and-deduction

model. Presenting itself, then, as both prototype *and* changeling, Shakespeare's *Hamlet* stages exactly the kind of epistemological mortification that Lacan would argue necessarily vexes *any* tradition based on the unquestioned authority of patriarchal Law. In short, the history of the play's construction as a "classic" revenge tragedy within a "tradition" – in terms of both critical and popular reception – replicates the dilemma that Hamlet is forced to face within the play itself, and that is: where do we locate the *origin* of a problem that needs to be redressed? For in asking whether 'tis better to suffer the requirements of a paternal mandate to revenge a particular crime or to take no arms against a more pervasive sea of troubles, Hamlet is asking no less a question than what kind of detective he is to be or not to be.

Which leads us back to the *noir*. If we accept Žižek's description of the *noir* universe, then we must conclude that *Hamlet* – and not Hammett – offers the first fully *noir* text in Western literature, and Prince Hamlet the first *noir* detective. Or, rather, the first *noir* re-venger. Situating a plot-driven classical revenge tragedy within the recursive circularity and ethical indeterminacy that characterize *noir*, Shakespeare's *Hamlet* is modernity's inaugural paranoid text.[6] By "paranoia," however, I don't mean an individual pathology in which someone imagines conspiracies or has delusions of persecution but, rather, paranoia in the literal Greek sense as a form of "overknowing", of surplus knowledge that leads, paradoxically, not to discovery but to undecidability. In the *noir* universe the paranoid is a man who always-already "knows too much" about what's really going on. The *noir* detective is less concerned with historical events – with what *happened* – than he is with ontologies – with the way things *are*. If the classic detective wants "just the facts", for the *noir* detective "the facts" are always less relevant than the sinister effects of a reality that acquires paranoid dimensions precisely the more one learns about "the facts".

In Shakespeare's *Hamlet* the Ghost is a "*father who knows*" and whose knowledge threatens the status of the symbolic mandate he imposes upon his son. The content of this knowledge consists not only of the "harrow[ing]" secrets of his purgatorial prison-house but, more disturbingly, of his "enjoyment" of the "blossoms" of his sin, for which, he tells Hamlet, he is "confined to fast in fires, / Till the foul crimes done in my days of nature / Are burnt and purged away" (1.5.16, 76, 11–13). At once delivering the injunction to "Revenge his foul and most unnatural murder" and revealing his own shadowy "double," the Ghost commands Hamlet to "Remember me" even as he makes the task impossible, speaking the paternal mandate from a corrupted enunciatory site that splits the integrity of the Law open to reveal its kernel of obscene enjoyment (ll. 25, 91). "This", Žižek argues, "is what is ultimately at stake in the *noir* universe: the failure of the paternal metaphor ... the emergence of the obscene father who supplants the father living up to his symbolic function" (*Enjoy* 159–60).

This disclosure, incommensurable with the idealized image Hamlet wishes to sustain of his father, makes identification with the paternal figure impossible. Sensing an excessively obscene presence in the surround before he even encounters the Ghost, Hamlet is casting about for a local habitation, a concrete cause. His ontological despair, already legible in his affective withdrawal from the "stale, flat, and unprofitable ... uses of this world" (1.2.133–34), signals his inability to integrate himself into the symbolic order, into the "intersubjective, 'public' ... space" that gives the subject his "ideal ego, the place from which he can see himself as someone 'who belongs'" (*Enjoy* 152). Hamlet attempts to respond to the Ghost's disclosure as a classic revenger, to gather facts in logic-and-deduction style. But the more he seeks to confirm the knowledge *he already has* of Claudius's guilt, the more he is paralyzed by the gravitational pull of another crime scene. For when the Ghost reveals the lurid details of his murder, he also makes "excessively *present*" to his son's imagination images of his own lascivious body, taken in postprandial concupiscence, "grossly, full of bread," and "barked about ... with vile and loathsome crust" (3.3.80; 1.5.71–72). Hamlet's subsequent disavowal of this "second" father fuels, I would argue, his compulsive commitment to a logic-and-deduction style that the Ghost's disclosure should have rendered unnecessary.

In other words, Hamlet now has "the facts," at least insofar as he knows that Claudius has committed regicide, fratricide, usurpation, and "damnèd incest" (l. 83). But Hamlet cannot act on this knowledge because action is impossible in a *noir* universe where what is at stake is not a local crime but rather the very status of the paternal logos itself. Unable to assume the symbolic existence that paternal identification confers but not yet physically dead, Hamlet (like the *noir* detective) finds himself *entre-deux-morts*, in the place "between two deaths." Incapable of narrativizing himself, of finding his place in the story, Hamlet literally "lack[s] advancement"

(3.2.322). "The time is out of joint", he says, "O cursèd spite, / That ever I was born to set it right!" (1.5.196–97). The shift from the classical to the *noir* universe instantiates a vertiginous jolt out of the sequential and into the synchronic. Within this multiplicitous miasma in which time cannot be accounted for, the whole meaning of solving a crime changes.

The figure of Claudius provides Hamlet with a temporary respite from the lassitude of *noir*, serving as the supplement who will embody the obscene enjoyment of the anal father. Like all good Derridean supplements, however, Claudius cannot contain everything he is supposed to stand for. There must be other sites of displacement. As Žižek points out,

> The failure of the paternal metaphor ... renders impossible a viable, temperate relation with a woman; as a result, woman finds herself occupying the impossible place of the traumatic Thing. The *femme fatale* is nothing but a lure whose fascinating presence masks the true traumatic axis of the *noir* universe, the relationship to the obscene father, i.e., the default of the paternal metaphor. ... The crucial point not to be missed here is that the *femme fatale* and the obscene-knowing father cannot appear simultaneously, within the same narrative space. (*Enjoy* 159–60).

As long as the real obscene father hovers unacknowledged in the *noir* background, Gertrude, as well as Ophelia, can take on for Hamlet the function of "traumatic Thing". With a circuit of disavowal which runs from the obscene father to Claudius to Gertrude to Ophelia to Gertrude and finally back to Claudius, we see Hamlet's desperate efforts to construct himself as a classic revenger in a world where corruption, crime, licentiousness, and decay can be seen everywhere *but* in the place of the Father.

For in Shakespeare's play, the King may be a thing that demands, but the King must not be a thing that *enjoys*. If he enjoys, he becomes a different kind of thing, something that produces *noir* paranoia because his authority is no longer guaranteed by disinterestedness. It is, therefore, no accident that in Shakespeare's play the only cure for the *noir* must come from outside the social formation, in the form of exogenous rule. Fortinbras (a true logic-and-deduction type) enters after the occupants of the *noir* universe are all dead. And his way will be paved not by Hamlet's "election" (5.2.66) but by Horatio's mediation. Charged by Hamlet with the task of telling Fortinbras "the occurrents, more and less, / Which have solicited" (ll. 310–11), Horatio – the literally nominated voice-of-reason (s) – has an impossible task. In the *noir* universe the story exists only in the gaps between causes and effects – a space that Horatio's philosophy cannot cope withal. Hamlet's story, such as it is, takes place in the interstices of an intersubjectivity that the play always already debars. No one in this play "knows" anyone else; and it is precisely this missing "intersubjective" knowledge, and not "occurrents" or events, that constitutes *Hamlet* as a *noir* tragedy. While Hamlet would, perhaps, have been better served by Habermas than by Horatio, the state of Denmark is best served by the latter, whose efforts can result only in a crude translation of a *noir* tragedy into a "classical" detective fiction – into a story of what "really" happened, both "more and less". By presenting us in *Hamlet* with two-fathers-in-one, Shakespeare undermines the structure of the social by making it impossible to separate the excrescences of paternal Law from those of state politics. There can be in Shakespeare's world no decay of the paternal logos which does not also dismember the body politic and erode the foundational authority of the state. With Horatio's "translation", then, the humiliated father may be erased, along with the subjectively mortified son, and paternal Law can be reinstated for a more suitable defender.

In his 1990 film version Franco Zeffirelli cinematically redistributes the "two fathers" – which in the *noir* bifurcate from the same figure – between the Ghost, who becomes the in-reserve, withdrawn father, guarantor of paternal Law, and Claudius, who becomes the "obscene-knowing father."

By cleaning up the king's body and downloading the "other" father into Claudius, Zeffirelli offers Oedipus as the logic-and-deduction answer to what in Shakespeare's play is a *noir* question. In Zeffirelli's version it is Claudius who looks "grossly ... full of bread" (3.3.80) and not the Ghost (played with St. Thomas More – like probity by Paul Scofield), who appears wan, gaunt, and elderly. Taking Hamlet's words literally – "My father, in his habit as he lived!" (3.4.130) – Zeffirelli's Ghost is dressed austerely in a monk's habit. In this way the film defenestrates the obscene-knowing aspect of the Father, retaining only an ascetic hologram that diverts our attention from the contradiction inherent in the paternal signifier.

By offering up Claudius as the anal father *manqué*, Zeffirelli underwrites Hamlet's own "necessary route through misrecognition." (Žižek, *The Sublime* 63) The "questionable shape" of the Ghost in Shakespeare's play becomes in Zeffirelli's film the unquestionable shape of Claudius's desire, as he – and not the Ghost – is assigned the role of "Master of Enjoyment." In Shakespeare's play, Claudius functions as Hamlet's *identified* symptom – the site at which the knowledge of "enjoyment," or the unseemly pleasure of "foul crimes", can be imagined without the subjective destitution of disidentification with the paternal. But in literalizing this symptomology, Zeffirelli falls for Shakespeare's *own* oedipal feint, taking it for the truth of Hamlet's desire by crudely parading it in the vaudevillian winks, heated glances, passionate kisses, and lubricious encounters between Gibson's Hamlet and Close's Gertrude.

Encouraged by Zeffirelli to cast our lot with the lad, we too can direct our loathing toward a corrupt Claudius because, while he may be lewd, he doesn't inspire paranoia, since (after all) he doesn't know anything that *we* don't know. His obscenity – predicated on the readily comprehensible and ultimately banal motivations of ambition, lust, and envy – *can* be contained within the confines of his overblown body. Neither spectral nor *noir*, it doesn't threaten the integrity of the symbolic order because we know what *his* enjoyment is about. We can attribute it, as Hamlet does, to a corrupt individual, leaving the paternal metaphor, the symbolic order, and by extension the state respectfully intact.

Finally, if the "beyond-reproach" paternal metaphor always contains its own obscene double, we must ask what happens when a culture no longer believes, however fetishistically, in the integrity of the paternal logos. To raise this question is not to nostalgize for a time when we all believed (if we ever believed) that father knows best. Rather, it is to observe the increasing difficulty the placeholders of paternal authority have in hiding their own obscene doubles, whether they are presidents of nations, of savings-and-loans, junk-bond kings, supreme-court justices, political-party leaders (or strategists), federal judges, angst-ridden filmmakers, priests, police officers, or football heroes. It is not for nothing that currently the most famous fathers in American mass culture are both absurd "masters" of enjoyment: the crude Al Bundy of "Married With Children" and the moronic Homer Simpson. Perhaps even more alarming than Žižek's notion of two fathers is the possibility that there might be only one left – the obscene father, the excrescence of a paternal logos that has deconstructed itself from the inside out.

One thing, however, seems clear: the paternal metaphor can no longer proclaim itself the guarantor of Law because it cannot sustain the fiction of its own disinterestedness. It cannot help but reveal the pleasure it takes in its experience of arbitrary entitlement at the very sites where it proclaims itself "beyond reproach." The *noir* detective learns to his disgust that the local crimes he uncovers originate in the very law that authorizes his actions – that the Name of the Father covers over a metastatic corruption that reproduces its crimes at precisely the same moment and in precisely the same way that it reproduces its authority. To wit, a preposterously illuminating anecdote: On 9 September 1994 Vladimir Zhirinovsky announced to the Russian news agency Interfax that he had a plan "to combat Russia's declining birth rate: He personally will father a child in every region of Russia in the coming year." Zhirinovsky, the fax stated, had given orders "to ensure that at least one child by the chairman of the Liberal Democratic Party of Russia personally [that is, himself] be born in each regional branch of the LDPR in 1995." It seems natural that, having posed naked in the shower for photographers, spread-eagled in the sauna, leering at strippers and cavorting with prostitutes (see the Sunday *New York Times Magazine*, 19 June 1994), Zhirinovsky should offer to repopulate Russia "himself." Crudely conflating the personal with the political by eliding the metaphoricity of political office – the fact that all politicians are placeholders – Zhirinovsky gives new meaning to the concept of the Fatherland. At a time when such a figure stands poised, among others to be sure, as a New World Master of fascist enjoyment, we cannot rope him off as merely an individual aberration. Rather, he should be seen as the obscene double of our own leaders, whose "terms compulsative" mandate a new world order structured as a forced choice. If we accept the proposition that *there are* always two fathers, then we can discern within postmodern diplomacy's paternalistic insistence on global free enterprise what Shakespeare's prophetic soul foreshadowed in *Hamlet*: the emergence of the *Noir* World Order.

NOTES

[Linda Charnes is Associate Professor of English, Renaissance Studies and Cultural Studies at Indiana University, Bloomington. She is the author of *Notorious Identity: Materializing the Subject in Shakespeare* (1993) and *Hamlet's Heirs: Essays on Inheriting Shakespeare* (2005), along with many articles on Shakespeare, psychoanalysis, and contemporary British and American culture. These include "The Hamlet formerly Known as Prince"

(2000), "We Were Never early Modern" (2000) and "The 2% Solution: What Harold Bloom Forgot" (2001).   Ed.]

1. Quotations of *Hamlet* follow the Oxford Shakespeare *Hamlet*.

2. Žižek, *The Sublime* 97–101 and passim.

3. Žižek discusses these terms in *Enjoy* 149.

4. Žižek, *Enjoy* 158–59. In the chapter "Why Are There Always Two *Fathers?*" Žižek mentions *Hamlet* only elliptically before returning to his discussion of Wagner's *Parsifal*. This seems to me to be a symptomatic near-oversight: Žižek notices that the Ghost's knowledge "concerns a dark, licentious side of the father-king who is otherwise presented as an ideal figure" (159); yet, like Prince Hamlet himself, Žižek proceeds to ignore the implications of this, arguing as he does that paranoiac *noir* emerges as a postwar phenomenon of the 20th century (cf. 149–52 passim).

5. For a thorough and useful discussion/analysis of the Western tradition of revenging, see John Kerrigan's rich study *Revenge Tragedy: Aeschylus to Armageddon*, especially chapters 5–7. See also Louise Schleiner, "Latinized Greek drama in Shakespeare's Writing of *Hamlet*"; and Fredson Thayer Bowers, *Elizabethan Revenge Tragedy 1587–1642* (1940; reprinted Gloucester, MA: Peter Smith, 1959).

6. Terence Hawkes sheds brilliant light on the strange and layered recursivity or backward narratologic of *Hamlet* in "*Telmah*".

2

Hamlet's Flesh: Lacan and the Desire of the Mother

JULIA REINHARD LUPTON AND KENNETH REINHARD

The opening line of Hamlet's first soliloquy, the formal vehicle for his famous "interiority", is fractured by a textual crux: "O that this too too *sullied* [or *solid*] flesh would melt, / Thaw, and resolve itself into a dew" (I.ii.129–30).[1] The Quarto reading ("sallied," a variant of "sullied") emphasizes the bad conscience of Hamlet, which bolsters Freud's Oedipal interpretation of the play, in which Hamlet's mourning for his father is tainted by his identification with Claudius. The Folio's "solid", on the other hand, supported by the soliloquy's language of dissolution, materializes the specific gravity of the flesh, its sodden resistance to the flights of fancy that "characterize" Hamlet; in this reading, the solidity of Hamlet's flesh rankly burgeons from the corporeality of Gertrude, whose bestial "increase of appetite" (I.ii.144) leads Hamlet to break into the famous *interruptio*, "Frailty, thy name is woman" (I.ii.146). A psychoanalytic philology might argue that both readings must be valid – not, however, as alternatives available for adjudication or compromise, but as rival readings "sullied" by their coexistence in mutual cancellation. Echoing anxiously through each other, the two words weigh down the symbolic agon of signification (the competing meanings of "sullied" and "solid") with the heaviness of the pure signifier (the near-homophony of the words), staging at the linguistic level the structural ambivalence in the soliloquy – as well as in the play and its psychoanalytic criticism – between mourning for the father and disgust with the mother.

Although both Freud and Lacan have been associated with readings of *Hamlet* that emphasize the father, we excavate the maternal remainders in Freud's coupling of *Hamlet* and *Oedipus Rex*. In this chapter, we unfold the implications of this reading through Lacan's emphasis on *Hamlet*'s alienation in the desire of the mother.

THE POUND OF FLESH

Lacan's discussion of *Hamlet* appears in "Seminar VI", titled "Desire and its Interpretation", a discourse whose title transcribes Freud's *Die Traumdeutung* (*The Interpretation of Dreams*) into a Lacanian register. Lacan's *interprétation* translates Freud's *Deutung*, and the German *Traum*, posited by Freud as the fulfillment of a wish, reappears as the French *désir*. Moreover, just as Freud's *Traumdeutung* couples *Oedipus* and *Hamlet* in an implicit theory of intertextual interpretation through repression and mourning, Lacan too takes *Hamlet* as the specimen Shakespearean drama of desire and interpretation. It is here that Lacan reformulates the cliché of romance, the "object of desire", as the "object *in* desire", not as separate from but constituted by desire. This paradigm, moreover, describes the place of literature "in" psychoanalysis: the status of Shakespeare as a discourse that both informs the rhetorical habits of psychoanalytic thought and is retroactively rewritten by it. Finally, if literature stands in the place of "the object in" the interpretive desire of psychoanalysis, the feminine gendering of that object inflects the critical allegories of desire and its interpretation – an object understood, however, not as the passive, "objectified" recipient of male desire but as the bearer of an alienating enjoyment.

Lacan defines the "object in desire" in the course of explaining the formula for fantasy, $ \Diamond a$:

> I express the general structure of the fantasy by $ \Diamond a$, where $ is a certain relationship of the subject to the signifier – it is the subject as irreducibly affected by the signifier – and where $\Diamond$ indicates the subject's relationship to an essentially imaginary juncture [*conjoncture*], designated by *a*, not the object of desire but the object in desire [*l'objet dans le désir*] ... This is our starting point: through his relationship to the signifier, the subject is deprived of something of himself, of his very life, which has assumed the value of that which

> binds him to the signifier. The phallus is our term for the signifier of
> his alienation in signification. When the subject is deprived of this
> signifier, a particular object becomes for him an object of desire. This
> is the meaning of $ ◊ a.
>
> The object of desire is essentially different from the object of any
> need [*besoin*]. Something becomes an object in desire when it takes
> the place of what by its very nature remains concealed from the
> subject: that self-sacrifice, that pound of flesh which is mortgaged
> [*engagé*] in his relationship to the signifier.   ("Desire" 28)

The formula of fantasy designates the relation of a subject split and
alienated by language to an object that promises to compensate for
that fundamental lack. At this point in Lacan's thought, the *a* functions as the imaginary substitute for the real substratum of living
being ("something of himself, of his very life") forever blocked by
the symbolic accession to language. Here Lacan associates the
barring of the subject with the phallus, the castrating mark of linguistic substitution, which guarantees that the object exists only *in*
desire, that is, as the opaque "juncture" of real loss and imaginary
reparation in the field of symbolic relations mapped by language;
later in Lacan's work, the affiliation of the *objet a* with the real is
increasingly emphasized over its primarily imaginary function in
"Seminar VI".

The Shakespearean "pound of flesh," on loan here from *The
Merchant of Venice*, emblematizes the bodily *physis* cut off by symbolic castration and imaginarily stitched by the endless string of
objects in desire. Lacan alludes to *The Merchant of Venice* when he
evokes the phallus through intimations of castration and circum-
cision, but recall that the flesh demanded by Shylock comes from
the breast:

> *Portia:* Therefore lay bare your bosom.
> *Shylock:*   Ay, his breast,
> So says the bond, doth it not, noble judge?
> "Nearest his heart;" those are the very words.
>   (IV.i.252–55)

Across the text of Shakespeare, Lacan's notion of the phallus is
here articulated as the permanent mortgaging of the flesh by language. The "pound of flesh," associated with the corporeality and
jouissance of the maternal bosom, is cancelled and phallicized by
its very weighing into pounds, measure for measure: "The subject
is deprived of something of himself, of his very life, which has

assumed the value [*pris valeur*] of that which binds him to the signifier." The subject's corporeal life disappears into its primitive valuation as the phallus, the value of value that underwrites the symbolic economy of linguistic substitution. Through the agency of the phallus, the signifier of the subject's "bond" to and by language, the annulled flesh is remembered as the imaginary object of exchange whose purchase promises to restore the Nature lost in its commodification. The *objet a* is neither referent (the "flesh" of the living being) nor symbol (the "pound" of phallic calculation) but the mask and index of the referent's cancellation by the symbol – in the Hegelian vocabulary of the early Lacan, the *objet a* is the imaginary consolation left over from the murder of the Thing by the Word.[2]

The metonymic links of the signifying chain are instituted by a primal metaphor: "the metaphor of the Name-of-the-Father, that is, the metaphor that substitutes this Name in the place first symbolized by the operation of the absence of the mother" (*Écrits* 200). The father's name – language, the agency of the phallus – replaces not (as one might expect), the body or presence of the mother, but rather, in Lacan's careful formulation, "the absence of the mother", the place of an initial symbolization that marks the loss of corporeal *jouissance* through the entry into language. The "image and pathos" of this doubled metaphor, extended and remembered by metonymic desire, resurfaces in the immobilizing object of fantasy: "The enigmas that desire seems to pose ... amount to no other derangement of instinct than that of being caught in the rails – eternally stretching forth towards the *desire for something else* – of metonymy. Hence its 'perverse' fixation at the very suspension point of the signifying chain where the screen-memory [*souvenir-écran*] is immobilized and the fascinating image of the fetish is petrified [*se statufie*]" (*Écrits* 167; translation altered).[3] The object is "in" desire in two senses: both as an interchangeable element produced in the metonymic train of associations that constitutes desire as "the desire for something else", and as the opaque blockage, the fantasmatic girl tied to the tracks, which derails that train with fixed and fixating metaphors of the maternal body in the melodrama of fantasy. As the return of metaphor within metonymy, the object operates both as the lure projected by desire to keep it moving and as the hypnotic "image of the fetish", which stalls and stills the cinematic movement of symbolization in the perverse freeze-frames of fantasy.

The object in desire, Lacan writes, is "petrified" or "statufied" [*se statufie*], a tombstone which fetishistically allegorizes "the absence of the mother", imagining her presence by symbolically commemorating her loss.

In "Seminar VI", Lacan derives "the absence of the mother" from the dialectic of need, demand, and desire: "It is insofar as the Mother, site of the demand for love, is initially symbolized in the double register of presence and absence, that she is in a position to initiate the dialectic; she turns what the subject is really deprived of – the breast, for example – into a symbol of her love" ("Hamlet, par Lacan" 39). The Other of demand, embodied by the mother or primary caregiver, is the locus of the child's first expression of need whose verbalization fundamentally alienates the particularity of bodily requirements into the universal demand for love. The difference between need and demand, Lacan writes elsewhere, is desire, "the power of pure loss [that] emerges from the residue of an obliteration" (*Écrits* 287). As the demand for absolute love, demand always exceeds what is expressed; in this difference, the Other emerges as lacking, as unable or unwilling to fulfill the desire left unexpressed in the demand.[4] Lacan calls this lack the phallus, the signifier without signified, which marks both what the Other cannot provide the child and what the child cannot fulfill in the Other. In this narrative, the "real privation" of the breast only becomes the initial site of symbolization through the intermediate moment of demand, which dialecticizes bodily privation into symbolic lack through verbalization. Hence the breast for Lacan is only an example rather than an essential origin or source of symbolization, whereas the phallus, as the signifier of the lack in the Other, is necessary and unconditional – not because of its physiological nature or naturalness, but, on the contrary, because of its arbitrary status by definition as the marker of the intrinsically nonquantifiable quantity, the x of the mother's desire.[5] Finally, the *objet a* of fantasy functions as both the denial and the reminder of this lack in the Other; in Lacan's algebra, the *Autre* of demand (A), is barred ($\bar{A}$) by the encounter with its lack (Φ), a decompletion of the Other as the set of all signifiers. This lack in the Other is fetishistically crystallized and compensated through the *objet a* of fantasy ($\$ \lozenge a$); through this object carved out of the Other, the fantasy both stages the subject's separation from the Other and re-covers their break. As Lacan says, "It is from the phallus that the object gets its function in the fantasy, and from the phallus that desire is constituted with the fantasy as its referent" ("Desire" 15). Whereas in fantasy the phallus is replaced by the *objet a*, the phallus as signifier of lack also maintains the desire which takes fantasy as its "referent" or stopgap.

The formula for fantasy, that is, also describes fantasy as formulaic, as the fixed, conventional, even clichéd narrative – the "formula romance" – which at once stages and delimits the parameters of desire by "adapting" it to a fixed set of relations between the barred subject and its fantasmatic object.[6]

THE OBJECT OF A *JOUISSANCE*

As Bruce Fink has argued, for Lacan, Hamlet's problem is Gertrude. Rather than identifying Hamlet with Claudius – in the Oedipal narrative established by Freud – Lacan emphasizes Hamlet's subjection to the desire of the mother:

> Our first step ... was to express the extent to which the play is dominated by the Mother as Other [*Autre*], i.e., the primordial subject of the demand [*la demande*]. ... This desire, of the mother, is essentially manifested in the fact that, confronted on one hand with an eminent, idealized, exalted object – his father – and on the other with the degraded, despicable object Claudius, the criminal and adulterous brother, Hamlet does not choose.
>
> His mother does not choose because of something present inside her, like an instinctive voracity. The sacrosanct genital object that we recently added to our technical vocabulary appears to her as an object to be enjoyed [*objet d'une jouissance*] in what is truly the direct satisfaction of a need, and nothing else.   ("Desire" 12–13)

Lacan locates the essential vacillation of Hamlet's will in the field of Gertrude's ambiguous desire; in Lacan's reading, we might say, Hamlet is "too much in the mother." Although Hamlet encounters something in Gertrude other than the two of them – the possibility of a third position opened up in the mother/child dyad by the dialectic of demand – this space does not operate as the symbolic lack of an imaginary phallus, but is overfull with the real phallus, the *objet d'une jouissance*, which, in the vocabulary of the Lacan of this moment, provides "the direct satisfaction of a need", rather than the deferral of a desire.

Through the dependence of Hamlet's desire on the desire – or rather the enjoyment – of the (m)Other, Hamlet's flesh feels "too

too sullied", because his mother's flesh appears "too too solid", insufficiently barred through castration (I.ii.129).

"The phallus", says Lacan, "even the real phallus, is a *ghost* [*ombre*]" ("Desire" 50). The "reality" of the phallus, that is, designates not its empirical manifestation in an actual penis (itself never more than a poor substitute for the phallus), but rather what Lacan calls a "phallophany", the nauseating emergence of the nonsymbolized phallus from behind the veils of signification in the field of the (m)Other's demand ("Desire" 48–49). The phallus, Lacan explains, "is this thing that is presented by Freud as the key to the *Untergang* of the Oedipus complex. I say *thing* [*chose*] and not *object*, because it is a real thing [*chose réelle*], one that has not yet been made a symbol, but that has the potential of becoming one" ("Desire" 46). This phallic thing is both too real, because it is the object of *jouissance*, and not real enough, because it fills out and denies the lack in signification. In Lacan's *Hamlet*, Claudius, the shameless and incestuous usurper, parades the real phallus enjoyed by Gertrude, an adulterous and adulterating union grotesquely literalized in the enigmatic interchange between nephew and uncle:

> *Hamlet*: Farewell, dear mother.
> *Claudius*: Thy loving father, Hamlet.
> *Hamlet*: My mother. Father and mother is man and wife, man
> and wife is one flesh; so my
> mother.
>
> (IV.iii.52–55)

In Hamlet's mock syllogism, the "flesh" of Claudius and Gertrude is joined in an antisacrament that corresponds to and replaces the dialectical union of the Pauline couple, joined in charity through the mediation of the Divine Third, with the mutated and contaminated fleshiness of the maternal body obscenely enjoying the real phallus. In *Hamlet*, Lacan says, "the Oedipal situation ... appears in the particularly striking form in the real" ("Desire" 51). Although in the Freudian staging of desire and its interpretation *Hamlet* offers a repressed, temporally remote version of *Oedipus Rex*, in Lacan's analysis, Oedipus is not so much distanced by repression as too close for comfort.

In Lacan's staging of the play, Ophelia is cast as the "object in desire" whose death provides Hamlet with some access to castration, and hence to the articulation of desire, through mourning. In acts 2 and 3, Ophelia, whom Hamlet rejects by equating her with the overbearing corporeality of his mother, comes to embody for Hamlet the flagrant grossness of the real phallus as the *objet d'une jouissance*. Tendentiously glossing her as "*O phallos*", Lacan comments that Ophelia is "exteriorized and rejected by the subject as a symbol signifying life ... the bearer of that vital swelling that he curses and wishes dried up forever" ("Desire" 23). In her death, Lacan argues, Ophelia is "reintegrated" as an object in desire: the graveyard scene "is directed towards that furious battle at the bottom of the tomb. ... Here we see something like a reintegration of the object *a*, won back here at the price of mourning and death" ("Desire" 24).

The object in desire is a dead object, a situation that defines the (masculine) structure of the obsessional neurotic, who can only desire something when it is radically unattainable: "Only insofar as the object of Hamlet's desire has become an impossible object can it become once more the object of his desire. ... [The obsessional neurotic] sets everything up so that the object of his desire becomes the signifier of this impossibility" ("Desire" 36). This condition of masculine desire, reworked in the poetics of the beautiful dead woman from Petrarch to David Lynch, has the further consequence of not only petrifying the feminine object, but also of deadening the male subject who identifies with loss.

The death of Ophelia stages Lacan's question, "What is the connection between mourning and the constitution of the object in desire?" ("Desire" 36). In order for the object to be "won back" as an object "in" desire, it must be killed and mourned, a process Lacan describes as the mobilization of the imaginary and symbolic orders in relation to a "hole in the real":

> Where is the gap, the hole that results from this loss and that calls forth mourning on the part of the subject? It is in the real ... Just as what is rejected from the symbolic register reappears in the real, in the same way the hole of loss in the real [*le trou de la perte dans le réel*] sets the signifier in motion. This hole provides the place for the projection of the missing signifier, which is essential to the structure of the Other. This is the signifier whose absence leaves the Other incapable of responding to your question, the signifier that can be purchased only with your own flesh and your own blood, the signifier that is essentially the veiled phallus.
>
> It is there that this signifier finds its place. Yet at the same time it cannot find it, for it can be articulated only at the level of the Other. It is at this point that, as in psychosis – this is where

mourning and psychosis are related – swarms of images, from which
the phenomena of mourning arise, assume the place of the phallus.
("Desire" 37–38, translation altered)

The "hole of loss in the real", evacuated by the occasion of
bereavement, Lacan says, reappears in the symbolic order, the field
of the Other, which is itself decompleted or barred by that loss;
normative mourning arises in turn as the installation of symbolic
and imaginary formations that both mark and mask loss, and in
the process (re)configure the object of mourning as an object "in"
desire. In the symbolic place cleared by real loss, the subject projects "the missing signifier", that is, the phallus that signifies the
lack in the Other, S(A̸).

The subject's access to the object as lost occurs only through a
third party: since Gertrude, as Lacan says in "Seminar X", demonstrates an "absence of mourning" (3 July 1963, 397), Hamlet's
mourning – and hence his desire – is also dysfunctional. "Swarms of
images" bordering on hallucination (the Ghost that his mother
cannot see) take the place of symbolic substitutes ("your father
lost a father; / That father lost, lost his" [I.ii.89–90]). The death
of Ophelia, as well as the murder of Polonius, are, according to
Lacan, ritual sacrifices in expiation of the unmourned loss of the
father, attempts to institute a lack that can be adequately mourned
("Desire" 39).

The object is constituted in desire through mourning, as a replay
and substitute for a loss that always exceeds, precedes, and
shadows the object "in question" – in the subject's question to the
Other.

If Gertrude holds the place of the *Autre* of demand in Lacan's
reading, the lack in the symbolic Other (the something rotten in the
state of Denmark), initially filled and filled up by Claudius as the
real phallus, is ultimately marked by the death of Ophelia and her
reconstitution in mourning as Hamlet's impossible *objet a*.

We would emphasize that, although Ophelia appears as the
means of Hamlet's separation from his mother through the acquisition of a new object – the "classical" Freudian narrative of Oedipal-
ization – Ophelia is nonetheless continually linked in the play to
Gertrude, and to Gertrude not as object of incestuous desire but as
maternal Other of demand.

Thus Hamlet's early conflation of Ophelia and Gertrude in the
fantasmatic projection of their voracious sexualities is born out in

Ophelia's erotic songs, which use the theatre of madness to stage the crossing of the Other of demand and the object of desire in the fundamental fantasy of Hamlet and *Hamlet*. In her mad scene, Ophelia insistently demands an audience not with Claudius but with Gertrude: "She is importunate, / Indeed distract", says the Gentleman to the Queen; "Where is the beauteous Majesty of Denmark?" cries Ophelia (IV.v.2–3, 21). Although the two women are separated out for Hamlet in the idealizing aftereffects of Ophelia's death, it is nonetheless Gertrude who narrates Ophelia's drowning, once again merging the two figures in the fluidly specular language of melancholy ("There is a willow grows askant the brook / That shows his hoary leaves in the glassy stream ..." [IV.vii.165–6]). At Ophelia's grave, Gertrude's elegiac substitution, "Sweets for the sweet", weaves the shattered signifiers of Ophelia's scattered flowers into the formal garlands of elegiac metaphor; and even as the lines promote the symbolizing work of mourning, their doubling, quasi-tautological equation also continues to manifest the intransigent link between Ophelia and Gertrude, object and Other, in the scene of Hamlet's desire. Finally, the two women are linked in death; Ophelia's garments, "heavy with their drink", pull her to her death (IV.vii.180); Gertrude dies by drinking from the poisoned goblet, as her last words obsessively reiterate: "No, no, the drink, the drink! O my dear Hamlet! / The drink, the drink! I am poison'd" (V.ii.315–16). Each dies "heavy with drink": echoing Hamlet's first soliloquy, we could say that Gertrude and Ophelia "melt, thaw, and resolve ... into a dew", condensing liquid and solid by virtue of their watery weightiness.[7]

NOTES

[Julia Reinhard Lupton and Kenneth Reinhard are Associate Professors of English and Comparative Literature at the University of California. They are co-authors of "Shapes of Grief: Freud, Hamlet, and Mourning" (1989) and *After Oedipus: Shakespeare in Psychoanalysis* (1993). Julia Reinhard Lupton has published *Afterlives of the Saints: Hagiography, Typology, and Renaissance Literature* (1996), and work on Shakespeare includes "Othello Circumcised: Shakespeare and the Pauline Discourse of Nations" (1997), "Creature Caliban" (2000) and "The Gertrude Barometer: Teaching Shakespeare with Freud, Eliot, and Lacan" (2001). Kenneth Reinhard is Director of the Center for Jewish studies at UCLA; his writings on psycho-analysis, literature and culture include "The Freudian Things: Construction and the Archaeological Metaphor" (1996), "The Jamesian Thing: *The Wings of the Dove* and the Ethics of Mourning" (1997) and "Coming to America: Psychoanalytic Criticism in the Age of Žižek" (2001).   Ed.]

1.   For the textual debate on the reading of Q2 "sallied" versus the Folio "solid", see Harold Jenkins's note to this line in the *Arden Hamlet* (436–38). References to *Hamlet* are to this edition.

2.   See Lacan, *Speech and Language in Psychoanalysis* 84, and Žižek, *The Sublime Object of Ideology* 131.

3.   See Malcolm Bowie's careful reading of the train imagery in this passage (*Lacan* 132–33). On the construction of the object out of metaphor and metonymy, see Jean Laplanche, *Life and Death in Psychoanalysis*, especially 66–84.

4.   For a clear account of demand in Lacan, see Elizabeth Grosz, *Jacques Lacan* 61–66.

5.   See J.-A. Miller, "To Interpret the Cause": "We do not know what she wants. And we do not know what and where she enjoys. The meaning of the phallus, in this sense is, precisely, to give an answer to this X ..." (46).

6.   Žižek defines fantasy: "What the fantasy stages is not a scene in which our desire is fulfilled, fully satisfied, but on the contrary, a scene that realises, stages, the desire as such ..." (*Looking Awry* 6).

7.   Alice Crawford pointed out to us the "drink link" between Ophelia and Gertrude.

3

Family Romance or Family History? Psychoanalysis and Dramatic Invention in Nicolas Abraham's "The Phantom of Hamlet"

NICHOLAS RAND

> A voice from another world ... demands vengeance for a monstrous enormity, and the demand remains without effect; the criminals are at last punished, but, as it were, by an accidental blow ... irresolute foresight, cunning treachery, and impetuous rage hurry on to a common destruction. ... The destiny of humanity is exhibited as a gigantic Sphinx, which threatens to precipitate into the abyss of scepticism all who are unable to solve her dreadful enigmas.
>
> A.W. Schlegel, *Lectures on Dramatic Art and Literature*

Nicolas Abraham's "The Phantom of Hamlet", written in 1975 as a sixth act to follow Shakespeare's *Hamlet*, is both intimately linked with and contrary to traditions of *Hamlet* criticism prevalent since the eighteenth century. His dramatic sequel reverses the effect of the final scenes of *Hamlet* by bringing the murdered Prince and the ghost once more on stage, and ends in the crowning of Hamlet as King of Denmark. This event follows an exchange among Hamlet, the ghost of his father, Horatio, and young Fortinbras. Assuming the role of psychoanalyst, Fortinbras investigates the probable reasons for the destruction of the royal family of Denmark (King

Hamlet, Claudius, Gertrude, Prince Hamlet) along with the House of Polonius (Polonius, Ophelia, Laertes). He questions the ghost's reasons for demanding vengeance and wonders why Hamlet's interview with the ghost throws the prince into confusion instead of spurring him to action. Fortinbras further suggests that the ghost's appearance itself, and not Hamlet's indecision, is the appropriate object of inquiry. Piecing together clues from the first act, young Fortinbras conjectures that the six characters who were killed or committed suicide in Shakespeare's tragedy were doomed by the devastating effects of secret crimes. The precise nature of the crimes comes to light when Fortinbras links the double poisoning of foil and drink in the duel of Hamlet and Laertes [act 5] to Horatio's account [act 1] of another duel, one that took place between Kings Hamlet and Fortinbras on the day of Hamlet's birth, some thirty years prior to the action of the play. In this duel, King Hamlet appears to have used a poisoned sword. Young Fortinbras seeks to discover the identity of the original poisoner and finds – in the actions of Laertes, and in the madness and suicide of Ophelia – sufficient evidence to surmise that the poisoner was their father, Polonius. Polonius, who served as instigator for two separate murders, those of King Fortinbras and King Hamlet, becomes one of the pivotal figures in Abraham's "Phantom of Hamlet." Abraham gives Polonius a political motive for his crime: the desire to avenge his country, Poland, which at various times had been conquered by both King Hamlet's Denmark and Fortinbras's Norway. These clarifications explain Hamlet's paralysis: because his father was himself a murderer, he cannot be avenged.

Shakespeare's *Hamlet* has been aptly called the "Mona Lisa" of literature. The play has enjoyed the same mixture of admiration and incomprehension as its pictorial counterpart. The placidly mysterious smile of Mona Lisa and Hamlet's tortured inaction have for centuries fascinated those who hoped to discover their essence or bring the clandestine core of their being to light. The comparison with Mona Lisa suggests that the character of Hamlet is an impenetrable surface whose features – perhaps through the utterly arresting finish of the depiction – fail to yield the depth requisite to make their humanity credible. Abraham responds to Hamlet's final plea:

> Horatio, I am dead.
> Thou livest; report me and my cause aright
> To the unsatisfied... .

O God, Horatio, what a wounded name,
Things standing thus unknown, shall live behind me!
If thou didst ever hold me in thy heart,
Absent thee from felicity awhile,
And in this harsh world draw thy breath in pain,
To tell my story.   [5.2]

At the start of "The Phantom of Hamlet," Fortinbras and Horatio, acting on Hamlet's behalf, make a pact to unravel the mystery. Fortinbras says:

This Prince to me, his successor, bequeathed
You, Horatio, his faithful witness,
His bosom friend, his heart's most inward ear,
Alert to secrets th' mind prefers to shun... .
I plead we may as one to daylight bring,
Amid the shapes which to our eyes appear,
The unseen web iniquity has cast.   [6.1]

Fortinbras, having been given Hamlet's "dying voice," opens the story sealed in Hamlet's final words: "the rest is silence" [5.2].

Transcending this silence through a psychological explanation for Hamlet's inaction was the aim of Sigmund Freud and Ernest Jones. The early psychoanalytic interpretation rests on a thematic comparison between *Oedipus Rex* by Sophocles and Shakespeare's *Hamlet*. Oedipus's unwitting parricide and incest with his mother are seen as the tragic fulfillment of a universal unconscious wish to eliminate the male child's rival for his mother's affection. Freud writes in *The Interpretation of Dreams* (1900):

Another of the great creations of tragic poetry, Shakespeare's *Hamlet*, has its roots in the same soil as *Oedipus Rex*. But the changed treatment of the same material reveals the whole difference in the mental life of these two widely separated epochs of civilization; the secular advance of repression in the emotional life of mankind. In the *Oedipus* the child's wishful phantasy that underlies it is brought into the open and realized as it would be in a dream. In *Hamlet* it remains repressed; and – just as in a neurosis – we only learn of its existence from its inhibiting consequences. Strangely enough, the overwhelming effect produced by the more modern tragedy has turned out to be compatible with the fact that people have remained completely in the dark as to the hero's character. The play is built upon Hamlet's hesitations over fulfilling the

task of revenge that is assigned to him; but its text offers no
reasons or motives for these hesitations and an immense variety of
attempts at interpreting them have failed to produce a result. ...
The plot of the drama shows us, however, that Hamlet is far from
being represented as a person incapable of taking any action. ...
What is it, then, that inhibits him in fulfilling the task set him by
his father's ghost? The answer, once again, is that it is the peculiar
nature of the task. Hamlet is able to do anything – except take
vengeance on the man who did away with his father and took that
father's place with his mother, the man who shows him the repressed wishes of his own childhood realized. Here I have translated into conscious terms what was bound to remain unconscious
in Hamlet's mind.   (*PF* 4: 366–67).

Both Freud and later Jones [in *Hamlet and Oedipus*, 1949] rely on
the twofold hypothesis that "Hamlet at heart does not want to
carry out the task" (Jones 45) of revenge, and that his countermo-
tive – the satisfaction of seeing his father dead – is entirely hidden
from him.[1]

"The Phantom of Hamlet", too, is infused with the Freudian idea
that Hamlet's hesitation has an unconscious psychological basis
which, though hidden, can be revealed. Yet the two interpretations
diverge because Freud and Abraham seek their explanations
for Hamlet's behaviour in different sources: Freud in universal infantile complexes and Abraham in the text itself. In Freud's view,
Shakespeare's *Hamlet* draws on a store of ideas absent from the
play (the "text offers no reasons or motives") but present in every
male child's mind. Hamlet, the would-be avenger, is a would-be
parricide whose long-dormant wish has become a harrowing
reality. The symptom of inaction becomes transparent once the infantile mental configuration is supplied, that is, once the general ap-
plicability of the Oedipus complex is recognized. The idea of
repression allows Freud to see the Oedipus complex at work even
though no trace of it can be found in the play. In Jones's words: "If
such thoughts had been present in [Hamlet's] mind, they evidently
would have been 'repressed', and all traces of them obliterated"
(70). Freud assumes that, due to repression, no reason can be given
in the play and therefore he seeks a solution outside it. Abraham
conjectures that the motive, though not stated, can be constructed
from the complex of events and forces in the tragedy. While for
Freud and Jones, Hamlet's inaction is readily understood as part of
a generalizable neurotic syndrome (resulting from an unresolved

Oedipus complex), Abraham sees Hamlet's symptom as a Sphinx-like riddle – to be answered with the aid of Shakespeare's text. The difference between the two conceptions affects the attitude adopted toward Hamlet. While Freud and Jones see Hamlet's predicament in his inability to acknowledge unconscious desires not to act, Abraham interprets Hamlet's confused hesitancy as the symptom of a genuine desire to act that has been inhibited or thwarted. For Freud and Jones, Hamlet is a typically duplicitous neurotic whose flight into illness guarantees the avoidance of unbearable fantasies; Abraham considers Hamlet's repeatedly stated perplexity a symptom of his being someone else's involuntary instrument. Based on his evaluation of hints found in the play, Abraham suggests that the source of Hamlet's behaviour is not himself but the secret influence of an other.

Once the idea that the *Tragedy of Hamlet* conceals a mystery is taken seriously, the psychoanalysis of the entire play (and not simply of the hero) can be founded on the following methodological premise: the plot, the characters, their speeches, their death, and even perhaps their names tacitly refer to unstated or concealed events and actions that took place before the first scene of the play. Shakespeare's tragedy is then symbolically viewed as a vast grave-yard scene in which the context for a hypothetical secret has remained buried.

In act I of *Hamlet*, the ghost's apparition is accompanied by a persistent need for secrecy. Horatio to Hamlet:

> Two nights together had these gentlemen,
> Marcellus and Bernardo, on their march ...
> Been thus encountered. A figure like your father, ...
> Appears before them, and with solemn march
> Goes slow and stately by them ...
> This to me
> In dreadful secrecy impart they did.
> [1.2]

Hamlet to Horatio, Marcellus, and Bernardo:

> I pray you all,
> If you have hitherto concealed this sight,
> Let it be tenable in your silence still,
> And whatsoever else shall hap tonight,
> Give it an understanding but no tongue;
> [1.2]

Dialogue between Hamlet and Horatio after the interview with the ghost:

> *Hor.*   What news, my lord?
> *Ham.* O, wonderful!
> *Hor.* Good my lord, tell it.
> *Ham.*   No, you will reveal it.
> *Hor.* Not I, my lord, by heaven ...
> *Ham.* How say you then? Would heart of man once think it? But
>   you'll be secret?
>
>   [1.5]

Hamlet bids his three companions swear and swear again:

> *Ham.* Never make known what you have seen tonight.
> *Both.* My lord, we will not.
> *Ham.*   Nay, but swear't.
> *Hor.*   In faith,
> My lord, not I ...
> *Ham.* Upon my sword.
> *Marc.*   We have sworn, my lord, already.
> *Ham.* Indeed, upon my sword, indeed.
>
>   [1.5]

Before they can consent to swear again, the ghost cries under stage:

> *Ghost.* Swear.
> *Ham.* ... Consent to swear.
> *Hor.*   Propose the oath, my lord.
> *Ham.* Never to speak of this that you have seen.
> Swear by my sword.
>
>   [1.5]

The ghost calls on them twice more. They repeat their vows of secrecy, yet upon entering the castle, Hamlet again says: "And still your fingers on your lips, I pray" [1.5].

What an extraordinary insistence on secrecy this is! It links Hamlet and the ghost of his father. But to what end? Shakespeare's play does not tell us explicitly. In the context of "The Phantom of Hamlet", the calls for secrecy signal the presence of a secret out of both Hamlet's and his companions' reach. Here, the excessive secrecy functions as the telltale symptom of a genuinely inaccessible secret. What the ghost tells Hamlet is but a part, itself merely the trace of a silence the ghost declines to break.

> I am thy father's spirit,
> Doomed for a certain term to walk the night,
> And for the day confined to fast in fires,
> Till the foul crimes done in my days of nature
> Are burned and purged away. But that I am forbid
> To tell the secrets of my prison house,
> I could a tale unfold ...
> Revenge his foul and most unnatural murder ...
> Murder most foul, as in the best it is,
> But this most foul, strange and unnatural.
>
> [1.5]

As before, even here insistence is a clue. The word "foul" recurs four times, once in self-reference to the crimes of the ghost, thrice referring to the murder committed by Claudius. Horatio completes the series of hints addressing the ghost:

> If thou hast sound or use of voice,
> Speak to me ...
> ... if thou hast uphoarded in thy life
> Extorted treasure in the womb of earth,
> For which, they say, you spirits oft walk in death,
> Speak of it. Stay and speak.
>
> [1.1]

The psychoanalyst-detective has a suspicion: the ghost walks with a secret, seeming to reveal one while withholding another. "Claudius is a murderer, let there be no secret! But why I am doomed to walk, none will ever know."[2]

In Abraham's fiction, Fortinbras the analyst contends that traces of King Hamlet's secret are scattered throughout Shakespeare's text. No more than traces; the "rest" unfolds as the invention of the psychoanalytic imagination. One clue is the "union" – the pearl. "Richer than that which four successive Kings / In Denmark's crown have worn" [5.2] – that Claudius dropped in Hamlet's poisoned cup. It tells of poison at the root of Claudius and Gertrude's union. Hamlet in act 5 says: "Here, thou incestuous, murd' rous, damned Dane, / Drink off this potion. Is thy union here? / Follow my mother" [5.2]. The poison-laden union bespeaks foul play in the union of lands that occurred when King Hamlet slew King Fortinbras, "who did forfeit, with his life all those lands / Which he stood seized of, to the conqueror" [1.1]. These facts and clues combine with invention in "The Phantom of Hamlet" to reveal a situation that remained out of reach for Shakespeare's Hamlet.

A situation concerning King Hamlet's duel with King Fortinbras of Norway can be imagined, given that the ghost's appearance evokes that contest in Horatio's mind: "Such was the very armour he had on / When he the ambitious Norway combated" [1.1]. The ghost intends to reveal his murder by Claudius, yet he comes dressed in the armour that is linked to his duel with the King of Norway.

> What may this mean
> That thou, dead corse, again in complete steel,
> Revisits thus the glimpses of the moon,
> Making night hideous, and we fools of nature
> So horridly to shake our disposition
> With thoughts beyond the reaches of our souls?
> Say, why is this?
>
> [1.4]

Nowhere in the play does Hamlet receive an answer. Fortinbras provides one in "The Phantom of Hamlet." "The story opens with a wager. With a wager it nearly ended. ... Of the two duels, fought thirty years apart, the second must include the first ... A memory must have inspired [Laertes] to anoint his sword with poison" [6.5].

Claudius and Laertes conspired to poison the naked sword and royal drink. Why resort to risky stratagems when Laertes was ready to avenge his father's murder openly by cutting Hamlet's throat in church? Why does the King bid Laertes keep close within his chamber and in secret requite Hamlet for his father? In *Hamlet* secrecy appears to outweigh the need for revenge. The venomous plotters Claudius and Laertes are heirs to King Hamlet and Polonius. Could their actions repeat their elders'? Was King Hamlet, murdered by Claudius, a secret murderer? Was Polonius, whose son proposes poison, in truth a poisoner? This is what young Fortinbras deduces in "The Phantom of Hamlet."[3] Fortinbras further imagines that Polonius successively served Kings Fortinbras, Hamlet, and Claudius, providing each in turn with his deadly in-struments.[4] But why Polonius, and how did he come to be associated with Kings Hamlet and Fortinbras? Listen again to Horatio speaking of the ghost in act 1, scene 1:

> Such was the very armour he had on
> When he the ambitious Norway combated:
> So frowned he once, when, in an angry parle,
> He smote the sledded Polacks on the ice.
> 'Tis strange.

[1.1]

In "The Phantom of Hamlet," Polonius – whose name means Poland – is assumed to be a compatriot of the "Polacks" attacked by King Hamlet. Moreover, young Fortinbras – "with conquest come from Poland" [5.2] – might well imagine that his own triumphant "Polack wars" are but the continuation of his father's, waged in competition with King Hamlet. Abraham hypothesizes that Polonius, caught between rivals equally bent on conquering his country, vowed to have revenge on both; he contrived to have King Fortinbras killed by old Hamlet and helped the latter perish at the hands of Claudius. What else might he have done, had he not himself been slain? Killed Claudius and had Laertes elected King?

Abraham's "Phantom of Hamlet" creates a prehistory for Shakespeare's *Hamlet* with the purpose of extrapolating *from the play* a fictive dramatic and psychological situation that motivates the symptom of Hamlet's blunted revenge. Abraham locates in the vengeful actions of Polonius the ultimate source of the drama.[5] From Polonius's scheming flows the rigged duel between Kings Hamlet and Fortinbras, resulting in the latter's murder. On the day of the infamous combat was born Prince Hamlet, the unwitting heir to a crime perpetrated in secret by his father. Hamlet's psychic inheritance of the secret occurs through the tacit transmission of his mother, whose thwarted love for the dead Fortinbras of Norway motivates her complicity in poisoning King Hamlet. Hamlet's haunting confusion or "phantom" is provoked by his unconsciously dawning yet incredulous suspicion that something shameful was left unsaid during the life of the deceased.[6] The Sphinx-like quality of Shakespeare's play is derived from the faint yet pervasive presence of a secret shared silently by some (Polonius, Claudius, Gertrude) and insidiously haunting others (Hamlet, Ophelia, Laertes).

Abraham considers the perplexity of readers to be an echo of the play itself. Hamlet's own dilatory speculation and bafflement at the absence of motive for his inaction are paralleled by the myriad efforts to interpret his predicament.

> I do not know
> Why yet I live to say this thing's to do,
> Sith I have cause, and will, and strength, and means
> To do't ...
>   How stand I then,
> That have a father killed, a mother stained,
> Excitements of my reason and my blood,
> And let all sleep
>
>   [4.4]

> O what a rogue and peasant slave am I!
> Is it not monstrous that this player here,
> But in a fiction, in a dream of passion,
> Could force his soul so to his own conceit
> That from her working all his visage wanned,
> Tears in his eyes, distraction in's aspect ...
>   And all for nothing? ...
>   What would he do,
> Had he the motive and the cue for passion
> That I have? ...
> Yet I,
> A dull and muddy-mettled rascal, peak
> Like John-a-dreams, unpregnant of my cause,
> And can say nothing – no, not for a king,
> Upon whose property and most dear life
> A damned defeat was made. Am I a coward?
> Who calls me villain, breaks my pate across,
> Plucks off my beard and blows it in my face,
> Tweaks me by th'nose, gives me the lie i' th'throat
> As deep as to the lungs? Who does me this?
>   [2.2]

Hamlet's question "Who does me this?" receives an answer in "The Phantom of Hamlet." By revealing a secret and inventing concealed dramas in King Hamlet, Gertrude, and Polonius's past, Abraham lends coherence to aspects of the play that have been repeatedly designated as inconsistencies.

Shakespeare's *Hamlet* is traditionally classified as a revenge tragedy. Yet, as our four-centuries-old fascination has shown, it is also a tragedy of enigma. Abraham's sequel proposes that the fateful acts happen before the opening but are never revealed to the hero. In this respect, *Hamlet* is radically different from *Oedipus*

Rex. While in *Oedipus Rex* – another revenge tragedy – the decisive act (the murder of Laius) also occurs before the opening, the play itself performs an investigation, the murderer is found, and the crime is avenged. In *Hamlet*, too, a murder has been committed before the first scene and an investigation carried out, through the ploy of Hamlet's *Mousetrap*, a part of the drama itself. The murderer is found – yet no revenge takes place. As in *Oedipus Rex*, our attention is gradually focused on the inquirer himself. In the ancient play, the process of self-discovery by Oedipus constitutes the plot, and the recognition of his identity coincides with the climax of the tragedy. In Shakespeare's *Hamlet*, the process of inquiry remains incomplete since the recognition of King Hamlet's murderer does not produce the clarity necessary for the play to reach its cathartic resolution. Whereas in *Oedipus Rex* the revelation sought is achieved, in *Hamlet* what persists, despite the investigation, is a bewildering sense of nonrevelation. "The Phantom of Hamlet" provides Shakespeare's play with a fictive structure of catharsis similar to that of *Oedipus Rex*. The inquiry is carried to the end until all the precipitating causes of the tragedy have been revealed or invented. "The Phantom of Hamlet" thus supplies the process of discovery exemplified in *Oedipus Rex* but mysteriously absent from *Hamlet*. By casting young Fortinbras as the analyst of secret dramas inherited from another generation, to which Hamlet's perturbed mind is an unwitting host, Abraham has created an emblematic expression of psychoanalytic inquiry into haunting. He has thereby altered the terms of *Hamlet* criticism, since the hero's inaction has ceased to be the main focus of the inquiry. Rather, Abraham sees in the general obscurity and structural unrest of the play a mark of the unspeakable secret that constitutes its unrevealed core.

NOTES

[Nicholas Rand is Professor of French at the University of Wisconsin-Madison, and is editor, translator and executor of the works of Nicolas Abraham and Maria Torok. His translation of Abraham's "The Phantom of Hamlet" appears in his Chicago edition of Abraham's and Torok's *The Shell and the Kernel*; he is the translator of their *The Wolf Man's Magic Word* (see Essay 8). He has published numerous articles and books with Maria Torok, including " 'The Sandman' looks at the 'Uncanny'" (1994) and *Questions for Freud: The Secret History of Psychoanalysis* (1997). Recent publications on psychoanalysis include "The Talking Cure: Origins of Psychoanalysis" (2001) and *Psychoanalysis and Literature* (2004). Ed.]

1. Jones sees in the potential reawakening of repressed infantile wishes (parricide and incest) the source of Hamlet's conflict: Hamlet is torn between filial piety and the murder of Claudius, the man who in broad daylight embodies desires which must remain unconscious. Killing his father's murderer would be tantamount to Hamlet's mental annihilation since such an act would expose thoughts he could not consciously tolerate.

2. This reconstruction of clues constitutes the groundwork of Abraham's premise: "The 'secret' revealed by Hamlet's 'phantom' ... is merely a subterfuge. It masks another secret, this one genuine and truthful, but resulting from an infamy which the father, unbeknown to his son, has on his conscience" ("The Phantom of Hamlet", *SK* 188–89).

3. Ophelia's madness – called "the poison of deep grief" by Claudius – combined with her suicide amid fantastic weeds, seems to Fortinbras a further conviction of Polonius. Let Polonius's foul deeds be seen the "dead man's fingers" (4.6) with weeds and flowers wrought confusion followed by death.

4. Claudius hints at the crucial role Polonius has played in his acquiring the crown. He displays gratitude when speaking to Laertes: "The head is not more native to the heart, / The head more instrumental to the mouth, / Than is the throne of Denmark to thy father" (1.2).

5. Abraham calls this the ultimate and abominable "Truth" of the play. The "truth" (in Abraham's cautionary quotation marks) is understood here as the wilfully concealed point of origin whose manifestations are consequently lies.

6. Elaborating on the interpersonal consequences of silence, the concept of the phantom is a direct extension of Abraham and Torok's work on secrets and crypts. See their *The Wolf Man's Magic Word: A Cryptonymy* and Abraham's "Notes on the Phantom" (*SK* 171–176).

Part II
E.T.A. Hoffmann, "The Sandman"; Sigmund Freud, "The 'Uncanny'"

Introductory Note

UNCANNY LITERATURE – FREUD AND THE "UNCANNY"

"The dimension of the uncanny, introduced by Freud in his famous paper, is located at the very core of psychoanalysis", says Mladen Dolar ("'I Shall Be With You'" 5).

One wouldn't have thought it from Freud.

Freud starts his essay of 1919, "The 'Uncanny'", by saying that the uncanny has "little to do" with psychoanalysis and belongs instead to "aesthetics". He writes: "It is only rarely that a psychoanalyst *feels impelled* to investigate the subject of aesthetics ... The writer of the present contribution, indeed, must himself plead guilty to a special obtuseness in the matter, where extreme delicacy of perception would be more in place. It is long since he has experienced or heard of anything which has given him an uncanny impression" (*PF* 14: 339, 340; my emphasis).

It hardly sounds like a promising beginning. Freud says that he feels "impelled" to investigate the uncanny – as if, driven, he is in the grip of the very thing that he is trying to investigate, as if he is somehow controlled "by" the uncanny rather than mastering its meaning himself. It is as if, strangely, the uncanny leads Freud away from himself, leads him astray – and as if it leads psychoanalysis away from itself, too, into aesthetics, into literature. Disconcertingly – "uncannily", even.

In fact, Freud never quite knows how to find his way about in the uncanny, never knows quite how to approach it. He argues that the uncanny belongs to aesthetics – and above all to literature – but devotes the first part of his essay to a conspectus of the dictionary definition of the word, namely, the range of meanings of the German word "unheimlich". It is only after this that he returns to the aesthetic – to E.T.A. Hoffmann's story "The Sandman", in fact – but then proceeds to enumerate instances of the uncanny from "real life" (*PF* 14: 373) that take him once more far from the field of aesthetics. It is as if Freud keeps getting distracted, keeps losing his focus – keeps taking his eyes off the "common core" (*PF* 14: 339) of meaning of the uncanny that he is seeking. It is almost as if Freud can't keep things in perspective – rather like the disoriented and mad student of Hoffmann's narrative itself, Nathaniel, who metaphorically loses his "eyes" in an uncanny play of disrupted perspectives. Towards the end of his essay Freud comes back to the question of literature, but, as we will see, it would be better to say that the question of literature *comes back to him*, returning like the repressed to haunt him and rob him (as Nathaniel is in the story) of his theoretical "eyes".

From the beginning, the uncanny is constituted in Freud's essay as a *division* of meaning. Indeed, Freud's excurse through the dictionary at the start yields less a "common core" of significance than a splitting of sense. He notes that though the German word "heimlich" designates the "homely", "tame" or "familiar" – everything that "belong[s] to the house" and is "intimate" (*PF* 14: 342) – and the "unheimlich" denotes the "opposite of what is familiar", the unknown or unfamiliar (*PF* 14: 341), there is a "shade[...] of meaning" of the "heimlich" that in fact *coincides* with its opposite, the "unheimlich" (*PF* 14: 345). This is when something is *too* cosy and intimate and, eerily, suggests something "withdrawn from the eyes of strangers, something concealed, secret"; in this way, the "heimlich" becomes "unheimlich". Freud comments, "Thus *heimlich* is a word the meaning of which develops in the direction of ambivalence, until it finally coincides with its opposite, *unheimlich*. Unheimlich* is in some way or other a subspecies of *heimlich*" (*PF* 14: 346, 347). To this extent, the word "heimlich" falls prey to its opposite, and becomes strangely "unheimlich" or *un*familiar to itself; as a linguistic effect it becomes, we might say, "uncanny" to itself. Julia Kristeva remarks that in Freud the uncanny designates the "immanence of the strange within the familiar" (*Strangers to Ourselves* 182–3), and to the extent that this is so *with the word* itself, Freud pursues his argument from the beginning in a field of linguistic and textual instability. The "uncanny" as a sign will not stay still; it is unstable, troubling, disturbing. It is uncanny. Like aesthetics, like literature, it seems that Freud is unable to hold the "uncanny" in place.

Freud notes admiringly that, in the field of literature, E.T.A. Hoffmann is the "writer who has succeeded in producing uncanny effects better than anyone else". But Freud rejects the psychologist Jentsch's view that Hoffmann's uncanny effects derive from his textual play with automata in which, says Freud, there is a doubt whether "an apparently animate being is really alive" (*PF* 14: 347). Instancing Hoffmann's 1816 tale "The Sandman", Freud argues that the uncanny in the story is embodied not by the automaton figure Olympia, but by the fantasy or nightmare figure of the tale, the "Sandman". This is because the Sandman, according to Freud, incarnates Nathaniel's infant or unconscious fears of castration. In Nathaniel's imagination, the Sandman – a figure from nursery tales who is supposed to throw "sand" in children's eyes as sleep descends on them – is reconfigured in frightening form as a monster who "tears out children's eyes" (*PF* 14: 348). Offering this reading, Freud believes that he is on secure ground, psychoanalytic (rather than aesthetic) ground, and asserts: "We know from psychoanalytic experience … that the fear of damaging or losing one's eyes is a terrible one in children … [it] is often enough a substitute for the dread of being castrated". He adds that there is a "substitutive relation between the eye and the male organ" (*PF* 14: 352), and in this vein reads "The Sandman" as if it were a psychoanalytic case study of castration anxiety, the main character Nathaniel amounting to no more than an imaginary patient on the analytic couch.

Here, it is as if literature did not exist, as if literature had disappeared into psychoanalytic theory.

Read in effect as a case history, it is as if "The Sandman" for Freud were not literature at all but psychoanalysis, as if psychoanalysis had absorbed fiction (or the aesthetic) into itself, annexed literature to theory and found its own truth in literature – but left literature alone. Literature (as Sarah Kofman, Hélène Cixous and Lis Møller point out in the following essays) gets forgotten. Literature gets written out, erased. Literature, one might say, gets repressed, along with the aesthetic.

Freud steers clear of the aesthetic, of literature, but at the same time he finds himself "impelled" towards it – uncannily.

But what is uncanny about "castration" for Freud? What is uncanny about the castration *anxiety* that, for Freud, haunts "The Sandman"? Castration inhabits the psyche – specifically, Nathaniel's in the story – because, says Freud, it is a fear that goes into repression but that "returns" to disrupt the self with dread, the repressed, the forgotten. It returns as a repressed fear which, for that reason, is at the same time *secretly* familiar; it returns as something familiar which is also strange to the self, a foreign yet intimate visitant, "uncanny". Freud says: "[the] uncanny is in reality nothing new or alien, but something which is familiar and old-established in the mind and which has become alienated from it only through the process of repression. This reference to the factor of repression enables us, furthermore, to understand Schelling's definition of the uncanny [cited earlier in his essay: 345] as something which ought to have remained hidden but has come to light" (*PF* 14: 363–4).

It seems, then, that one *always knew* the uncanny, but at the same time that one *never* knew it; in fact, one cannot know the uncanny because its effect is to bring back the familiar in the idiom of the strange, the alien, the other. One cannot *recognize* or embrace the uncanny object; instead, one is disturbed by its *power to disturb one's power to recognize it.*

Elizabeth Wright argues that surrealism promotes an aesthetic of the uncanny. She says that the surrealist painters "specialize[d] in the uncanny object" because they took the familiar world and defamiliarized it, presenting the viewer with, for example, a watch that melts (Salvador Dali), a pipe that proclaims that it is "not" a pipe (*Psychoanalytic Criticism* 134), a closed door with a "vaguely human" shape puncturing it (René Magritte). These objects, says Wright, wrest the familiar world into the unfamiliar, the known into the unknown, the habitual into the strange. In the uncanny, she says, "the *unheimlich* object threatens us in some way by no longer fitting the context to which we have been accustomed", and she adds: "[t]he familiar, the *heimlich*, is the result of the apparently successful orderings we have made of the world", but the *unheimlich* "defies the normality of seeing" and disturbs habitual perceptions in the name of the unknown, the unpresentable ("The Uncanny and Surrealism" 265, 277). This means that the "narcissistic gaze" (*Speaking Desires* 25) of the subject or viewer is disrupted, that the self loses its bearings and hold upon the world. It is hardly surprising, then, that Freud loses his way, too, in the uncanny, that he cannot find his way about in it. No one can. As Françoise Meltzer says, the uncanny is when "one is ... 'not at home' (*unheimlich*) in one's recognized world" ("The Uncanny Rendered Canny" 231).

In a strange foreshadowing of Dolar's point with which we began – namely, that the "dimension of the uncanny is … at the very core of psychoanalysis" – Freud says during the course of his essay that he "should not be surprised to hear that psychoanalysis, which is concerned with laying bare … hidden forces, has itself become uncanny to many people for that very reason", and adds that he has "heard this view expressed by [a] patient's mother long after her recovery" (*PF* 14: 366). Thus, although he professes himself "obtuse" (*PF* 14: 340) when it comes to uncanny feelings, Freud regards his own new science, psychoanalysis, as living and breathing the very air of the uncanny. In this way, psychoanalysis is not just a theory of the uncanny but itself *an uncanny theory*; it introduces the strange or the unconscious into the familiar, the other or the alien into the self. In psychoanalysis and in the uncanny, we might say, we *are* strangers to ourselves.

If psychoanalysis is uncanny – and its discovery of the unconscious is uncanny – it is nevertheless the case that Freud regards psychoanalysis as his "home", as the familiar, the *heimlich*. Freud feels himself at home there – rather than in the aesthetic, where he is unsure how to find his way about. After he has completed his reading of "The Sandman" – a psychoanalytic showcase for the uncanniness of castration, he thinks – Freud lists a number of other instances of the uncanny (doubts about whether something is animate or inanimate, effects of doubling, and of "involuntary repetition"), and pronounces them to be "difficult to judge" psychoanalytically. From there, he turns to the idea of "presentiments" which "come true" as a source of the uncanny, and says, "And now we find ourselves on *familiar* ground". This is the familiar ground of the psychoanalytic theory of primary narcissism and of the infantile "omnipotence of thoughts" (*PF* 14: 354–61 – my emphasis), where the uncanny arises from something happening *now* (a thought that comes true) which actually belongs to the stage of infantile narcissism when thoughts did, in fact, come true (according to the infant).

Freud is glad, it seems, to find himself back here on "familiar ground": on the familiar ground of established psychoanalytic theory. Yet he keeps losing directions to his own theoretical home, keeps straying – as he strayed, indeed, in the story he recounts in "The 'Uncanny'", in the bordello area of an Italian town and returned to the same place three times without knowing where he was, strangely and uncannily (*PF* 14: 359). And, in "The 'Uncanny'" itself, Freud keeps returning to the same place – to the aesthetic, to literature – uncannily, without knowing where he is. Freud keeps coming back to literature, but does not know how to hold the uncanniness of the literary, of the aesthetic, in place. Uncanny literature inhabits Freud's theory of the uncanny like a stranger.

At the beginning of the final section of his essay, Freud says, "In the course of this discussion the reader will have felt certain *doubts* arising in his mind", and adds later: "nearly all the instances that contradict our hypothesis are taken from the realm of fiction, of imaginative writing. This suggests that we should differentiate between the uncanny that we actually experience and the uncanny that we merely picture or read about" (*PF* 14: 368, 370 – my emphasis). Freud instances the fact that although, in real life, immediate wish-fulfilment based on the omnipotence of thoughts would certainly be uncanny, in much literature – and he mentions fairy stories – it would not be in the least be uncanny (*PF* 14: 369). In fairy stories, that is, thoughts can produce the realities that they configure without any uncanny effects following (anything can happen, so to speak). But if the writer "pretends to move in the world of common reality" – that is, if he appears to accept what Freud calls "the conditions operating to produce uncanny feelings in real life" – the situation becomes troubled, unstable, indeterminate. For what the writer can do, Freud remarks, is generate "everything that would have an uncanny effect in reality", but can also "increase his effect and multiply it far beyond what could happen in reality". This means, says Freud, that "[w]e react to his inventions as we would have reacted to real experiences", yet "by the time we have seen through his trick it is already too late and the author has achieved his object" (*PF* 14: 374). We think we are in reality – or that we are governed by the protocols of reality – but find we are in fiction. We don't know where we are: it is uncanny ...

Freud observes, candidly, that an "*aesthetic* inquiry" into the problem of the uncanny would in fact "open the door to doubts about what exactly is the value of our general contention that the uncanny proceeds from something familiar which has been repressed" (*PF* 14: 370). For in the "tricks" or games or ruses performed by literature the uncanny can, it seems, be produced *apart* from any actual or real return of the "repressed" – whether it is a repressed "complex" or a "surmounted" mode of thought, as in the case of the omnipotence of thoughts (*PF* 14: 374–5). In literature, that is, the uncanny can be generated by the pure operation of a *textual effect that suspends the distinction between imagination and reality*, and renders this distinction indeterminate. Freud himself says it, before he gets to the last section of his essay. "An uncanny effect", he writes, "is often and easily produced when the distinction between imagination and reality is effaced" (*PF* 14: 367). When we do not know if we are in the imagined or the real – whether we are in a world of truth or fiction – we are in the uncanny. And it is literature that has the ability to visit this uncertainty upon us the most effectively, Freud says. It is uncanny.

But what, then, of Freud's "general contention" that "the uncanny proceeds from something familiar which has been repressed", the main theoretical claim of his essay? What if an "*aesthetic* inquiry" should cast "doubt" on *that* claim? What if that claim belonged itself, strangely, to *literature* as well as psychoanalysis, to *fiction* as well as reality, a fiction that here would be Freud's own, psychoanalysis's own? Perhaps, in the end, what is "uncanny" about psychoanalysis is that it remains haunted by the repressed possibility that its own "truths" *may* be forms of fiction – the truth or the fiction of "castration" included – and that literature inhabits the body of its discourse as the uncanniest of guests.

The essays in this section display the "uncanny" power of literature to subvert the "common core" (*PF* 14: 339) of meaning that Freud pursues in "The 'Uncanny'", and the uncanniness of psychoanalysis itself insofar as it is a discourse dedicated to the encounter with strangeness. In Essay 4, Sarah Kofman interrogates Freud's reading of the uncanny in Hoffmann in order to situate the question of *fiction* within it. In Derridean style, she finds fiction operating as a strange "supplement"[1] within Freud's analytic argument; fiction, she argues, generates effects of uncanny excess and doubling that make it escape from Freud's grasp. Though Hoffmann's text "authorizes an analytic kind of reading", says Kofman, Freud's essay reduces Hoffmann's fiction to a "truth exterior and anterior to it" (*Freud and Fiction* 160, 159): the truth of castration. Yet Kofman employs Freud "against" Freud in order to argue that the theme of castration in his text masks the ubiquity of the death instincts in his theory: a ubiquity that is marked in "The 'Uncanny'" as a return of the repressed. In this way, Kofman uses Hoffmann to mount a "Freudian" reading of Freud, a reading that shows Freud to be uncomfortably implicated in the force of his own insights.

The subversive power of fictionality in relation to Freud's bid for analytic mastery is also examined by Hélène Cixous in Essay 5.

Cixous shows how "The 'Uncanny'" entails the *repetition* rather than resolution of the uncanny effects of "The Sandman"; and she foregrounds the textual strategies of Freud's essay in order to demonstrate that, against his own will, Freud is a *practitioner* of the uncanny as much as a theorist of it. Freud is an artist as much as an analyst of the uncanny. If literature and psychoanalysis are shown to transgress on each other's territory in Cixous's essay, Lis Møller (Essay 6) takes this further by showing how "The Sandman", in deconstructive style, suspends its narrative figures undecidably, and uncannily transgresses the opposition of truth and fiction. Møller examines Freud's reading of Hoffmann's tale in terms of its own privileged analytic figure, the disembodied "eye", and shows that while the eye "constitutes the point of departure of [Freud's] psychoanalytic interpretation ... [it] at the same time confronts us with that which this interpretation ignores or excludes". In her argument, fiction again becomes something that opens psychoanalysis up to the uncanny strangeness of the other, to that which is within the gaze of psychoanalysis but also exceeds it.

NOTE

1. Derrida's influential account of the logic of supplementarity is excerpted in *Acts of Literature* (76–109).

4

The Double is / and the Devil: The Uncanniness of "The Sandman"

SARAH KOFMAN

UNITY, MULTIPLICITY OF THE UNCANNY

"The 'Uncanny'", written a year before *Beyond the Pleasure Principle*, is set against a background of war,[1] death, the death instinct. The uncanny can also give rise to a masochistic type of pleasure, a satisfaction (*jouissance*) arising from the very source of anxiety itself; a pleasure which also leads back to the death instinct since it is linked to return and repetition. Thus, by extension, there is no aesthetic feeling in which the death instinct is not implicated. What traditional aesthetics wishes to disguise behind a rigid distinction between two types of feeling is that death is always already at work in the "positive", that Eros and the death instinct are indissociable. Every pleasure is "mixed". Thus, by giving the uncanny more than marginal consideration, Freud "uncannily" blurs the limits of the positive and negative.

Freud does not really say all this: he says it without saying it, implicitly. It is written on the reverse of the text: the indissoluble union between Eros and the death instinct is inscribed within the Freudian text – itself particularly "uncanny".

In effect, the desire for unity which drives the investigation finds itself under attack at every turn from the need to introduce distinctions and divisions: even if, by several *tours de force*, Freud tries to erase these differences in favour of unity. Firstly there is a duality at the level of *method*: two types of analysis are used; a linguistic analysis of the notion of the *Unheimlich* and an analysis of all the properties, things, impressions, experiences and situations that give rise to *Unheimlichkeit*. A clever trick in presentation allows this duality to be reduced to unity and Freud to assert that the results of both analyses are identical: the order of exposition is not faithful to the order of invention. The linguistic analysis, which comes first, has, in fact, been carried out after the analysis of examples. The selection of linguistic material is determined by the latter which cannot, therefore, serve to confirm the results obtained by the linguistic method.

In the third part of the essay, Freud replies to a number of objections which threaten to destroy the unity he has obtained by these methods. The most important objection? That the proposed definition of the uncanny is not convertible: "It may be true that the uncanny [*Unheimlich*] is something which is secretly familiar [*Heimlich-Heimisch*], which has undergone repression and then returned from it, and that everything that is uncanny fulfils this condition. But the selection of material on this basis does not enable us to solve the problem of the uncanny. For our proposition is clearly not convertible" (*PF* 14: 368). A series of examples can, in effect, run counter to the psychoanalytic definition: all the themes used to support the hypothesis are capable of having different effects. Fairy tales, in particular, by situating themselves straight away in the realm of animism, the realm of the omnipotence of thoughts and desires, never give rise to feelings of uncanniness, despite the fact that they make frequent use of motifs considered to be particularly uncanny. Another objection: it is difficult to dismiss the factor of uncertainty (decisive in Jentsch's definition) as "negligible", given its prime importance in producing the uncanny feelings associated with death.

Despite these objections, Freud *wants* to retain the proposed definition without qualifications, without leaving any remainder for the aestheticians:

> It is evident therefore, that we must be prepared to admit that there are other elements besides those which we have so far laid down as determining the production of uncanny feelings. We might say that these preliminary results have satisfied *psychoanalytic* interest in the problem of the uncanny and that what remains (*das Rest*) probably calls for an *aesthetic* enquiry. But that would be to open the door to

> doubts about what exactly is the value of our general contention that
> the uncanny proceeds from something familiar which has been
> repressed. (370)

The objections disappear once an initial distinction is introduced:
between works of *fiction* and *real* life. Most of the examples which
weaken the psychoanalytic hypothesis are taken from the realm of
fiction.

The uncanny in fiction "merits in truth a separate discussion"
(372). It includes every instance of the uncanny that occurs in real
life and more besides: a fictional supplement that psychoanalysis
must take into account and by which it does not want to be
outdone. Here the distinction between two types of *Unheimlichkeit*
cannot be upheld without qualifications:

> For the realm of phantasy depends for its effect on the fact that its
> content is not submitted to reality testing. The somewhat paradoxical
> result is that *in the first place a great deal that is not uncanny in
> fiction would be so if it happened in real life: and in the second place
> that there are many more means of creating uncanny effects in fiction
> than there are in real life.* (372–3; Freud's italics)

From this there follows a further distinction: between works of
fiction whose conventions admit animistic beliefs and those which
claim to situate themselves in the realm of everyday reality. Works
of the first kind would not produce uncanny feelings because there
would be no conflict over whether "things which have been 'surmounted' and are regarded as incredible may not, after all, be possible" (373). The key example: fairy tales. However, this is not
self-evident and we can ask ourselves whether here Freud is not, in
fact, revealing a "predilection for smooth solutions and lucid expo-
sitions" (372). In effect, his line of argument could be that of a rationalist who is unaware of the full extent of unconscious forces
and has not yet surmounted his belief in the omnipotence of judgement and reason: "In fairy stories feelings of fear – including therefore uncanny feelings – are ruled out altogether. We understand
this, and that is why we ignore any opportunities we find in them
for developing such feelings" (376). "We adapt our judgement to
the imaginary reality imposed on us by the writer ... In this case too
we avoid all trace of the uncanny" (373–4).

When the author of a work adopts realist conventions, everything
that in real life gives rise to feelings of uncanniness has the same

effect in the fictional work. This effect is, however, intensified by the poetic licence granted the writer to include "events which never or rarely happen in fact."

But if all fiction, as fiction, is not subject to reality-testing,[2] the preceding distinction becomes arbitrary: consequently the uncanny effect produced in this case is not pure; the reader is mystified and resents the author for "in a sense, betraying us to the superstitiousness which we have ostensibly surmounted; he deceives us by promising to give us the sober truth and then after all overstepping it."

The way for the writer to avoid incurring the reader's resentment? To keep him or her in the dark for as long as possible about "the precise nature of the presuppositions on which the world he writes about is based" (374).

Freud's conclusions are the outcome of a thematic interpretation which makes a false economy on the specificity of fiction and the story's narrative structure. In "The Sandman", the narrative structure is particularly complex and inseparable from the "themes" explored.

THE WRITER'S EYE-GLASS: THE IMAGINARY AND THE REAL

The complexity of the tale: it begins with an exchange of letters between Nathaniel, Lothario and Clara (two characters to whom Freud pays hardly any attention); it continues with a direct address by the author to the reader; finally it unfolds according to the most banal narrative conventions. The presence of several characters who have very different perspectives on Nathaniel's story from his own, a point of view that is at times contradictory, at times satirical, helps to prolong the "intellectual uncertainty" until the very end of the story. If Nathaniel's fiancée Clara's perspective is, as her name suggests, "clear", simple, realist; if her point of view is also shared by her brother Lothario, and the rest of the entourage, a sensible and reasonable point of view that contrasts with Nathaniel's – Nathaniel the dreamer, the visionary, the madman who confuses the imaginary and the real, who sees double – it is nonetheless not described as the perspective that contains the truth, and the reader can no more identify with Clara than with Nathaniel. Moreover, Hoffmann's treatment of the realist perspective is tinged with irony and it seems as if he inclines more towards the visionary perspective, which is also his own. Yet this is not presented as being a "true" perspective either. The fact that the conclusion of the story seems to endorse Nathaniel's version of events is not decisive: what happens here is perhaps an "uncanny" coincidence between fantasy and reality. But above all, contrary to what Freud says, the ending remains ambiguous and the reader's doubts are not resolved. Freud's summary says that Clara, from the top of the tower where she and Nathaniel have climbed, sees a curious object moving along the street. Nathaniel examines this object through Coppola's spy-glass and, on recognizing Coppelius,[3] is seized by a fit of madness. In Hoffmann's version, all that is described is the approach of an indistinct form, sufficiently vague for everyone to project their own fantasies onto it: "Then the loving pair ... gazed out at the fragrant woodland and at the blue mountains that rose like a giant city beyond. 'Just look at that funny little grey bush that seems as if it is coming towards us.'" Nathaniel takes the spy-glass from his pocket and, more than the appearance of Coppola, it is the use of this telescope that triggers off his madness. Through the spy-glass, it is the face of Clara, the fiancée he thought that he would finally be able to marry, which appears terrifying to him, a veritable Medusa's head, as he imagined her in his poem. This is why he tries to throw her off the tower: "Nathaniel reached into his side-pocket; he found Coppola's telescope and gazed through it. Clara was standing before the glass! Then a spasm shuddered through him; pale as death, he stared at Clara".[4]

"Nathaniel looked into Clara's eyes, but it was death which gazed at him mildly out of them" ("The Sandman" 105, end of the poem).

Through a spy-glass one's view of the real can only be deformed. The German word is: *Perspektiv*. The different characters the writer creates are so many different perspectives on the real. Even the eye of the person who sees clearly is a lens or a telescope. Coppola, the spectacle dealer, calls his spectacles "lovely eyes". One eye does not see more truthfully than another, even if one eye is never the same (or as good) as another: certain perspectives can be worth more than others, one leading to a happy marriage (hence Clara's "happy-end"), another to madness and death; but neither can be more truthful. What seems interesting and *unheimlich* in Hoffmann's text (which is Nietzschean *avant la lettre*) is that it shows that it is not a case of madness on one side and reason on the other but that their limits are not clearly defined, each being a matter of perspective. A blurring of the limits between the normal and the pathological, the imaginary and the real, places "The Sandman" among works producing uncanny effects of the first type rather than the second. But polemics prevents Freud from recognizing this: faced with Hoffmann's intentional undecidability, he opts for Nathaniel's point of view: the reader is not, he says, the superior and rational person he or she thinks. Without a doubt. But this does not mean that Nathaniel's visions are not the product of "fantasy".

The shifting of fixed margins and limits seems, for Hoffmann, to be literature's essential function. It is the artist's privilege not to imitate a pre-existing reality, but to represent the real through a multiplicity of distorting eye-glasses, each constitutive of a different reality. In a work of fiction, each of the characters is an external projection of the artist's multiple visions. Freud knew that Hoffmann considered his fictional characters to be images derived from impressions received before the age of two years and preserved in the camera obscura of his unconscious until they were later developed.

Nathaniel's "madness" is subject to the same processes as Hoffmann's notion of literary "creation": both are subject to an inner compulsion attributed to an external force:

> he spoke continually of how each of us, thinking himself free, was in reality the tortured plaything of mysterious powers: resistance was vain; we had humbly to submit to the decrees of fate. He went so far as to assert that it was folly to think the creations of art and science the product of our own free will: the inspiration which alone made creation possible did not proceed from within us but was effectuated by some higher force from outside.   (103)

A strong inner compulsion which obliges the author to describe to others his bizarre, magnificent, terrifying visions in glowing colours but without finding words that are adequate to the task: "every word, everything capable of being spoken seemed ... colourless and cold and dead" (100). A discrepancy between the dead and deadly word and the fiery vitality of the vision that explains the structural complexity of the story. Hoffmann first of all sketches a rough outline of his inner vision – the letters at the beginning of the story. He then adds more and more glowing colours to reproduce as faithfully as possible "the picture ... come forth [from his] heart". The only reason that the expression of the vital vision, an expression which his "strong compulsion ... to speak about Nathaniel's unhappy life" necessitates, is expressed in writing rather than verbally is the absence of a listener.

But why should this initial sketch take the form of an exchange of letters? In what sense is the letter of a letter different from that of a direct narrative mode? For Hoffmann the epistolary mode is decisive at this point to get the reader to accept the fantastical account which follows, which is "as much as a poet [can] do". Thus it is really the form of the narrative and not the theme in itself which plays the decisive role in the production of effects.[5] In order to create an effect of uncanniness right from the beginning, this beginning must be striking, original and gripping. This excludes any beginning that is too prosaic: "Once upon a time", or one that is likely to create a comic effect ("Go to the devil! cried the student Nathaniel"). Beginning with an exchange of letters avoids the problem of finding the right beginning since, in effect, it is "not to begin at all" (100–1). There can be no instance of the uncanny that does not always already imply repetition. Moreover, what the letter expresses, not literally but implicitly, on the reverse of the text, is what is proper to writing itself: the letter of writing literally never begins but is always a repetition of an originary repetition, a double and thus triple writing: the exchange of three letters. And it continues. Writing's supplementarity indefinitely calls forth supplementarity because there has never been an originary model perfectly present and complete, because without writing the inner visions in all their "colours and light and shade" remain vague, indefinite, evanescent. If these visions were so glorious, so vivid, why would there be any need to resort to a double regarded as inferior and deadly? Mimesis is necessary and originary because life always already implies death and needs the mortal supplement to be fixed and take form. Hoffmann does not really say all this: while rejecting a mimesis that is the double of a pre-existing external reality, he seems to suppose the existence of an internal vital reality which serves as a model. On the other hand, death is originarily inscribed within his text, by the very fact that it begins with the absence of a beginning. The necessity of writing and not just of narrating out loud is essential; writing is not a mere substitute for speech. It indicates that life must necessarily always pass through death. Thus Nathaniel wonders why he writes down his childhood memories in a letter to Lothario instead of recounting them to him on his imminent return home: "But why am I writing you all this? I could have told you about it better and at greater length face to face

– for you must now learn that I shall be with you in a fortnight's time (99)."

It could be said that through writing Nathaniel constructs rather than recollects his memories: it is impossible to distinguish the narrative of his childhood memories from that of his fantasies, the tale of the past from the imagined story of the future. The narration of his childhood memories is already literature, just as the fictional poem in which he imagines his future is a self-punishing repetition of the past. The function of both is the same: firstly, to rekindle in glowing colours what has already begun to fade from the imagination: "The figure of the repulsive Coppelius had, as Nathaniel himself was constrained to admit, grown dim in his imagination, and in his tales, where Coppelius appeared as a malign agent of destiny; it often required an effort to bestow life and colour upon him" (104–5). Secondly, to enable him to master, by symbolically repeating them, his terrifying visions; to master the future by predicting it, but also, sadomasochistically, to anticipate it, since the future he imagines will, in fact, be realized in an amazing coincidence between fantasy and reality:

> At length he hit on the idea of making his gloomy foreboding that Coppelius would disrupt the joy of his love into the subject of a poem: he depicted himself and Clara as united in true love but now and then it was as if a black hand reached out over them and erased their feelings of joy; at last, as they were standing before the marriage altar, the terrible Coppelius appeared and touched Clara's lovely eyes, which sprang out like blood-red sparks, singeing and burning onto Nathaniel's breast. Coppelius then seized him and threw him into a flaming circle of fire [etc ...]. While Nathaniel was composing his poem he was very quiet and self-possessed: he polished and improved every line, and the constraint of metre made it possible for him not to rest until everything was clear and harmonious. Yet when he had finished the poem and read it aloud to himself, he was seized with horror, and exclaimed: "Whose dreadful voice is this?!" Before long, however, it again seemed to him no more than a good poem, and he came to think that Clara's cold disposition would certainly be inflamed by it, although at the same time he had no clear notion of what Clara's becoming inflamed might lead to or of what purpose could be served by distressing her with horrible images prophesying a terrible destiny and the destruction of their love.   (105–6)

Nathaniel's literary activity, which implicitly illuminates Hoffmann's own, is inseparable from the other "themes" of the story, those of

the Sandman and the fear of losing one's eyes. It is significant
that literature is conceived as painting, as a *visionary* literature.
Nathaniel's literary activity is inseparable from his relations with
women: what he seeks in a woman, whether it is Clara or Olympia,
is a docile and passive listener for his poems: a strictly narcissistic
pleasure: "From the profoundest depths of his writing desk,
Nathaniel fetched up everything he had ever written: poems, fantasies, visions, novels, tales, daily augmented by random sonnets,
short stanzas, canzoni, and he read them all to Olympia without
wearying for hours on end. And he had never before had so marvellous an auditor" (117). An overwhelming literary output which
repeats the symbolic activity he carried out as a child during the
periods when Coppelius did not visit his father: when he would
draw pictures of the Sandman in numerous different forms: "On
tables, cupboards, and walls everywhere in the house ... the
strangest and most hideous pictures" (88).

Not only does this activity enable him to master his terror of the
Sandman by drawing derisory caricatures of him, it is also a means
of masochistic self-torture: a pleasure stemming from beyond the
pleasure principle, one that is highly prized by our hero. While the
Sandman is a hideous, terrifying, anguishing, *unheimlich* figure
whose presence he consciously flees, unconsciously he desires it. At
night he summons the Sandman back in his dreams: "When I heard
the sound of clumping coming up the stairs in the evening I trem-
bled with fear and terror ... I was the first to run into the bedroom
on the nights he was coming, and his fearsome apparition tor-
mented me till dawn" (87).

Nathaniel's extreme taste for tales of witches, goblins and evil
creatures of all kinds, and the fact that he prefers his nurse's sadistic
account of the Sandman to his mother's more reassuring version,
also stems from the same pleasure in the negative. The perception
of the real is always anticipated by him in an ill-fated form: the fantasized double doubles the real, gives it its particular colouring: thus
when Nathaniel, hoping to catch a glimpse of the Sandman, discovers only the lawyer Coppelius, he endows him with all the
Sandman's terrifying features and creates a picture of him that
could not possibly correspond to any real being. "The Sandman,
the terrible Sandman, was the aged advocate Coppelius, who sometimes comes to lunch with us. But the most horrible of forms could
not have aroused in me a more profound terror than did this
Coppelius" (89).

Fantasy and reality coincide because reality is always structured by fantasy, because it has never been present as such. Thus it is impossible to establish fixed, definite boundaries between the real and the imaginary: a blurring of distinctions that is particularly likely to produce uncanniness, according to Freud (*PF* 14: 367).

A reading of "The Sandman" cannot therefore ignore the presence of repetition and doubling in all its multiple forms, which is an important factor in producing an impression of uncanniness. If the fear of losing one's eyes reinforces this effect, then it cannot perhaps be dissociated from the effect of doubling, from Nathaniel's fantasies and literary activity. There is no need to refer to the general symbolism of dreams and myths to understand the anxiety Hoffmann's text arouses if we take into account not one theme in isolation but the way it is connected with the others. Thus the Olympia episode and its effect is inseparable from the uncanny effect produced by the Sandman and also from the problem of the double.

THE ANIMATE AND THE INANIMATE: DIABOLICAL MIMESIS

For Freud the uncanny effect produced by the Olympia episode is in some sense negligible. The impossibility of deciding whether she is animate or inanimate produces only limited uncertainty and the uncanny impression which is produced by this uncertainty is very different from the uncanniness of the rest of the text. In fact, the doll is only another form of the double and the uncertainty she creates can hardly be distinguished from that produced by literature and painting as doubles. As imitations, the latter also create an illusion of life. Thus Nathaniel, through the fatal power of writing, can make Clara burst into tears, terrify her merely by reading her his poems. Fiction has a greater effect on him than life, and gradually replaces it: from being a mere representation of life it ends up taking its place, bringing madness and death in its wake. Literature as a mimesis which becomes a substitute for life is a perversion belonging to the creature who rivals God: a diabolical mimesis.

The sensible Clara, who prefers life to its double, does not fall victim to the illusion, she does not confuse the animate and the inanimate: "Fantasists enjoyed little success with her: for, although she did not say very much ... her bright eyes and that subtle ironical smile told them: 'Dear friends! How could you believe of me that I should regard your transient poetic fancies as real beings, possessing life and action?' For this reason Clara was stigmatised by many as cold, unfeeling, prosaic" (102). In conformity with a whole philosophical tradition, Clara both rejects the double as inferior to life and distinguishes two types of mimesis: a bad mimesis whose effects are harmful and whose products carry the mark of the devil: they cause boredom and horror; and a good, divine mimesis which brings joy and life:

> In former days he had a great gift for lively and cheerful stories, which he would write down and Clara would listen to with the most heartfelt enjoyment; now his tales had grown gloomy, incomprehensible and formless, so that even if Clara considerately refrained from saying so he could nevertheless sense how little they appealed to her. Clara found boredom almost unendurable: when she was bored, the most unconquerable weariness of mind she felt appeared in how she spoke and in the look in her eyes. (104)

Bad mimesis makes Nathaniel forget the living presence of Clara and turn instead to dead representatives. Nathaniel's perversion is illustrated by his indifference to Clara's charms, the fact that he prefers his dead fiancée to his flesh and blood one, and his failure to distinguish between the living and the dead. In the grip of the demonic power that has entered his life, all his values undergo a transmutation: he takes Clara for a "lifeless, accursed automaton" (106) and wants to marry Olympia. The Olympia episode cannot, therefore, be treated in isolation from the rest: it is the inverted image of Nathaniel's relationship with Clara, illustrating in capital letters the power the double exercises over the hero. Nathaniel prefers the automaton to the living woman because he flees the latter, with whom he could begin a sexually productive activity. What he wants is a frigid, lifeless woman, a mirror of himself, who will listen to his poems without growing weary: "O lovely, heavenly woman! ... O heart in which my whole being is reflected!" (114). Nathaniel's narcissism makes him unfit for object-love, for forbidden love. The correlative of his narcissism is his "creative" activity, the production of doubles, a substitute for procreation.

If, in an important note, Freud does mention Nathaniel's narcissism and sees in Olympia Nathaniel's double, he nonetheless does not develop this idea at all in terms of his general interpretation and, above all, he does not connect narcissism and doubling with literary "creation". In fact, it is Nathaniel's love for his "creatures" that makes him confuse the animate and the inanimate: it is he himself who gives life to his works, who lends his *eyes* to his mirror-image. Olympia's expressionless eyes come to life only when he reads her his poems: "And he never before had so marvellous an auditor: she did not sew or knit, she did not gaze out of the window, she did not feed a cagebird, she did not play with a lapdog ... She sat motionless, her gaze fixed on the eyes of her beloved with a look that grew ever more animated and more passionate" (117).

Nathaniel brings Olympia to life at the expense of his own: Coppola can only create Olympia by stealing Nathaniel's eyes just as the Sandman must tear out children's eyes in order to feed his own children.

Thus eyes, in Hoffmann's tale, are the life principle – but the principle of an arificial life: the hero can only create narcissistically through his eyes, not procreate through his genitals. It is not coincidental that his way of estranging Clara and breaking off his engagement is to read her his poems. If, in the story, the eye is a substitute for the sex, this must be understood literally and not symbolically. Nathaniel can only create by artificial means, by mimesis, by mimicking or doubling life: a power of representation, of vision, of division which belongs to the death instincts, not to Eros. The eye is a diabolical source of life: a demonic power of doubling. Indeed, one could almost say the opposite to Freud, that for Nathaniel to lose his eyes would mean the recovery of his sex.

But Freud, who only takes the "theme" of eyes into account in relation to the Sandman episode, regards the fear of losing one's eyes as a symbolic substitute for the fear of castration: he sees the Sandman as a substitute for the castrating father who always intervenes to spoil love.

PRIMAL SCENE AND SATANIC SORCERY: THE DEVIL'S ARTIFICES

The double is neither living nor dead: designed to supplement the living, to perfect it, to make it immortal like the Creator, it is always "the harbinger of death" (*PF* 14: 357). It disguises, by its perfection, the presence of death. By creating what he hopes are immortal doubles, man tries to conceal the fact that death is always already present in life. The feeling of uncanniness that arises from the double stems from the fact that it cannot but evoke what man tries in vain to forget.

The scene which Nathaniel witnesses as a child from behind the curtain is especially *unheimlich* because it is the spectacle of an attempt to create life from inert matter; a vision capable of castrating whoever witnesses it, because it reveals the indissoluble bond between life and death. Thus Nathaniel can prefer artistic, narcissistic creation, producing doubles he thinks are immortal, to procreation. His artistic activity can therefore be interpreted as a consequence of this vision. But we can go even further: the sorcery scene mimics by simulacrum the primal scene,[6] of which it cannot fail to remind us. Nathaniel is not a hidden witness, as he desires, at his own conception, but he is present at the conception of another being, a creation for which his eyes are necessary. The artificial creation of a double is thus reminiscent of the procreation of a sister or brother whose birth robs the child of something fundamental. Thus the spectacle can only give him a masochistic pleasure. There are several indications in the text to the effect that the sorcery scene is a diabolical reenactment of the primal scene. It always occurs at night, in ritualistic fashion, at the same time; it is linked with certain specific sounds – the heavy thudding steps of a man coming up the stairs and characteristic creakings. Most of its elements are inverted: it involves two men and results in an unnatural creation; the silent and motionless father plays a passive role. The two protagonists undress and put on black smocks rather than white ones – "night" wear. It all takes place as if Nathaniel, anxious to possess the supreme knowledge of how children are created, finds the answer to his curiosity by fantasizing a Promethean type of magical creation from which women are excluded. A forbidden knowledge for which he will necessarily be punished. Nathaniel expects to be punished, he always already predicts it and awaits it in fear and trembling. At this point we should read the complete text:

> At the risk of being discovered and, as I firmly believed, severely punished, I remained there listening, with my head stuck through the curtains. My father received Coppelius solemnly. "Up! To work!" Coppelius cried in a hoarse, growling voice, and threw off his coat. My father slowly and gloomily removed his dressing gown and both clad themselves in long black smocks. I did not see where they got them from. My father opened the folding doors of a wall-cupboard; but I saw that what I had for so long taken to be a wall-cupboard was, rather, a black cavern, in which there stood a small hearth.

> Coppelius approached it and a blue flame flickered upon the hearth. All kinds of strange implements lay around. Good God! As my father bent down to the fire, he looked quite different! A dreadful convulsive pain seemed to have distorted his gentle, honest features into a repulsive devil mask. He looked like Coppelius. The latter seized the glowing tongs and with them drew brightly glowing substances out of the thick black smoke and began vigorously to hammer away at them. I seemed to see human faces appearing all around, but without eyes – instead of eyes there were hideous black cavities. "Eyes, bring eyes!" Coppelius cried in a dull, hollow voice. Gripped by wild terror, I screamed aloud and fell out of my hiding place onto the floor. (90–1)

The child's expectation that he will be punished could only be so strong because it evokes an earlier punishment, that punishment suffered, or fantasized, for having spied or having wanted to spy on the primal scene. The father would then have intervened and threatened the child with castration. The latter's present fear of losing his eyes is not a substitute for the fear of castration, but it cannot fail to evoke it: it is the self-punishing repetition of the fear of castration, in a more sadistic form, since it is linked to the loss of life and the fragmentation of a living whole. The sorcery scene is therefore the "real" return of another scene which was perhaps only fantasized. But with the primitive fantasy always doubling present perception, it is difficult to distinguish what part each plays. In this case, what produces the uncanny is overdetermined: it is the sorcery scene, *unheimlich* in its own right because connected with the problem of the double; it is the return of the castration fantasy in the guise of the more anguishing fragmentation fantasy; but, above all, it is the coincidence of fantasy with the real.

Hoffmann, for whom the function of literature is the blurring of all boundaries and margins, for whom the real is a double of the imaginary, in a certain sense, authorizes an analytic kind of reading – a reading in which he himself is implicated.

On the other hand, however, Freud, by making a thematic reading of the text, by extracting from it an ultimate signified, the castration complex, responsible for the effect produced, seems trapped within the "traditional logic of the sign". He turns the text into a paradigmatic illustration of a truth exterior and anterior to it. The text thus called to witness is reinscribed in the process of analytic truth.

In turn, by taking the Freudian reading to its limit, by substituting the death instincts for the castration complex, have I simply replaced one theme with another, or have I "surmounted" this kind of reading?

If one accepts the theory of the death instincts, it perhaps becomes pointless to oppose castration and the death instincts, since the latter become the condition of the former which, consequently, cannot play the role of a theme or an ultimate signified. With the theory of the death instincts, the work can no longer be the secondary illustration of an originary model full of sense, because such a hypothesis scotches any identity and plenitude of meaning and turns the text into an originary double. With the notion of the death instincts understood as a principle of general economy, the distinction between the imaginary and the real is replaced by problematics of a simulacrum without an originary model. A "diabolical" literature is no longer a literature of illusion or deception: it mimics the double as illusion by giving rise to "effects" of sense and themes, in a mood of simulacrum and derision; introducing within the text a structure of duplicity which does not allow itself to be reappropriated into, or mastered by, a problematics of truth or falsehood.

NOTES

[Sarah Kofman (1934–1994) was Professor of Philosophy at the University of Sorbonne, Paris, and the author of more than twenty books on philosophy, art, literature and psychoanalysis. One of France's most important contemporary thinkers, she published widely on the "question of woman" in the Western tradition. Her writings on Freud and psychoanalysis include *The Childhood of Art: An Interpretation of Freud's Aesthetics* (1970), *Freud and Fiction* (1974), *The Enigma of Woman: Woman in Freud's Writings* (1980) and "Conversions: *The Merchant of Venice* under the Sign of Saturn" (1988). Ed.]

1. At the very beginning, Freud alludes to the war which has prevented him from studying foreign literature in any depth (*PF* 14: 340). Also, in more general terms, the *"unheimlich"* character of the Freudian text (which is so wily and perverse that it concludes by according fiction a privileged character while at the same time, on the level of its analyses, it ignores the specificity of literature) leads one to conclude that a fundamental conflict is being played out within it.

2. Fictional conventions permit the adult to be a child once more: for the duration of his or her reading, the adult is spared the effort of having to adapt to the real. The pleasure in magical and extraordinary events consists of this additional saving of psychic energy.

3. For the relationship between Coppelius and Coppola, Freud refers us to the following etymology: "Frau Dr Rank has pointed out the association of the name with *Coppella* – crucible, connecting it with the chemical operations that caused the father's death; and also with '*Coppo* – eye-socket'" (*PF* 14: 352).

4. "The Sandman" 123. Kofman cites the translation of "The Sandman" in R.J. Hollingdale's (trans.) *Tales of Hoffmann* (1982): to preserve the integrity of her discussion, page references to Hoffmann's tale in Essay 4 are to this edition [Editor's note].

5. If one is concerned to preserve the opposition between form and subject matter that is at work in the Freudian text.

6. For the Freudian primal scene (the child's viewing of its parents' copulation) see Part III on *The Wolf Man* [Editor's note].

5

Fiction and its Phantoms: A Reading of Freud's "Das Unheimliche" (The "uncanny")

HÉLÈNE CIXOUS

These pages are meant as a reading divided between literature and psychoanalysis, with special attention paid to what is produced and what escapes in the unfolding of a text, sometimes led by Freud and at other times by his double. Indeed, Freud's text may strike us to be less a discourse than a strange theoretical novel. There is something "savage" in the *Unheimliche*, a breath or a provocative air which at times catches the novelist himself-off-guard, overtaking him and restraining him. Freud and the object of his desire (i.e., the truth about the *Unheimliche*) are fired by reciprocal inspiration. As a commentary on uncertainty, with its tightly drawn net mended by its plots and their resolutions, this long text of Freud employs a peculiarly disquieting method to track down the concept *das Unheimliche*, the Disquieting Strangeness, the Uncanny. Nothing turns out less reassuring for the reader than this niggling, cautious, yet wily and interminable pursuit (of "something" – be it a domain, an emotional movement, a concept, impossible to determine yet variable in its form, intensity, quality, and content). Nor does anything prove to be more fleeting than this search whose movement constitutes the labyrinth which instigates it; the sense of strangeness imposes its secret necessity everywhere. The ensuing unfolding whose operation is contradictory is accomplished by the author's double: Hesitation. We are faced, then, with a text and its hesitating shadow, and their double escapade. As for plots, what is brought together here is quickly undone, what asserts itself becomes suspect; each thread leads to its net or to some kind of disentanglement. In the labyrinthian space, many characters alluded to as witnesses and well-informed persons appear and are quickly relegated to the corner of some street or paragraph. What unfolds without fail before the reader's eyes is a kind of puppet theatre in which real dolls or fake dolls, real and simulated life, are manipulated by a sovereign but capricious stage-setter. The net is tightly stretched, bowed, and tangled; the scenes are centered and dispersed; narratives are begun and left in suspension.

Freud considers the *Unheimliche* as, at the same time, a "domain" and a "concept", an elastic designation. The fact of the matter is that the "domain" remains indefinite; the concept is without any nucleus: the *Unheimliche* presents itself, first of all, only on the fringe of something else. Freud relates it to other concepts which resemble it (fright, fear, anguish): it is a unit in the "family" but it is not really a member of the family. Freud declares that it is certain that the use of the *Unheimliche* is uncertain. The indefiniteness is part and parcel of the "concept". The statement and its enunciation become rejoined or reunited. *The statement cannot be encircled*: yet Freud, arguing for the existence of the *Unheimliche*, wishes to retain the sense, the real, the reality of the sense of things. He thus seeks out "the *basic* sense". Thus the analysis is anchored, at once, in what is denoted. And it is a question of a concept whose entire denotation is a connotation.[1]

In the third paragraph, Freud rigorously refocuses the relation between aesthetics and the medico-psychological disciplines. He underscores the repressive limits of aesthetics which convey ideological implications. Aesthetics deals with *positive* and casts aside contrary sentiments (ugliness as a positive value has scarcely a place in this tradition). Then, there appears the neuro-psychiatric study of E. Jentsch.[2] Freud considers it both interesting and deceptive; as an insufficient yet respected precursor, Jentsch will represent, henceforth, the "layman's" attitude, which is "intellectual" and indeed antianalytical because of its phenomenological approach to strangeness. Freud offers, straightaway, a subjective explanation for Jentsch's failure: he has not sufficiently delved into literature; he concerns himself only with everyday experience. Thus he loses "all claim to priority". Literature is the objective of psychoanalytical inquiry. A hierarchy is created through the system of priorities.

Freud calls upon what has, as yet, received no theoretical attention, notably upon "sensibility," and, more precisely, his own, because it is exemplary and different from the average sensibility, and "singularly insensitive" to the *Unheimliche*. Assuming the personality of "the author of this essay", Freud brings Jentsch into relief here and enters the scene in a double role: actor and "mechanician," analyst and subject of analysis. "It is long since he had experienced or heard of anything which had given him an uncanny impression". When the subject is so questioned by the author's undertaking, it gives rise to astonishment since what was familiar to him is now peculiar or strange to him. Things no longer *know* how to reach him. ... He must, thus, go to them; it is in this way that the scholar pushes himself forward and comes to life again so that the *representation* which replaces the experience may emerge. This enables him to examine the states which he studies by experimenting upon himself. What had been lost returns first, and the procession of ghosts is clandestinely ushered in. Then, as if in reaction to a private desired return which rejects melancholy, Freud reverts to the universal, or nearly so; he calls out "to the majority of men", to a nearly impossible consensus, as if the *Unheimliche* were recognized in the same way by everyone. A rather paradoxical hope, one might think, since it is in the nature of the *Unheimliche* to remain strange. But hope should not be repelled. The pathetic feature of the risk that props the scientific upon the unscientific recalls the divergence in the makeup of the *Unheimliche* – the familiar and the strange – which Freud posits as the cornerstone for his research. Just as the still undetermined *Unheimliche* benefits from the status of concept, so too is the nonscientific clothed with the dignity of the scientific.

In this equivocal area, in which the author admits that he is the hesitant subject of his inquiry, the text bifurcates toward the choices in method, thus making indecision the occasion of some progress. Bifurcation: "Two courses are open to us at the start". Each produces in a different manner the same result, which starts the process over again; one (linguistic experience) or the other (everyday experience) or the two. From one ambivalence to another, or else language as a general [phenomenon], or else the world as a series of individual cases; nevertheless, these two methods are proposed to us although the choice has been made by

Freud and the method already followed. Freud assigns us an *inverted* order in relation to the one he has followed. After the event, the history of the inquiry presents itself by the other method, as if he had wanted to begin by the undecided element in the *Unheimliche* which is lodged in language.

The choice of "a suitable example":[3] we find ourselves back at the crossroads, and we take the one that goes through the world. Once again, we allude to Jentsch's opinion in order to outstrip it immediately. Instead of a dictionary, we now have a split scene of animated "objects" – Freud's summary of Jentsch's position as essentially a little raised stage or setting. The "author" introduces here the preoccupation of the theatre, everything which the theatre represents as an image of living and what life is able, as a canvas, to hide from theatrics. On the stage and the stage of the stage, the relationship between Freud's discovery concerning scientific truth and the mechanics of fiction may be brought out. Freud's own text, here, functions *like* a fiction: the long work on personal pulsations, the dramatic redistribution upon such and such an approach, the suspense and surprises and impasses; all of that seems a part of the special work of fiction, and the "author" takes advantage of the narrator's privileges to which the analyst cannot consent. "Better than anyone else", says Freud, it is the writer who consents to give birth to the *Unheimliche*. The writer is also what Freud wants to be. Freud sees in himself the writer, the one whom the analyst must question concerning the literature which psychoanalysis must understand in order to know itself. He is, in his relationship to the writer, as the *Unheimliche* is in its relationship to the *Heimliche*. In his strangeness with respect to creation, he feels himself "a case". The enigma of the *Unheimliche* has a literary answer, claims Freud in the manner of Jentsch, and this is his most reliable answer.

Scarcely does he appropriate Jentsch's example (in the manner of children: this doll belonged to me) when he declares himself the true master of the method since his predecessor did not know how to make proper use of it. The way in which he misappropriates betrays a stinging boldness and the ploy of a fox! On the one hand, Freud quotes the Jentsch citation about the Sand-Man beginning with the character of the automaton, the doll Olympia. At the same time, he discards Jentsch's interpretation. The latter links the *Unheimliche* to the psychological manipulation of Hoffmann, which consists in producing and preserving uncertainty with respect to the true nature of Olympia. Is she animate or inanimate? Does Freud regret the psychological argument? So be it. He takes advantage of it to displace the *Unheimliche* of the doll with the Sand-Man. Thus, under the cover of analytical criticism and uncertainty, the doll which had been relegated to the background is already, in effect, in the trap. Its repression will be accomplished, moreover, with the approval or the complicity of the reader, of whom Freud, henceforth, is well aware. His real and persistent concern with the reader's point of view, his attention to and his demand for communicability, which proceed from his well-known need to share [with the reader], to guide, to teach, and to justify himself before him – this pedagogical procedure that we find throughout his discourse upon occasion may appear to be encouraging the obvious. "I hope that most readers will agree with me", says the orator who takes no risk whatsoever without making an alliance or returning to it. The dialogue entered upon with the reader is also a theatrical artifice in which the answer precedes and envelops the question. From then on, it is a matter, without further delay, of turning the episode involving Olympia into satire, thus managing to eclipse and obscure it. We get sand thrown in our eyes, no doubt about it.

Next comes Freud's narration of the Sand-Man and the account is faithful (or so it would seem); it is not a paraphrase. Freud delights in having to rewrite the tale structurally, beginning with the *centre* designated as such a priori. The whole story is recounted then by the Sand-Man who tears out children's eyes. Given the fact that Freud's approach is that of inverted repetition, one sees how he rewrites the tale for demonstrative purpose: a reading that is reclosed as that in the *Unheimliche* is now closed on the *Heimliche*. The reader gets the impression that Freud's narrative is not as *Unheimliche* as he claims: is that new element which should have remained hidden doubtless too exposed here? Or did Freud render uncanniness something too familiar? Was the letter stolen? The two versions of the Sand-Man have to be read in order to notice what has been slipped into one version from the other. As a condensed narrative, Freud's story is singularly altered in the direction of a linear, logical account of Nathaniel and strongly articulated as a kind of "case history", going from childhood remembrances to the delirium and the ultimate tragic end. All through the story, Freud intrudes in various ways: in one instance to bring the fantastic back to the rational (the *Unheimliche* to the *Heimliche*); in another instance, he intrudes to establish explicit liaisons which are not conveyed as such in the text. These interventions, in effect, constitute a redistribution of the story while they tend to attenuate, to the point of effacement, the characters who represent the *Heimliche*, like Clara and her brother. He minimizes the uncertainty revolving around Olympia, thus pushing Olympia toward the group of the *Heimliche* and clearly diminishing the texture of the story by trimming, in particular, the discontinuity of the exposition, the sequence, the succession of narrators, and points of view. These interventions organize a confrontation between the Sand-Man and Nathaniel which is much more sustained and obsessive but also less surprising than in the original version. If the reader's eye is applied to the satanic eyeglass of the optician (by Hoffmann – Freud suggests – an action which betrays a number of intentions on the part of the "author"), the function of the eyeglass as it is replayed by Freud constitutes a disturbing complexity: it seems to eradicate the doubt concerning the author's intention. Does it, indeed, lead us toward real life or toward the fantastic? *No more doubt* (there is repetition and insistence on Freud's part concerning the rejection of doubt): by a series of abrupt thrusts, Freud jumps from one effect to the other (giving the appearance of going from cause to effect) until reaching "the point of certitude", of *reality*, which he wishes to establish as the cornerstone upon which he may found his analytical argument. We are obliged to accept this "conclusion" with its retroactive effects, or to get out of this venture without loss. Let us play: let's concede that there is a real sequence and not only a semblance of sequence in such a peremptory declaration.[4] And let's rely on the logic of "consequently": we do not question, like Freud, that Coppola may be Coppelius, thus the Sand-Man in reality; and we believe Nathaniel not to be delirious but clairvoyant. Let us accept these effects (and also this fictional unity of the reader and the analyst), and this "art of interpretation", but not without keeping the secret desire to *unmask* what should not have remained hidden in such a selective reading. Freud pruned the story of its involved narrative structure, of the heterogeneity of its points of view, of all "superfluous" detail (the "operatic" aspect of the account with its choruses of students and villagers and the retinue of mediations which are more or less useful to the plot), pruned it of any meaning which did not seem to contribute to the thematic economy of the story. But should not this gesture of the cutting of such Hoffmannesque trees (Freud, moreover, complains of their thickness) be underscored? For it is indeed a question of *cutting* rather than one of summarizing, as if insisting that the presence of eyes contaminated the sight that reads the text. The role of pantomime, so striking in Hoffmann's story, is precisely the element that accounts for the charm of this creative work, this springing from the *Erinnerung* through the epistolary account up to the carnival scene, this extreme interiorization of subjects and reduplication of an ordinary reality by an extraordinary one (which *prohibits* reading the story exclusively in one or the other worlds). This pantomime that obliges the reader *in fact* to appreciate this superb creation from the real and imaginary axes is categorically expelled by Freud. Therein springs that debatable proceeding of intellectual uncertainty which leads him to dance between psychology and psychoanalysis. The rambling demonstrability turns back attentively to what is at stake, and reflects Freud's constraint: decreeing, for example, that uncertainty on such and such a point is not as uncertain as that: Coppola = Coppelius. But this is so by paronomasia. Rhetoric does not create the real. To perceive identities is reassuring, but perceiving "incomplete" identities is another matter. In his reduction of "intellectual uncertainty" to a rhetorical uncertainty, Freud appears to be playing on the velvet of lexicography. Because Jentsch's *vocabulary* is answerable to psychology, Freud allows himself the possibility of completely excluding this uncertainty insofar as it would be "intellectual". When the *Unheimliche* forces back the Jentschian motif, is there not, in fact, *a repression of the repression*? Does not Jentsch say more than what Freud wishes to read?[5]

Eyes in one's pockets: It is up to us to read *in its ambiguity* Freud's phrase and what it censures: "This short summary leaves, I think, no doubt. ..." Do we understand by that, Hoffmann's story or the story that is quickly recounted? But it is precisely the short summary that displaces and engenders doubt. Thinking about this method of telling as a deformation of the thought in the text in the manner in which we speak of thought in a dream, Freud "relates", in fact, how he would have deciphered the puzzle of the dream. His elaboration *begins*, in reality, from a conclusion which returns the analysis to the still intra-analytical circle. This is a conclusion that cuts two ways. (1) The expulsion of "intellectual uncertainty" allows the prescription of an analytical interpretation; and the minimizing of Olympia leads to the focus on Nathaniel. (2) In this narrative of the Sand-Man, Freud plays up the fear of becoming blind and its substitute so that the Sand-Man is cut off from view by the reducing equation: Sand-Man = loss of eyes (yet it is not so simple as this). Thus, in one stroke, the two great and extraordinary figures are supplanted, and with them, Hoffmann's theatre: one half of the text is eliminated. Only the eyes remain: Freud's terrain is now less mobile; we are on territory which is very much reinforced by observations and theoretical knowledge ("to learn", "learned"). On the one hand, the fear of the loss of sight is a fact of daily experience which clichés underscore, and that is a *familiar* fear. Moreover, examination of three formations of the unconscious (dreams, phantasms, myths) shows that this fear hides another, that of castration. Oedipus, who is summoned briefly here, gives testimony that enucleation is an attenuation of castration. And castration, enucleation, and Oedipus assert themselves here without our being sure, however, of their position relative to the whole in which they are constituted. *If* one articulates the implication, the accent is placed on castration rather than on Oedipus; analysis of the *Unheimliche* can thus pass for analysis of the nuclear Oedipus-castration question. Freud, moreover, has not elaborated directly concerning the complex articulation of the Oedipus-castration: the boy is led to liquidate his Oedipus because of the castration complex that has the bearing of something forbidden.

Freud starts from the fear the boy experiences of seeing his penis removed. But we should thus examine this principle, for it is a fact that Freud never abandoned (or wanted to abandon) the sexual character of castration; we should likewise examine here the return to the father which the castration myth implies. In point of fact, the entire analysis of the *Unheimliche* is characterized (we shall see this more and more clearly) by Freud's *resistance* to castration and its effectuality.

For Freud, castration must be the point of its own enigma: enucleation is nothing but an attenuation of castration; there is a "substitutive relation between the eye and the male member." How can we reinforce by a rational point of view this affirmation which Freud soon recognizes as a debatable one? Indeed, one might reverse the terms (castration as an attenuation ...) or make them equivalent: enucleation or castration. Freud, then, leaves one nonproof for another, by affirming that the secret of castration does not refer to another secret more profound than that which is articulated by anguish: the fear of castration refers back to castration and, at the very least or most, to its process of substitution (the relationship of substitution, *Ersatzbeziehung* of the penis to the eye and to other organs). *Kein tieferes Geheimnis*: "no secret anymore profound", says Freud: the "very obscure sentiment" of resistance to the threat of castration is the same for all of the presentations of the loss of an organ. Freud's theoretical work is concerned with the quality of the *fear* that is elicited. Attention is thus focused on this strong and obscure sentiment which is the uncanny element of anxiety.

What lies on the other side of castration? "No meaning" other than the fear (resistance) of castration. It is this *no-other-meaning* (*Keine andere Bedeutung*) which presents itself anew (despite our wish to underplay it) in the infinite game of substitutions, through which what constitutes the elusive moment of fear returns and eclipses itself again. It is this dodging from fear to fear, the unthinkable secret since it does not open on any *other* meaning: its "agit-ation" (Hoffmann would say "*Unruhe*") is its affirmation. Even here, isn't everything a repercussion, a discontinuous spreading of the echo, but of the echo as a displacement, and not in any way as a referent to some transcendental meaning? The effect of uncanniness reverberates (rather than emerges), for the word is a relational signifier. *Unheimliche* is in fact a composite that infiltrates the interstices of the narrative and points to gaps we need to explain. This is what Freud underscores with a kind of relentlessness in the guise of urgent questions which are in fact tantamount to emphatic propositions: yet the "question" *why* (a mask for *because*) obligates the theory to account for the "arbitrary" characteristics of the story. What then appears as a shadow in the Freudian argument is the "arbitrary" requirement concerning meaning: a relation of reciprocal guarantee sets up, here, its mirroring effect. The hypothesis aimed at filling the gaps (these "become filled with meaning") derives from a refusal to admit the insignificance of certain characteristics. Without this hypothesis, the narration would be castrated. The fear of castration comes to the rescue of the fear of castration.

Note to Olympia; or the other story of the Sand-Man: In the form of a note, Freud, in fact, gives us a second narrative which would presumably be only the "reestablished", first and original version, closer to the interpretation of a case than to the displacement wrought by the creator's imagination beginning with these elements. It is no longer a question here of the Sand-Man, but rather of its analytical version. Coppelius is designated here as the redoubtable father ...

It follows that if in the ordering of this new text, a dismembered, tightened-up, and reassembled Olympia takes on a new importance, she is, at once, retrieved by the interpretation: "she can be nothing else than a personification of Nathaniel's feminine attitude toward his father in his infancy", says Freud. To be sure! Homosexuality returns in reality under this charming figure. But Olympia is more than just a detached complex of Nathaniel. If she is no more than that, why are not the dance, the song, the mechanisms, and the artificer brought back into the game or theorized upon by Freud? What are we expected to do with these puppets which have haunted the stages of German romanticism?

Again, the beautiful Olympia is effaced by what she represents, for Freud has no eyes for her. This woman appears obscene because she emerges there where "one" did not expect her to appear, and she thus causes Freud to take a detour. And what if the doll became a woman? What if she *were* alive? What if, in looking at her, we animated her?

Superannuated, isolated from the scene, the doll comes out ... between two acts.

Toward a Theory of Fiction: Fiction is connected to life's economy by a link as undeniable and ambiguous as that which passes from the *Unheimliche* to the *Heimliche*: it is not unreal; it is the "fictional reality" and the vibration of reality. The *Unheimliche* in fiction overflows and comprises the *Unheimliche* of real life. But if fiction is another form of reality, it is understood that the secret of the *Unheimliche* does not refer to a secret more profound than that of the *Unheimliche* which envelops the *Unheimliche*, just as death overflows into life.

What is fiction in reality? This is a question which haunts the accesses to the Freudian text, but without entering them. Freud writes, "Fiction presents more opportunities for creating uncanny sensations than are possible in real life." The analysis returns to another object, the one which it has come up against unceasingly without ever exhausting it: *fiction*. It is not merely a question here of examining the enigma of the *Unheimliche* but also of the enigma of fiction as such, and of fiction in its privileged relationship to the *Unheimliche*. Fiction (re) presents itself, first of all, as a Reserve or suspension of the *Unheimliche*: for example, in the world of fairy tales the unbelievable is never disquieting because it has been cancelled out by the convention of the genre. Fictional reality, then, is interrupted. Or fiction can also multiply the uncanny effect by the interruption in the contract between author and reader, a "revolting" procedure in the author's estimation, which allows us to wander until the end, without any defence against the *Unheimliche*. That is only possible provided the Surmounted One[6] is never completely surmounted. The impossible could then represent itself as the possible (let us distinguish here between absence in reality through impossibility and absence through death). The impossible is not death, and death is not impossible. For Freud, the variations of the Surmounted only stem, in fact, from mystification. A false death. The *true* secret of fiction rests somewhere else. Fiction, through the invention of *new* forms of *Unheimliche*, is *the very strange thing*: if one considers the *Unheimliche* as a fork of which one branch points in the direction of the uncanny and the other in the direction of an anxiety, one sees, at the extreme end of the uncanny, fiction pointing toward the unknown: what is newest in the new, through which it is in part linked with death.

As a Reserve of the Repressed, fiction is finally that which resists analysis and, thus, it attracts it the most. Only the writer "knows" and has the *freedom* to evoke or inhibit the *Unheimliche*. In other words, only the writer has the freedom to raise or to repress the Repression. But this "freedom" defies all analysis; as another form of the *Unheimliche* it is like that which should have "remained … hidden." Still, this fiction does not escape the law of representation, and is mysterious to everything else but itself.

From our point of view, as unflaggingly disquieted readers, we cannot help but think that Freud has hardly anything to envy in Hoffmann for his "art or craftiness" in provoking the *Unheimliche* effect. If we experience uneasiness in reading Freud's essay, it is because the author is his double in a game that cannot be dissociated from his own text: it is such that he manages to escape at every turn of phrase. It is also and especially because the *Unheimliche refers* to no more profound secret than itself: every pursuit produces its own cancellation and every text dealing with death is a text which returns. The repression of death or of castration betrays death (or castration) everywhere. To speak of death is to die. To speak of castration is either to surmount it (thus to cancel it, to castrate it) or to effect it. "Basically" Freud's adventure in this text is consecrated to the very paradox of the writing which stretches its signs in order to "manifest" the secret that it "contains". As for solitude, silence, and darkness, which have always been there since childhood, "we can only say that they are actually elements in the production of that infantile morbid anxiety from which the majority of human beings have never become quite free." So, of the

Unheimliche (and its double, fiction) we can only say that it never completely disappears ... that it "re-presents" that which in solitude, silence, and darkness will (never) be presented to you. Neither real nor fictitious, "fiction" is a secretion of death, an anticipation of nonrepresentation, a doll, a hybrid body composed of language and silence that, in the movement which turns it and which it turns, invents doubles, and death.

NOTES

[Hélène Cixous is a Professor of English Literature at the University of Paris VIII, Vincennes, where she founded the "Centre d'Études Féminines" in 1974. A prolific feminist writer, she has published many works of literary criticism, philosophy, drama and fiction. Her writings bearing on Freud, femininity, literature and psychoanalysis include "The Laugh of the Medusa" (1975), "Sorties" (1975), "Castration or Decapitation?" (1976), the novel *Portrait du Soleil* (1974) and the drama *Portrait de Dora* (1976; see Essay 11). A selection of her work across the many genres in which she has written appears in *The Hélène Cixous Reader*, edited by Susan Sellers (1994). Ed.]

1. In semantics, *denotation* signifies the "literal" or dictionary definition of a word, while *connotation* designates the range of "figural" associations that a word possesses [Editor's note].

2. Cited by Freud (*PF* 14: 340); the study appeared in 1906. Freud's connection with his predecessor is fascinating; it would seem likely, despite appearances to the contrary, that *Das Unheimliche* has something to do with "intellectual-ness".

3. The form and structure of Cixous's text, as will be clear to the reader, mimes and doubles that of Freud's "The 'Uncanny'" – a strategy that generates an effect of "uncanny" echoing between the two essays. The disorientation that this brings about has to do in part with Cixous's refusal to give page references to most of the citations she makes from Freud's essay; thus the reader has to have the diction and style of Freud's text in mind so that the uncanny play of mimicry and questioning being pursued by Cixous can unfold between the texts [Editor's note].

4. Freud, 352: "the conclusion of the story makes it quite clear that Coppola the optician really *is* the lawyer Coppelius and also, therefore, the Sand-Man. There is no question, therefore, of any intellectual uncertainty here ..."

5. Cixous seems to be saying that Jentsch's psychological reading represses the element of castration that, for Freud, is the crucial motif of

"The Sandman": castration is repressed in Jentsch by the theme of "intellectual uncertainty". But Freud represses uncertainty itself in his drive to know the uncanny [Editor's note].

6. Freud says that one source of the uncanny is the infantile belief in the "omnipotence of thoughts" (*PF* 14: 362–3); he argues that, despite being "surmounted" (370), these beliefs can return later in life with the uncanny stamp of familiarity *and* strangeness [Editor's note].

6

"The Sandman": The Uncanny as Problem of Reading

LIS MØLLER

The most concise exposition of the basic ideas of what I have been calling "psychoanalytical textual archaeology" is to be found in Freud's essay "The 'Uncanny'", in connection with his interpretation of E.T.A. Hoffmann's narrative "The Sandman", which it singles out as the chief literary example of the uncanny. "Hoffmann's imaginative treatment of his material", writes Freud, "has not made such wild confusion of its elements that we cannot *reconstruct* their original arrangement" (*PF* 14: 353; my italics). This observation, marking the beginning of a long footnote, sums up the premise of traditional psychoanalytic literary criticism: the idea of an original text, distorted through the author's poetic treatment, but nevertheless still retrievable. According to this, Freud's analytical version of "The Sandman" is, by the same token, the "original" version – a text that exists prior to the narrative itself. Psychoanalytic literary criticism presents itself as the undoing of the author's imaginative distortion and the reconstruction, from the traces left behind, of the "original arrangement" of the elements. The psychoanalytic reader restores the latent, uncensored version of the text.

As a reader of "The Sandman", Freud adopts an authoritative stance that reduces Hoffmann's story to an object of psychoanalytic knowledge. Analyzing is represented as a regressive movement from textual surface to psychic depth, conceived of in terms of a

97

movement from obscurity and "wild confusion" to coherence and intelligibility. "Freudian method", claims Frederick Crews, "invariably turns up traces of themes that Freudian doctrine declares to lie at the roots of psychic life, and those themes typically subvert the intended ... meaning of a text ... and replace it with a demonic excavated content"(*Out of My System*, xiii). This characterization seems indeed to apply to Freud's interpretation of "The Sandman". As the analysis proceeds, it is only the substitution of the manifest text with its latent, fantasmatic content that allows us to comprehend the quite unparalleled atmosphere of uncanniness this narrative evokes; it is only this substitution that allows us to account for those aspects of the story that seem "arbitrary and meaningless" (*PF* 14: 353).

Yet the most striking insight of "The 'Uncanny'" is Freud's suspicion that his analytical reconstruction has in fact failed to explain the uncanniness of "The Sandman" – indeed, his haunting suspicion that the uncanny is precisely that which evades textual archaeology. Taken out of its context and isolated from the theoretical discussions that frame it, the interpretation of Hoffmann's narrative is an instance of psychoanalytic criticism in its most reductive and dogmatic form. What is so remarkable about "The 'Uncanny'", however, is the fact that Freud calls into question the basic assumptions on which his interpretation depends, as he allows himself to be haunted by that which his interpretation excludes. The major insights of "The 'Uncanny'" emerge not from his reconstruction of Hoffmann's narrative, but from the analytical space, which is the space of encounter of two voices, psychoanalysis and literature.

"The Sandman" is an enigma Freud sets out to solve, but that which is enigmatic appears to be inextricably bound up with those aspects of the story that are set off by his reading – those aspects for which his archaeological reconstruction cannot account. The enigma lies in between, as it were. It is this "in between" that my reading will address: the space that opens between "The Sandman" and Freud's psychoanalytic interpretation of the narrative. The focus of my reading is the figure of the "eye" in Hoffmann's story – the eye that constitutes the point of departure of the psychoanalytic interpretation, but which at the same time confronts us with that which this interpretation ignores or excludes. In agreement with Sarah Kofman and other critics who have commented on "The 'Uncanny'",[1] I stress that what is dismissed by Freud as "irrelevant" (351) to the understanding of the uncanniness of "The Sandman" is precisely that which has to do with the problem of fiction and fictionality.

This applies first of all to the theme of Clara/Olympia, or life-as-death and death-as-life, which appears to be bound up with the theme of poetic creation, and, secondly, to the role of the narrator and the narrative frame of the story. But what Freud has excluded from his interpretation of "The Sandman" returns, itself almost uncannily, in the theoretical framework of his reading, in the concluding discussion of the uncanny and fictionality which, in fact, comes to query his interpretation of the uncanniness of Hoffmann's story. As pointed out by several readers, Freud ultimately arrives at an understanding of the uncanny that calls in question the assumption that uncanniness derives from the latent content, uncovered by psychoanalytic interpretation. Indeed, he arrives at a definition that calls in question the assumption that the uncanny is an effect of content at all. In the following, I explore the transformations Freud's understanding of the uncanny undergoes. My main intention, however, is to show how this elaboration of the theory of the uncanny problematizes an archaeological reconstruction of Hoffmann's text and thus gives rise to a new understanding of reading in psychoanalysis.

To Freud, the eye in Hoffmann's narrative is a metaphor of sexual difference. The eye represents the male organ, the organ the Oedipal father threatens to remove. The preciousness of the eye and the dread of having no eyes, that is, the preciousness of masculinity and the dread of being castrated, are the emotional poles between which "The Sandman" is suspended and from which this story derives its uncanniness. The figure of the eye is conceived of in terms of the dichotomy of masculinity and castration (femininity), possession and lack, presence and absence. But if one reads "The Sandman" rather than just Freud's summary of the narrative, it becomes clear that this dichotomy of possession and lack does not wholly capture the complex workings of the figure of the eye.

First of all, let us pursue the dichotomy of eyes and "no eyes" or "lack of eyes" that Freud has recognized in Hoffmann's narrative. In "The Sandman", possession of eyes is linked with life and warmth while lack of eyes connotes death and coldness. Nathaniel does not understand that Olympia is a dead automaton, until he sees her face with empty sockets. Lack of eyes turns Olympia's beautiful face into a hideous mask of death: "he had seen but too plainly that Olympia's waxen, deathly-pale countenance had no

eyes, but black holes instead – she was, indeed, a lifeless doll".[2]
Without her lover's animating glance, Olympia's hands and lips are
cold as ice; her very body radiates coldness – a coldness that is described as a "horrible deathly chill" (135). In contrast, Nathaniel's
mother and Clara, the women of flesh and blood, are associated
with revivifying warmth. Following Coppelius's attack, the child
Nathaniel falls into a state of unconsciousness, a "sleep of death"
(*Todesschlaf*); his mother's "gentle warm breath" (115) returns him
to life. Similarly, Clara raises her fiancé from the sleep of death that
follows his encounter with the eyeless Olympia. As Clara stoops
over him, Nathaniel feels "an indescribable sensation of pleasure
glowing through him with heavenly warmth" (142).

There is nothing very remarkable about this opposition of eyes/
life/warmth and no eyes/death/coldness, and I should not dwell on
the subject, except that the existence of this dichotomy in "The
Sandman" constitutes a third term: one which destabilizes the conventional opposition of life and death as it blurs or effaces the
boundary between the two. The static dichotomy of eyes and empty
orbits is set in motion through the appearance of a special kind of
eyes: detached eyes, bodiless eyes, so to speak; eyes that do not
belong unequivocally to one character, but circulate between different characters. The critics who have dealt with "The Sandman"
and "The 'Uncanny'" have not, I think, made it sufficiently clear
that the detached eyes constitute a third term that Freud's binary
scheme fails to master.

The theme of detached eyes is of course associated with the doll
Olympia, whose eyes are said to have been stolen from Nathaniel.
But Coppola's spectacles are also bodiless eyes of a sort. "Pretty
eyes," cries the optician as he offers his wares for sale, "Pretty
eyes!" And he goes on to cover Nathaniel's table with glasses.

> A thousand eyes stared and quivered, their gaze fixed upon
> Nathaniel; yet he could not look away from the table, where
> Coppola kept laying down still more and more spectacles, and all
> those flaming eyes leapt in wilder and wilder confusion, shooting
> their blood-red light into Nathaniel's heart.   (131)

At the sight of the optician's "eyes" a great terror seizes Nathaniel.
And yet, quite ironically, he purchases another bodiless eye, namely
Coppola's pocket telescope, which eventually will seal his fate.

Possession of eyes is coupled with warmth, lack of eyes with
coldness. As the passage quoted above indicates, bodiless eyes are

associated with fire, flames, and "bleeding sparks, scorching and burning" (127). "Circle of fire! of fire!" cries Nathaniel, as he sees Olympia's eyes – his own torn-out eyes – lying "upon the ground, staring at him" (141). Fire, in "The Sandman", figures as an agent of fatal transformations, crossings, and reversals. Fire turns everything into its opposite. Hidden in his father's study, the child Nathaniel sees his father bending over a blue flame. The flame transforms his "mild features" into "a repulsive, diabolical countenance. He looked like Coppelius" (115). Later, the father dies in an explosion; he burns to death in his study as he, together with Coppelius, is engaged in some strange experiments. "On the floor of the smoking hearth lay my father dead, with his face burned, blackened and hideously distorted" (116). But "when, two days afterwards, my father was laid in his coffin, his features were again as mild and gentle as they had been in his life" (117). Thus fire appears to be a delusive medium; in the glow of the fire, the good father resembles the wicked Coppelius. Or is it rather that fire affords Nathaniel a glimpse into his father's true – demonic – self?

According to Freud, it will be remembered, Nathaniel's father and Coppelius are nothing but the two figures into which the father imago has been split. Fire, then, is a fundamentally ambiguous force. So are, in fact, the bodiless eyes. "Spyglass" is the English translation of *Perspektiv*; and the ambiguity of this term is indicative of the equivocal quality of the bodiless eye. Is the pocket telescope, which Nathaniel purchases from Coppola, an eye that enables one to spy on that which cannot be seen with the naked eye? Or is it a glass, a mirror in which one sees oneself? Is the bodiless eye a distorting medium, or does it provide supreme insight? There are no final answers to these questions. In Hoffmann's narrative, the bodiless eye is a disruptive term that cannot be placed. The bodiless eyes are neither eyes nor no eyes – or both eyes and no eyes. They are related to insight as well as to blindness, to life as well as to death.

Nathaniel directs the telescope toward Olympia's window. "Never in his life has he met a glass which brought objects so clearly and sharply before his eyes" (132). In this respect, the bodiless eye is the vehicle of perverted desire. For Nathaniel is a voyeur, obsessed with that which is concealed behind closed doors and drawn curtains. In his second letter to Lothair, Nathaniel relates how he has peeped into Professor Spalanzani's room. This scene is itself but a repetition of the traumatic childhood scene Nathaniel had related in his first letter. Driven by an urge to see the Sandman, the child sneaks into his father's study and hides behind a curtain. From his hiding place, the child sees his father and the awful lawyer Coppelius engaged in mysterious experiments. In so many ways this scene is the key to the riddle of the bodiless eyes and thus to the fate of Nathaniel. But what was it the child saw that night in his father's study? In order to answer this question, we have to read the scene through the grid of other, subsequent incidents, since the traumatic scene appears to be nothing but a primal scene, which, like the Wolf Man's primal scene, is only understood after the fact.

Peeping into Professor Spalanzani's room, Nathaniel sees a young woman: Olympia, Spalanzani's daughter. Her face is like an angel's, but her eyes are strangely empty, "indeed there was something fixed about her eyes as if, I might almost say, she had no power of sight" (122). Only too late will Nathaniel learn that Olympia is also the offspring of Coppelius/Coppola. In the childhood scene, Coppelius pulls Nathaniel out from his hiding place and threatens to rob him of his eyes: " 'Now we have eyes enough – a pretty pair of child's eyes', he whispered, and, taking some red hot grains out of the flames with his bare hands, he was about to sprinkle them in my eyes" (115). This scene prefigures the fight between Spalanzani and Coppelius/Coppola that Nathaniel witnesses. The two men are fighting over Olympia, the automaton they together have created, "a work of twenty years" (141). Coppelius runs off with the wooden doll; Spalanzani throws Olympia's torn-out eyes at Nathaniel, "the eyes stolen from you ... there you see the eyes!" (141). Taken together, these fragments form a pattern. The scene Nathaniel witnessed that night in his father's study was a scene of conception. Peeping through the curtain the child saw his father and Coppelius attempting to create life out of matter. The kind of life that is the outcome of such a process is Olympia: the "child" of Spalanzani and Coppola/Coppelius who comes to life as Nathaniel's eyes are inserted in the automaton.

The torn-out eyes engender an artificial, fictitious, supplementary life that is neither life nor death. According to Freud, the theme of Olympia – the theme of the confusion of the living and the dead, of the real and the artificial – cannot be held responsible for the un-canniness of Hoffmann's narrative, because "the author himself treats the episode of Olympia with a faint touch of satire and uses it to poke fun at the young man's idealization of his mistress" (227). But satire, in "The Sandman", is less unequivocal than Freud is prepared to recognize. Far from being an independent theme, which might be separated from the theme of the Sandman, the theme of Olympia permeates the entire narrative.

The confusion of life and death associated with Spalanzani's automaton is bound to be repeated, even after the truth of Olympia has been disclosed. Toward the end of the story, Nathaniel, who has been reunited with Clara, is enjoying the view from a tower together with his fiancée. Suddenly he cries out "wooden doll" (144) and, apparently in a fit of madness, tries to hurl Clara from the tower. This scene is in fact the repetition in reverse of the scene of animation, that is, Nathaniel's animation of Olympia. From the top, Clara's attention is drawn to a curious object appearing in the distance. "Nathaniel mechanically put his hand into his breast pocket – he found Coppola's telescope" (143). Freud, in his interpretative summary of the narrative, misreads this passage when he assumes that it is the sight of the dreaded Coppelius that brings about Nathaniel's final fit of madness. "We may suppose", he writes, "that it was his [Coppelius's] approach, seen through the spy-glass, which threw Nathaniel into his fit of madness" (351). But it is not Coppelius, the castrating father, whom the young man sees through the pocket telescope; it is *Clara*: "Clara was in the way of the glass" (143). And just as the spyglass once showed him the doll Olympia transformed into a living woman, so does the telescope now transform Clara into a dead automaton, a "wooden doll." When the truth of Olympia was revealed to Nathaniel, the young man fell into a state of madness. The same thing happens now.

> Clara was in the way of the glass. His pulse and veins leapt convulsively. Pale as death, he stared at Clara, soon streams of fire flashed and glared from his rolling eyes, he roared frightfully, like a hunted beast. Then he sprang high into the air and, punctuating his words with horrible laughter, he shrieked out in a piercing tone, "Spin round, wooden doll! – spin round!"   (143–44)

A crowd has gathered below the tower, and from this crowd Coppelius suddenly emerges. Nathaniel stands still, catches sight of the lawyer, and with the words "Ah, pretty eyes – pretty eyes!" (144) he flings himself over the parapet.

The price of wanting to kindle life is death. But not even death can bring to an end the pattern of repetition that governs the narrative. As it turns out, Nathaniel's failure to establish the distinction

between the living and the dead, the real and the artificial, is conta-
gious. The reaction of the population of the small university town
to the story of Olympia is emblematic of this effect. As it becomes
publicly known that Spalanzani's daughter was in fact an automaton, a "pernicious mistrust of human figures" (142) begins to
prevail. A deep uncertainty over-spreads and contaminates everything. From now on, all ladies fear being mistaken for dead wooden
dolls – and all young men secretly suspect their sweethearts of being
automatons. As Olympia is now being associated with mechanical
perfection, there is no way of proving one's humanity except
through artificial, mechanical, *im*perfections.

In spite of themselves, Nathaniel's fellow townsmen, one might
say, inherit the young poet's perverted preference for the artificial.
Paradoxically, then, Olympia was all too human, precisely because
she was a mechanical doll. "It is all an allegory – a sustained
metaphor" (142), contends the professor of poetry and rhetoric.
But an allegory for what? For the artificiality of human life? For the
fact that life is smitten with death? In this case, Coppola's spyglass
would not be the deceptive, distorting medium it gave the impression of being. The demonic bodiless eye provides an insight, though
it is not the knowledge Nathaniel had hoped for. Nathaniel's fatal
confusion of an automaton with a human being has revealed a horrifying fact. The crossing of the borderline between life and death
has always already taken place; the opposition of life and death, of
eyes and no eyes, has always already been undermined. As lifeless
works of art are animated through projection, so is life itself
marked by death. This, indeed, may be the content of Nathaniel's
final mad vision. What he saw as he looked at Clara, the embodiment of life, through Coppola's spyglass was that which Freud, at
this point in his analysis, is not prepared to see: the uncanny return
of Olympia in Clara, the encroachment of the artificial on the real,
the encroachment of death on life. What was prefigured in his poem
had come true to him: "Nathaniel looks into Clara's eyes, but it is
death that looks kindly upon him from her eyes" (127).

Situated on the borderline between eyes and no eyes, (in)sight
and blindness, life and death, the bodiless eye blurs or effaces this
boundary. There is not life on one side and death on the other, but
rather life-in-death and death-in-life. There is not insight on one
side and blindness on the other. Rather, there is the absence of any
stable and secure position from which one can distinguish truth
from falsehood. The bodiless eye is a figure for this ambiguity or

uncertainty, just as it is the figure for the impossibility of mastering the narrative. For Coppola's spyglass is not only associated with Olympia, Spalanzani, and Coppelius/Coppola's oeuvre, and with Nathaniel's demonic poem; ultimately, the bodiless eye becomes a metaphor for "The Sandman" itself. As readers of this story, says Freud, we perceive that Hoffmann "intends to make us, too, look through the demon optician's spectacles or spy-glass" (351). And to look through this demonic spyglass is to be smitten with Nathaniel's fatal desire as well as with the uncertainty, the "pernicious mistrust", that is the target of the narrator's satire. Only when it is too late will the reader discover that Hoffmann's labyrinth of mirrors has numerous entrances, but no exit.

Thus from the very beginning, the narrative raises the question of point of view: Should we read the story of the Sandman through the eyes of Nathaniel or through the eyes of Clara? Is the demon other or is he a projection of forces within one's own self? Are we in the realm of the supernatural or are we dealing with phantoms of the self? What is real and what is imaginary? Does Nathaniel's childhood recollection account for what really happened? Or is truth rather to be sought in Clara's analytical reconstruction? Having posed these questions of how to read, the text introduces a third pair of eyes, those of the narrator. Though if we expect the narrator to provide us with the insight that allows us to distinguish between the real and the imaginary, between truth and delusion, we are disappointed. All that a poet can do, we find, is to present life as "a dull reflection in a dimly polished mirror" (124). The eye of the narrator is nothing but yet another (distorting?) mirror that reflects the ambiguity of the initial positions.

Freud's Oedipal reading of "The Sandman" is based on a double negligence: the neglecting of the theme of Olympia (or of Olympia/ Clara) and the neglecting of the narrative frame or of narration itself. The theme of Olympia is in fact inseparable from the problem of the narrative structure and the narrative dynamics of "The Sandman". This is, first of all, because Olympia is the embodiment of the desire for insight, the desire for mastery, the desire to create, to produce life. In this respect, Olympia is bound up with the narrator's desire to tell and to animate through his telling. Secondly, it is because the uncertainty to which Olympia gives rise permeates the entire narrative. Olympia is a problem of reading for which there is no irreversible solution – a problem of reading passed on from Nathaniel to the narrator and finally to the reader. As I have suggested above, what Freud excludes from his interpretation is precisely that which would have allowed him to see "The Sandman" not as an example of the uncanny, not as an object of a psychoanalytic explanation, but as an implicit *theory* of the uncanny. From this perspective, his misreading of the final madness scene – that is, his confusion of the return of the wooden doll Olympia in the body of Clara with the return of the castrating father – is symptomatic: the theme of Olympia is that which does not quite fit in with Freud's Oedipal approach to "The Sandman"; indeed, it constitutes a threat to his wish to master the text and therefore must be overlooked, if not repressed or negated.

Having completed his interpretation of "The Sandman", Freud attempts to apply his theory of the uncanny to the theme of Olympia, and, rather than confirming his theory, the theme of Olympia induces him to reexamine the problem of the uncanny.

The theme of Olympia is a disruptive force. Olympia is associated with the "uncertainty" Freud has so vehemently rejected, with death – or rather with life-in-death and death-in-life – as well as with the desire that is so compulsively transmitted or transferred. It is the theme for which Freud's textual archaeology cannot account. But it is also the theme his argument runs up against; the theme that brings back what he has excluded from his interpretation of "The Sandman", and which ultimately obliges him to reconsider his initial definition of the uncanny, as well as the question of what is involved in a psychoanalytic reading.

Freud's argument compels a return to the question posed by "The Sandman" itself: the question of how to read. We have seen how Freud in his definition of the uncanny expressly ruled out the hypothesis of "intellectual uncertainty". His discussion of unintended recurrence of the same and of "our relation to death", however, will lead him to include in his own argument the explanation he has rejected. Are we, he writes, "after all justified in entirely ignoring intellectual uncertainty as a factor, seeing that we have admitted its importance in relation to death?" (370). Indeed, the factor of "intellectual uncertainty" becomes the primary concern of the final part of the essay, in which Freud, precisely because of the factor of uncertainty, will be obliged to consider the uncanniness of fictional texts as a separate case and, ultimately, to recognize that the uncanny has a privileged relation to literature or fictionality.

After having related and analyzed various instances of the uncanny, Freud arrives at the remarkable conclusion that he has not been able to solve the problem of the uncanny.

> It may be true that the uncanny (*unheimlich*) is something which is secretly familiar (*heimlich-heimisch*), which has undergone repression and then returned from it, and that everything that is uncanny fulfils this condition. But the selection of material on this basis does not enable us to solve the problem of the uncanny. For our proposition is clearly not convertible. Not everything that fulfils this condition – not everything that recalls repressed desires and surmounted modes of thinking belonging to the prehistory of the individual and of the race – is on that account uncanny.   (368).

The uncanny effect, then, does not derive from any particular content or subject matter.

For almost every example adduced in support of the theory of the uncanny as return of the repressed, one may be found that rebuts it. And, notably, it transpires that "nearly all the instances that contradict our hypothesis are taken from the realm of fiction, of imaginative writing" (370). It is the threat of being castrated that "gives the idea of losing other organs its intense colouring", claimed Freud in connection with his interpretation of "The Sandman". "We shall venture, therefore," he concluded, "to refer the uncanny effect of the Sand-Man to the anxiety belonging to the castration complex of childhood." He now admits that not all fictional texts that deal with dismembered limbs are on that account uncanny. Fairy stories "are crammed with instantaneous wish-fulfilments which produce no uncanny effect whatever. ... Fairy tales quite frankly adopt the animistic standpoint of the omnipotence of thoughts and wishes, and yet I cannot think of any genuine fairy story which has anything uncanny about it." The coming to life of an inanimate object and the reanimation of the dead have been represented as an uncanny theme. But again: "things of this sort too are very common in fairy stories" (369) and therefore not in themselves uncanny. Fiction is par excellence the site of the uncanny, since, as Freud observes, "there are many more means of creating uncanny effects in fiction than there are in real life" (373). Yet fiction is that which his argument incessantly comes up against; fiction is that which frustrates his attempt to arrive at a stable and consistent definition of the uncanny.[3]

The imaginative writer, says Freud, has "this licence ... that he can select his world of representation" so that it either coincides with the known reality or departs from it. "We accept his ruling in every case." In fairy tales the world of reality is left behind from the very start. Despite their subject matter, fairy tales are not uncanny, for they are entirely set within the realms of the imaginary; we know for certain how to read them. The writer can also choose a world of representation that is less imaginary than the world of fairy tales and yet differs from reality by admitting supernatural beings such as demonic spirits or ghosts. "So long as they remain within their setting of poetic reality, such figures lose any uncanniness which they might possess" (373). Referring to the supernatural apparitions in *Hamlet* and *Macbeth*, Freud points out that the reader adapts his judgment to the imaginary reality the writer has imposed on him: "In this case too we avoid all trace of the uncanny" (374). For the feeling of uncanniness "cannot arise unless there is a conflict of judgement as to whether things which have been 'surmounted' and are regarded as incredible may not, after all, be possible" (373). "Thus we see", Freud concludes, "how independent emotional effects can be of the actual subject-matter in the world of fiction" (376). This statement, which marks a return to the surface of textuality, is implicitly a withdrawal from textual archaeology.

Freud's desire to explain everything – or, more specifically, his desire to accommodate the theme of Olympia within the psychoanalytic interpretation of "The Sandman" – has prompted a supplementary treatment of the uncanny which, rather than elaborating on his initial definition, has shown the archaeological approach to the uncanny in literature to be untenable. In his attempt to apply to other instances of the uncanny the hypothesis of an infantile factor, derived from the Oedipal reading of the theme of loosing one's eyes, he has launched an inquiry into the uncanny that once again confronts him with problems he believed he had solved.

In light of Freud's concluding remarks, the figure of the eye in "The Sandman" assumes a new importance to the theory of the uncanny. An uncanny effect, it is maintained, "is often and easily produced when the distinction between imagination and reality is effaced" (367). Ambiguously poised between seeing and blindness, between truth and deceit, the detached eye in Hoffmann's narrative is the figure of such effacement. Situated on the surface, the eye is the boundary between inside and outside, self and other; it is precisely the collapse of this boundary that "The Sandman" enacts.

As a vehicle for perpetual crossings, the eye – the detached eye – disturbs the dichotomy between life and death and prevents us from establishing a clear distinction between the real and the imaginary world. The eye, therefore, is the figure of the textual undecidability that is the basic premise of the uncanny effect – whatever its source in the unconscious may be.

Freud began his essay by presenting "The Sandman" as an *unheimlich* story which, once it had been analyzed, would confirm the psychoanalytic theory of the uncanny. But rather than being an object passively awaiting psychoanalytic excavation and reconstruction, Hoffmann's narrative turns out to be a highly complex work that offers resistance to the Freudian approach. The point of departure of the psychoanalytic interpretation was the assumption of a "substitutive relation between the eye and the male organ", and between the fear of losing one's eyes and the anxiety of castration. "The 'Uncanny'" ends by showing that this assumption does not explain the uncanny effect. The interpretive pattern Freud applies to Hoffmann's narrative has already been undermined by the text itself. By constructing a system of binary oppositions destabilized through the appearance of a third term, "The Sandman" escapes Freudian systematics. On the level of that which is narrated, this third term is the bodiless eye, the telescope that generates the fictitious, supplementary life of Olympia, the life that is neither/nor and both/and. On the level of narration the third term is the third point of view, the narrator who renounces authority and thus disturbs the reader's expectation of a singular solution.

In the context of "The 'Uncanny'", "The Sandman" is itself a disruptive term that problematizes Freud's archaeological reconstruction, as it returns to haunt his argument. But from the failure of Freudian archaeology something else has emerged: an understanding of textuality and uncanniness that belongs neither to Freud nor to Hoffmann, but to both.

NOTES

[Lis Møller is Associate Professor of Comparative Literature at the University of Aarhus, Denmark. She is the author of *The Freudian Reading: Analytical and Fictional Constructions* (1991), and has published books and articles on psychoanalysis, literary theory and nineteenth-century literature. Her most recent English-language publications include "Repetition, Return, and Doubling in Henrik Ibsen's Major Prose Plays" (2001) and

"Thomas De Quincey's Arabesque Confessions" (2002). She is editor, with Marie-Louise Svane, of *Romanticism in Theory* (2001).   Ed.]

1. Along with Kofman's and Cixous's discussions, excerpted in this volume, Møller lists the following "brilliant poststructuralist and deconstructive readings" of Freud's "The 'Uncanny'" and Hoffmann's "The Sandman": Weber (1973), Mehlman (1975), Hertz (1979) and Wright (1998; 128–34). We might add Rubin (1982), Meltzer (1982) and Wright (1999; 18–30) [Editor's note].

2. "The Sandman" 141. Møller cites the translation of "The Sandman" in J.M. Cohen's (ed.) *Tales from Hoffmann* (1951): to preserve the integrity of her discussion, page references to Hoffmann's tale in Essay 6 are to this edition [Editor's note].

3. This is Cixous's point. It is not merely the question of examining the enigma of the uncanny, she says, but also of examining the enigma of fiction, "and of fiction in its privileged relationship to the *Unheimliche*" (Essay 5).

Part III
Sigmund Freud, *The "Wolf Man"*

Introductory Note

CONSTRUCTING AND DECONSTRUCTING THE WOLF MAN

Sergei Constantinovitch Pankeiev: the "Wolf Man". He was Freud's most celebrated, perhaps most enigmatic patient.

Freud called him the "Wolf Man" after a dream the boy had when he was 4. Little Sergei dreamed that he woke one summer night, watched his window open by itself and saw a group of white wolves sitting in a walnut tree outside, looking at him fixedly. Terrified, he screamed and woke up.

The wolf dream became the analytic centre-piece of Freud's most elaborate and theoretically revealing case history, *From the History of an Infantile Neurosis* (completed in 1914, and published in 1918). The Wolf Man was analyzed by Freud from 1910–1914, and again from 1919–20. He arrived in Freud's consulting room at the age of 23 in a state of crippling dependency; he needed an enema every day from a valet in permanent attendance on him, and was attended by a private doctor. As Peter Brooks points out in Essay 7, Pankeiev had been in and out of sanatoria from the age of 21, but had gained no relief from his obsessive and hysterical symptoms. He had suffered and manifested symptoms, in fact, all his life. His family reported that at the age of $3\frac{1}{2}$ his behaviour changed from docility to difficulty and fits of screaming, and Freud records that at 4 the dream of the wolves led to an animal phobia that, after a period of schooling in the Bible from his mother, produced a full-scale obsessional neurosis with a religious basis that lasted until the boy was 10. The obsessional neurosis subsequently modulated into a devotion to all things military, and the Wolf Man's health col-

lapsed finally when he suffered a breakdown precipitated by gonor-
rhoea at the age of 17.

Freud interprets the Wolf Man's neuroses and phobias as symptoms of his disturbed sexual life, and charts his history in relation
to what he sees as the *traumatic* sexual meaning of the wolf dream.
Freud says that the dream is charged with repressed significance,
and that what is repressed is a *memory*. The dream, he says, is in
fact "another kind of remembering" (*FR* 419; *PF* 9: 285). This
points to the reason why the *Wolf Man* has become a *cause célèbre*
in psychoanalytic theory, for Freud interprets the wolf dream as
enshrining a "primal scene" that was forgotten but that occurred
when Sergei was just $1\frac{1}{2}$. He says the primal scene is dreamed
rather than remembered and takes its traumatic effect in a *deferred*
moment: not at the time of its occurrence but later. This is the
Freudian concept of "deferred action" or *nachträglichkeit*, what
Jean Laplanche has translated into English as "afterwardsness".[1]
Here an event happens that is not itself traumatic, but becomes
so when it is retroactively charged with trauma at a later time.
Furthermore, in the case of the Wolf Man, the "primal scene" is
symptomatized in the patient's phobias. Freud says that because the
primal scene is unavailable to memory it can be approached only
through a work of analytic construction. He says: "scenes ... like
this one ... which date from such an early period [in the patient's
history] ... are as a rule not reproduced as recollections, but have to
be divined – constructed – gradually and laboriously from an aggre-
gate of indications" (*FR* 419; *PF* 9: 284–5). As products of "construction", these scenes are in effect analytic inventions designed to
account for the patient's symptoms: they are belated fictionaliza-
tions of a scene of origin for the subject's illness. In the case of the
Wolf Man, the "primal scene" is famously one of coitus *a tergo* –
from behind – between his parents. Freud thinks that Sergei woke
up in his cot one summer afternoon when just $1\frac{1}{2}$ and witnessed his
parents' sexual intercourse, half-undressed and in white under-
clothes. He believes Sergei's mother's genitals and father's organ
were clearly visible to him, and that although he "received the impressions when he was one and a half ... his understanding of them
was deferred" (*FR* 411; *PF* 9: 269): deferred, that is, until he was 4,
the time of the dream.

Because of repression, Freud says, the primal scene is distorted by
the dream: thus the opening of the window in the dream disguises
Sergei's opening eyes in the scene (*FR* 408–9; *PF* 9: 265), the

wolves' attentive gaze conceals his *own* looking at his parents' love-making, the immobility of the animals masks the "violent motion" of the scene he actually witnessed (*FR* 409; *PF* 9: 266), and the *whiteness* of the wolves disguises the whiteness of his parents' undergarments in the scene (*FR* 411; *PF* 9: 269). Sergei's "deferred" understanding of the scene as sexual, Freud says, results from events in the intervening time in which, at $2\frac{1}{2}$, he excitedly witnesses a maid kneeling and scrubbing the floor in the same posture as his mother in the primal scene, wets himself and, thinks Freud, is jokingly threatened with castration for it (this is the "scene with Grusha", *PF* 9: 331, 336); the period from the age of $3\frac{1}{4}$ in which he is "seduced" by his older sister when she takes his penis in her hand and tells him sexual stories about his nurse or "Nanya" (*PF* 9: 248); the "castration" threat from his Nanya at 3 after he has turned his affection from his sister to her and plays with his penis in front of her (*PF* 9: 253); and his witnessing on trips made with his father of "large white [sheep] dogs" like the wolves in the dream who were most likely, Freud says, to be seen not just working but copulating *a tergo* too (*FR* 424; *PF* 9: 292), replaying the position of his parents in the primal scene.

This history of infant sexual experience and observance up to the age of 4 enables a belated or *deferred* reading by the Wolf Man of the forgotten primal scene; for the scene is now flooded with traumatic sexual meaning and erupts in the anxiety dream of the white wolves. What is activated in the dream is both the boy's castration anxiety – his sight of his mother's genitals, Freud argues, is reseen belatedly as evidence of "castration" in the light of threats he received later (*PF* 9: 355) – and a flurry of libidinal identifications on his part with both of his parents, both active and passive. Indeed, the Wolf Man's history is seen by Freud *as* a story of multiple and unstable sexual identifications, in which the subject identifies by turns with passive and aggressive, heterosexual and homosexual, feminine and masculine positions, at once in symptom and fantasy. Freud writes: "it was not only a single sexual current that started from the primal scene but a whole set of them ... his sexual life was positively splintered up by it" (*FR* 414; *PF* 9: 275–6).

This "splintering" of the Wolf Man's sexual life into multiple identifications – what Freud calls his "unbridled instinctual life" – imposes a peculiar burden on the analyst writing the case history: a burden of *narration* in which, seeking a "general perspective" (*PF* 9: 345), Freud finds himself continually hampered by fragments, discontinuities, contradictions and undecidables in the story. Freud acknowledges that his analysis, despite or may be because of the wealth of information at his disposal about the Wolf Man's sexual history, is "disjointed", with his "exposition showing corresponding gaps" (*PF* 9: 345); as Linda Ruth Williams says, "Like *Dora*, this is also a fragmented text" (*Critical Desire* 133). Indeed, the *Wolf Man* is as notable for its analytic or interpretive inconclusiveness as for its theoretical instructiveness. Freud *wants* to finalize and formalize the case history in terms of its closure in a cure and its textual closure, too, saying of the Wolf Man in a later text: "When [the patient] left me in the midsummer of 1914, with as little suspicion as the rest of us of what lay so shortly ahead [i.e. the First World War], I believed that his cure was radical and permanent" (*SE* 23: 217). However, the "cure" proved neither radical nor permanent. Freud notes that in 1919 the Wolf Man was back in his consulting rooms, destitute and stateless now in the wake of World War I and the Russian Revolution, in order to "master a part of the transference that had not been resolved"; but even here the Wolf Man's psychoanalytic story was not over. In the mid 1920s – October 1926 to February 1927 – he was analyzed again, this time not by Freud but one of his disciples, Ruth Mack Brunswick, due to continuing "paranoid" interruptions in his health. Speaking of this period of his patient's history, Freud refers to the Wolf Man's "perennial neurosis" (*SE* 23: 218): in fact, the Wolf Man continued to enter into analytic and quasi-analytic relationships throughout his long life (he died in 1979), a history meticulously and valuably documented by one of his later analysts and friends, Muriel Gardiner, in *The Wolf-Man and Sigmund Freud* in 1972.

The fact that the Wolf Man was, as Nicolas Abraham and Maria Torok put it, "bewitched by some secret" – a secret that, indeed, *remained* undisclosed – ensured that his story had a rich afterlife, way beyond his association with Sigmund Freud. Abraham and Torok comment: "Just think of Freud and his Wolf Man. From 1910 well into Freud's extreme old age, the case of this enigmatic Russian ... never stopped haunting him, drawing from him theory upon theory because he could not discover the key to the poem" (*SK* 140). "Theory upon theory" is drawn from Freud by the Wolf Man, they say; and, indeed, a remarkable feature of the *Wolf Man* as a case is that its history of reinterpretation strangely rehearses the structure of its *meaning*, its meaning, that is, as *nachträglichkeit* or "deferred action". Insofar as the Wolf Man and his case "haunt"

Freud, they could be said to repeat and renew themselves uncannily within Freud and psychoanalysis itself like a traumatic scene of *deferred interpretation*, an unlaid phantom or ghost of meaning, something that is returned to like the "primal scene" in the case but that always at some level remains missing, absent, undisclosed.

Freud's most famous "return" to the primal scene in the case itself is his reinterpretation in the second draft of the paper of the very *reality* of that scene. Having insisted for most of the text *on* the reality of the primal scene (it was part of his contemporary disagreement with Jung and Adler), Freud entertains the possibility that the scene *may* be a structure of fantasy, that it may have been constructed retrospectively by the patient rather than have been an observed event – the sight of the copulating white dogs, he thinks, may have been "transferred" on to a non-sexual scene of togetherness between the Wolf Man's parents witnessed when he was younger (*FR* 424; *PF* 9: 293). Freud says with disarming theoretical candour that the question of whether primal scenes are "real memories or phantasies" is in fact undecidable, not capable of being determined, and he concludes: "I intend on this occasion to close the discussion of the reality of the primal scene with a *non liquet* ['It is not clear']" (*FR* 426; *PF* 9: 295). As Nicholas Rand points out, the model of reading that operates in the *Wolf Man* thus oscillates vertiginously between asserting the "primacy of trauma or ... fantasy" (*WMMW* lv); or as Jonathan Culler puts it, the question that cannot be determined is whether we are dealing with a "primal event ... [or] a trope, a transference" (*The Pursuit of Signs* 180). For Rand, this means that any reading of the *Wolf Man* must stake out its territory in the space "*between* fantasy and trauma, fiction and reality" (my emphasis, *WMMW* lvi); another way of putting this would be to say, as Lis Møller does, that the *Wolf Man* "deconstructs the dichotomy of real event and fantasy and allows for the coexistence of different and mutually exclusive readings" (*Freudian* 82).

Peter Brooks, in "Fictions of the Wolf Man: Freud and Narrative Understanding" (Essay 7), sees this aporia or interpretive undecidability in the case as part of the moment of Freud's cultural modernism, and argues that psychoanalytic narrative is part of the general crisis of cultural and psychological narration that characterizes the modernist era. He says that in the *Wolf Man* Freud finds detection and its narration to be "complex and problematic, like the plots of modernist fiction, and indeed inextricably bound up with the fictional" (Essay 7). The undecidability of the primal scene would be the privileged example of that inextricability. Brooks says that the Freudian view of events as taking on "traumatic significance by deferred action (*Nachträglichkeit*) or retroaction ... working in reverse sequence to create a meaning that did not previously exist" (Essay 7), radically disorganizes our sense both of linear temporality and narrative causality; for it suggests that stories are written *backwards* rather than forwards. Brooks views psychoanalysis and the genre of the case history it invents as manifestations of the secularization of human narratives that begins with the Enlightenment period and Romanticism, moves through the 19th century, and results in the decline of the "sacred masterplot" (*Reading for the Plot* 268) of collective myth or narrative, the grand story underwritten by God or nature. He says that although psychoanalysis shares the 19th century's "privileging of narrative explanation" (Essay 7), it also radically undermines confidence in that model, suggesting that the "closure demanded by narrative understanding – the closure without which it can have no coherent plot – is always provisional, as-if, a necessary fiction" (Essay 7). In the case of the *Wolf Man*, indeed, the deferment of the Wolf Man's meaning – both that of his own story and the story of his psychoanalytic interpretation – is exemplary of the open-endedness of psychoanalytic narrative, for the Wolf Man as a subject of psychoanalysis is constituted in an endless transcription and retranscription of an inaccessible scene of origin, together with the "splintered" effects of that origin.

The most impressive post-Freudian meditation on this inaccessible origin and its effects is Nicholas Abraham's and Maria Torok's remarkable study of the Wolf Man case, *The Wolf Man's Magic Word: A Cryptonymy*, published in 1976 (excerpts from Chapters 1 and 2 of this text are included in Essay 8). Abraham's and Torok's study consists of a reading of the Freudian case history, of the Wolf Man's appearance elsewhere in Freud's writings, and of the complex history of the Wolf Man in the wake of Freud. Their "Introduction" to the text, entitled "Five Years with the Wolf Man", speaks of their "numerous rereadings" and "renewed returns" to the "same documents" (Essay 8) – these documents being Freud's case history itself, the Wolf Man's letters to Freud, Ruth Mack Brunswick's "A Supplement to Freud's 'History of an Infantile Neurosis'" of the 1920s, the Wolf Man's own "Memoirs" written late in his life, the Wolf Man's correspondence with Muriel Gardiner, and his late dialogues with Karin Obholzer. So many "returns" to the "same documents", so many *deferred effects* of his story, we might say, and of the texts that try to tell his story. For Abraham and Torok, it is as if there was some kind of ghost or phantom – like the phantom of *Hamlet* (as we saw in Part I) – walking through the books and pages of the Wolf Man's history, refusing to speak its meaning, insisting on keeping the story open, refusing to let the Wolf Man's story be laid to rest. The Wolf Man's story is haunted; it encloses or encrypts a ghost.

And Abraham and Torok do find a kind of ghost,[2] or a kind of crypt, in the life of the Wolf Man: and they find it in what they call the Wolf Man's "magic word". But what is this "magic word" that belongs to the Wolf Man? Where does its "magic" reside? What "crypt" is buried in him? Retheorizing the Freudian notion of re-pression, Abraham and Torok argue that what is repressed or buried in the Wolf Man and his story is not traumatic castration anxiety, as Freud would have it, but rather a *word*: and, specific-ally, a word of *desire*, a word of *pleasure*, a *libidinal* word. That word is *tieret*. It is a Russian word (the Wolf Man was native Russian), and it means "to rub". Employing an analytic procedure they call "anasemia" – in which words or fragments of words are led "'back up [and] toward' (from the Greek *ana*) ... earlier sources of signification (*semia*)" (Rashkin, *Family Secrets* 43) – Abraham and Torok find that in the Wolf Man's nightmare of the wolves, in the dreams he relates to Ruth Mack Brunswick, and in the text of his entire life, a group of "repressed pleasure-words" (Essay 8) are buried or encrypted, with *tieret* the most significant of them. Starting from something that Freud notes in his text but fails to analyze, namely, that the Wolf Man was *multi-lingual*, Abraham and Torok begin to "hear" (*WMMW* 34) a constellation of Russian and English words interred or encrypted within the Wolf Man's German. They hear, that is, behind the German words he spoke to Freud, Russian homonyms from his native language, along with English words from his experience with his English governess in his "*English* nursery" (*WMMW* 31). In a remarkable effect, they disin-ter or decrypt an entire vocabulary of trans-lingual homonyms and homophonies that, for them, point not to the Wolf Man's witness-ing of a scene of coitus between the parents, but rather to a scene of seduction of the Wolf Man's sister by his father. In the wolf dream, for instance, they hear the Russian word *siestorka*, or "sister", hidden behind the idea of the "pack of six" wolves in the dream – a "sixter" (or sister) of wolves, they suggest (Essay 8) – and they use the verbal and symptomatic textures of the Wolf Man's later analysis with Ruth Mack Brunswick in the 1920s to read, in a kind of deferred analytic effect, what Brunswick calls "new material of great import, hitherto forgotten memories, all relating to the complicated attachment of the [Wolf Man's] preschizophrenic sister to her small brother" (Gardiner, *The Wolf-Man and Sigmund Freud* 263), material buried in the Wolf Man himself and in Freud's text.

The Wolf Man's sister – older than him, intellectually gifted, sexually precocious – is a key figure, of course, in the Freudian case history itself, being credited with "seducing" the Wolf Man when he was $3\frac{1}{4}$. But Abraham and Torok insist – as Freud cannot because of his fixation on castration – that the Wolf Man's desire is not to do with phallic, but with sister loss. The word *tieret*, they argue, is the "magic word" that both "expresses" the Wolf Man's desire – that is, his desire to be "rubbed" by the sister (*tieret*) – and buries that desire in a crypt in his psyche. For, as well as a "pleasure-word", *tieret* is a "*taboo word*" (Essay 8), and this taboo derives from the Wolf Man being called to bear witness, Abraham and Torok say, to *a scene of family scandal*, to the scene of an "*alleged seduction of the daughter by the father*" (Essay 8), a scene of sexual rubbing and of inadmissable pleasure: *tieret*. A prohibition and a desire, then, are encrypted in the "magic word".

The word is repressed, but it continues, say Abraham and Torok, to articulate both what the Wolf Man hides from himself during his life (namely, the father's seduction of his loved sister) *and* to articulate the thing he most desires (to be part of that scene himself, to identify with the desiring father in relation to the sister, to identify with the sister as the favourite of the seducing father). Articulating both a prohibition and a pleasure, the word *tieret* must be kept secret by the Wolf Man at all costs; it must be encrypted, interred, denied. But the cryptic or "magic" word appears in the Wolf Man's life where it cannot be noticed, where it can give pleasure but not reveal itself, where it can keep itself secret in order to ensure that the crypt remains intact. Thus Abraham and Torok point to the Wolf Man's compulsive falling in love with women positioned on all fours, as in the "scene with Grusha" in the Freud case (*PF 9*: 329–36), where "Grusha" is found squatting to scrub or to *rub* the floor: *tieret*. And they point to the Wolf Man's unnamed appearance, too, in Freud's late essay "On Fetishism" (1927), where Freud refers to a man, unmistakably the Wolf Man, whose "fetishistic precondition" for sexual arousal was a bizarre "shine

on the nose" (*PF* 7: 351): and, again, they hear encrypted here
the taboo words "'to rub', 'to shine'" (*SK* 154), or to polish, in this
case the "nose". *Tieret.*

But does the scene of seduction, or "rubbing", between the
daughter and the father actually take place? Is this in fact the Wolf
Man's "true" primal scene? For Abraham and Torok, the paternal
seduction scene is undoubtedly witnessed to by the Wolf Man's
"word", but they suggest that this scene might be just as much *produced* by the word as represented by it. The taboo word is a libidinal counter of pleasure and of prohibition, and its presentation of a
"true" event is both asserted and denied by the Wolf Man. The
Wolf Man, Abraham and Torok say, at once "claims and denies"
(*WMMW* 46) the truth of the paternal seduction scene, wanting it
and not wanting it, and in fact *living* the undecidability of the two
alternatives. The seduction scene is asserted as reality *and* as fiction
by the Wolf Man, but his libidinal history will not say which it is.

For Jacques Derrida, in his introduction to and interpretation of
Abraham's and Torok's *The Wolf Man's Magic Word* (Essay 9),
the Wolf Man's secret or "crypt" never appears as a *presence*; its
phantomatic status materializes, instead, what he calls "the *cryptic*
structure of the ultimate 'referent'". Derrida is interested in the
unplaceable and unlocatable structure of the crypt that is interred in
the Wolf Man's psyche and speech. His title, "*Fors*", already hints
at this unplaceability of the crypt: *fors* incorporates the sense of
something belonging both to the inside (as in the "French expression *le for intérieur* ... the inner heart") and something belonging to
the outside (as in the *fore*-word to a text, something exterior to
another text – see "Translator's note", *WMMW* xi–xii). The crypt,
then, is both interior and exterior to the Wolf Man's self; it occupies an *unassignable* place within and without the walls of his identity. In this way, the Wolf Man is a subject-in-deconstruction; for,
insofar as he is inhabited by a "cryptic" otherness, the boundaries
of his identity are indeterminable. Derrida emphasizes that the crypt
is constructed and maintained through a play of language, or rather
of *languages*. There are, he points out, "three languages that are
building it": Russian, English, German. This, of course, means that
there is no *one* language in which the crypt resides; instead, it is
dispersed or disseminated trans-lingually. This is why Derrida
speaks of Abraham's and Torok's *mots anglés*, or "angled words";
the crypt is verbally confected on the basis of the "angles" or the
skewed conjunctures between the Wolf Man's three languages. At

the same time Derrida puns in French on the phonetic identity between *anglés* and *anglais* (English), thereby reminding the reader that it is in the *angles* between the Wolf Man's adult languages (Russian and German) and his infant or "nursery" language (English), that the crypt is preserved. The impossible portmanteau word "anglish" – used by the translator, Barbara Johnson, to translate Derrida's pun into English – emphasizes the fact that, for Derrida, Abraham's and Torok's Wolf Man is always in a place, or "no-place", *between* languages. His magic word is located in a "babel of tongues" (*WMMW* 35).

The enigmatic or elusive topos of the Wolf Man's crypt does not mean, however, that his analysis is impossible or unthinkable. Rather, the crypt becomes the *condition* of the Wolf Man's analysis; it makes his story possible, keeps it at once open and closed, and keeps interpretation alive. Jacques Derrida – like Sigmund Freud, Ruth Mack Brunswick, Muriel Gardiner, Nicolas Abraham and Maria Torok – becomes another scribe in the "immense polyphonic poem" of the Wolf Man's biographical and textual history, a history that reveals how life can be lived as a rich and cryptic fiction, and a rich and cryptic fiction can be lived as one's truth.

NOTES

1. For Laplanche's account of his translation of Freud's term, see his "Notes on Afterwardsness" (*Jean Laplanche* 217–223).

2. In his "Foreword" to *The Wolf Man's Magic Word*, Derrida says that "the words 'ghost' and 'haunting' are sometimes unavoidable in designating the inhabitants of the crypt within the Self", though strictly speaking the ghost in Abraham and Torok belongs to "a parental unconscious". Here, I use the word "ghost" in what Derrida calls the "wider sense ... of the inhabitant of a crypt belonging in the Self" (*WMMW* 118, 119).

7

Fictions of the Wolf Man: Freud and Narrative Understanding

PETER BROOKS

Sergei Pankeiev, otherwise known as the Wolf Man, died in the Vienna Psychiatric Hospital at the age of ninety-two on May 7, 1979. The event passed without much public notice. No doubt most presentday readers of Freud's classic case history of the Wolf Man, *From the History of an Infantile Neurosis*, published in 1918, have assumed that its subject long since passed away, or at least vanished from the context of the narratable into the vague and uninteresting realm of "real life." He had become fixed as a literary figure, a textual creation, evoked to represent a certain psychological configuration, an exemplary biography. The Wolf Man, however, in 1971 published his own memoirs, including his reminiscence of the remarkable Dr. Freud, thus offering a curious moment of reversal, as if the object of investigation in the detective story had suddenly taken over the narrative from the detective himself. Yet he called his memoirs *The Wolf-Man by the Wolf-Man*, signing his own version of his life's story with the name he had been assigned by Freud in the case history, the name derived from his most famous traumatic dream, itself using as its representational material derivatives from fairy tales: a symbolic fictional construct at several removes from "reality" which he yet assumed as his public identity. His identity remained to the end of his life inextricably bound up with his role as the most famous "case" of psychoanalysis, with a biography written by Freud that was essential to a certain conceptual moment and theoretical construction in Freud's thought.[1]

However much for us as readers the Wolf Man belongs to the pages of Freud's case history, he had, of course, his "own" histories. He lived through the individual and collective disasters of two world wars, the Bolshevik Revolution in his native Russia, the Nazi *Anschluss* in Austria, economic inflation, devaluation, and destitution, his wife's suicide, the demise of his two principal psychoanalysts, Freud and Ruth Mack Brunswick, and the persistence to the end of evident obsessional traits. The outer history of the Wolf Man was all too closely intertwined with the cataclysmic political history of twentieth-century Europe; while his inner history, as we know from Freud's case history, remained resolutely fixed on the past, caught in the labyrinth of personal disasters that Freud traces back to his patient's second year. The place of this inner story, this "history of an infantile neurosis", within the context of the experience of modern political and social history already suggests an elusive and particularly "modernist" issue of meaning and understanding. In particular, the case history within history, and personal history within the case history, pose forcefully major questions about the nature of historical and narrative understanding, suggesting both the necessity and the limits of narrative meanings, and the complexity of our uses of narrative plot.

Let me lay out briefly the salient points of personal and general history. The Wolf Man was born on Christmas Day, 1886, according to the Julian calendar used in Russia (January 6, 1887, by the Gregorian calendar), the son of a wealthy Russian landowner and liberal political leader. He arrived in Vienna in January, 1910, a severely debilitated young man accompanied by his valet and his personal physician; he carried a letter of introduction to Freud, who immediately won his confidence, and began analysis. He had spent the previous two years in and out of various sanatoria, undergoing hydrotherapy and every other cure within the arsenal of German alienists, but without remission in his obsessive and hysterical symptoms. It was in a Munich sanatorium that he had fallen violently in love with his nurse, Therese, whom he pursued to her room and besieged with requests for a rendezvous, to become her lover in a brief, stormy, interrupted affair. By 1911, Freud considered the analysis well enough begun to permit the Wolf Man to see Therese again; and in 1914, she came to Vienna, and the couple received Freud's permission to marry at the completion of analysis. This appeared to be at hand: the Wolf Man, preparing to return to Odessa, called upon Freud to bid him goodbye on June 29, 1914. The day before, the Archduke Franz Ferdinand had been shot at Sarajevo. Neither the Wolf Man nor Freud foresaw the consequence: that for the next five years there could be no communication between them. By spring 1918, Odessa was occupied by German troops. Then came the collapse of the Central Powers, the October Revolution, and the arrival of the Red Army. In 1919, the Wolf Man managed to escape from Odessa and make his way along the Black Sea to Rumania, thence to Austria. On very bad advice, he equipped himself for exile by buying an equal number of German marks and Austrian crowns, which by the time of his arrival were close to worthless. His immense fortune had indeed vanished to nothing, and when he returned to Freud in the fall of 1919 to resume analysis of some previously unanalyzed material, he was unable to pay him. Freud undertook this new analysis gratis because the Wolf Man – whose case history he had in the meantime written (in 1914–15), then published with two important bracketed additions (in 1918) – had proved to be so valuable to the progress of psychoanalysis. The Wolf Man indeed became a kind of ward of the Vienna psychoanalytic community, living off its annual dole, a collection undertaken by Freud from among his wealthy patients and disciples that would itself play an important role in the later analyses carried out by Ruth Mack Brunswick, which would be concerned with elements of the transference unresolved in the original analysis. Eventually, the Wolf Man found employment as an insurance agent and lived a petit-bourgeois existence, complete with Sunday painting, in a state of relative peace which was, however, shattered for some time by Therese's suicide shortly following the *Anschluss*. While at times ostensibly skeptical about the lasting therapeutic benefits of psychoanalysis – and himself never wholly free from neurotic obsessions, particularly in his erotic life – he remained a devout admirer of Freud, one who had evidently absorbed the lessons of psychoanalysis so well that they informed his entire world view. He wrote papers on the psychoanalytic study of art and continued to talk of his own biography, his relation to figures past and present, in a nuanced and well-mastered psychoanalytic vocabulary. He was frequently visited by Freud's disciples, and apparently to the last received a small stipend from the Freud Archives, of which indeed he could be said to have constituted a living part.[2]

When he first came to Freud in 1910, the Wolf Man was emblematic of one aspect of European high bourgeois culture in its finest flowering: the morbid narcissism of its most sensitive and artistic souls, those debris of capitalist and imperialist grandeur who perhaps in some measure legitimized empire building and public affairs through the implicit equation of their incapacity to participate with sickness. Dependent on his valet and his personal physician in all the routines of daily life (including dressing in the morning and receiving his regular enema for his hysterical constipation), the Wolf Man reminds us of the decadent des Esseintes, hero of Huysmans's *A Rebours*, indeed of a whole line of valetudinarian heroes reaching back to Villiers de l'Isle-Adam's Axel, who some years earlier had spoken the celebrated slogan: "Live? Our servants will do that for us." The cast of characters that moves through his years in the German sanatoria – French princesses, Russian counts, merchants from Hamburg, an occasional spinster from Boston – evokes nothing so much as Thomas Mann's *The Magic Mountain*, with its microcosm of European civilization on the brink of its destruction in the Great War. The Wolf Man's pursuit of Therese has much of the grotesque pathos of Hans Castorp's courtship of Clavdia Chauchat. In his memoirs, the Wolf Man compares his love for Therese, who reminds him of a Leonardo painting, to Swann's passion for Odette, who reminded *him* of a Botticelli painting, in Proust's *Recherche*. Like the novels of Mann and Proust, the Wolf Man's story seems to draw up the balance sheet of European high bourgeois culture at the moment of its apparent triumph as it blindly prepares its self-immolation. By the time of his return to Freud, the social order that produced the Wolf Man, and his story, had been shattered, the "proud tower" of European civilization lay in fragments, its advanced culture stunned by reversal.

Like the two great representative novels of European Modernism that I have evoked, the story of the Wolf Man contains within it the outline of a "standard" nineteenth-century narrative – the story of a coherent individual in society and within history – yet, again like these novels, so complicated and undermined by the process of its telling that the apparent premises of the nineteenth-century narrative mode are put into question. In a manner yet more radical than Mann's or even Proust's – perhaps more nearly approaching Faulkner's – Freud's case history involves a new questioning of how life stories go together, how narrative units combine in significant sequence, where cause and effect are to be sought, and how meaning is related to narration. The case history of the Wolf Man's story, itself embedded in modern history, suggests a paradigm of the status of modern explanation, which must on the one hand see itself as narrative, concerned with a set of histories and the mediations among them, and on the other hand recognizes that the traditional tenets and the very authority of narrative have been subverted, that the bases of explanation have been radically problematized. The Wolf Man himself, in his memoirs, provides an explicit link between Sherlock Holmes's search for explanation and Freud's:

> Once we happened to speak of Conan Doyle and his creation, Sherlock Holmes. I had thought that Freud would have no use for this type of light reading matter, and was surprised to find that this was not at all the case and that Freud had read this author attentively. The fact that circumstantial evidence is useful in psychoanalysis when reconstructing a childhood history may explain Freud's interest in this type of literature.   (Gardiner 146)

Freud apparently was fully aware of the analogies between psychoanalytic investigation and detective work. Faced with fragmentary evidence, clues scattered within present reality, he who would explain must reach back to a story in the past which accounts for how the present took on its configuration. The detective story exhibits a reality structured as a set of ambiguous signs which gain their meaning from a past history that must be uncovered so as to order the production of these signs as a chain of events, eventually with a clear origin, intention, and solution, and with strong causal connections between each link. The figure of the detective may be seen as an inevitable product not only of the nineteenth century's concern with criminal deviance, but also, more simply, of its pervasive historicism, its privileging of narrative explanation, accounting for what we are through the reconstruction of how we got that way.

Working to trace the etiology of neurosis, Freud occupies this same ground. In his earliest case histories – those in the *Studies on Hysteria* (1895) – he almost explicitly assumes a Holmesian posture, pressing his patients for the symptomatic clues, reaching back to uncover a moment of trauma, a scene of crime that makes sense of all subsequent events. As he finishes his preliminary exposition of the Wolf Man's symptoms, he again sounds like the detective making out his *aide-mémoire* of the facts in the case:

"Here, then, in the briefest outline, are the riddles for which the analysis had to find a solution. What was the origin of the sudden change in the boy's character? What was the significance of his phobia and of his perversities? How did he arrive at his obsessive piety? And how are all these phenomena interrelated?" (*PF* 9: 245–6) Yet with the case of the Wolf Man, Freud will discover "detection" and its narrative to be extraordinarily more complex and problematic, like the plots of modernist fiction, and indeed inextricably bound up with the fictional. I want to consider how the narrativity of the structure of explanation deployed in this nonfictional genre, the case history, necessarily implicates the question of fictions through the very plotting of that narrativity and what this implies about the nature of modernist narrative understanding.

Freud encounters not only a problem in investigation but also a problem of exposition, of writing, which he alludes to at the start of his second chapter, where he confesses that he is "unable to give either a purely historical or a purely thematic account" of his patient's story; that he can write a consecutive "history neither of the treatment nor of the illness" (240), but must combine different stories and methods of presentation.

Attempting to "unpack" Freud's two either/ors here, we find four separable elements in his material and his account: (1) the structure of the infantile neurosis (the history of the neurosis); (2) the order of event in the past providing the cause of the neurosis (the etiology of the neurosis); (3) the order of emergence of past event during the analysis (the history of the treatment); (4) the order of report in the case history.

It may be helpful here to refer once again to the Russian formalist distinction between *fabula*, or story, and *sjužet*, or plot – a distinction that itself belongs to a modernist awareness and, in its application to Freud's case history, suggests how we read even this kind of biographical account with certain narrative expectations. In Freud's text, the *sjužet* must ultimately be the fourth in the series of elements I identified: the order of report of the material that constitutes the "case" of the Wolf Man.[3] But this *sjužet* will alternately choose its *fabula* from among the three other elements, sometimes presenting the history and structure of the infantile neurosis, sometimes tracing the events that caused it, sometimes following the course of the analysis and the way event emerged during it. The "ultimate" *fabula*, one might say, is element number 2, the etiology of the infantile neurosis; but in the presentation, element number 1, the way the neurosis manifested itself and evolved, can serve as its *sjužet*, and so can element number 3, the way the events of child-hood emerged during the analytic sessions. The history of the neu-rosis, element number 1, can in turn be *fabula* to element number 3 as *sjužet*. The elements occupy shifting positions in relation to one another, as the "story" and its "plotting", and it must be the task of the fourth element, the writing of the case history itself, to recover the other elements in their complex interrelationship. Freud evokes frequently the problems of exposition and explanation which this situation poses: he notes, for instance, the limitations encountered in "forcing a structure which is itself in many dimen-sions" onto a two-dimensional plane (308). He must manage to tell, both "at once" and "in order", the story of a person, the story of an illness, the story of an investigation, the story of an explanation; and "meaning" must ultimately lie in the effective interrelationship of all of these.

One can trace this issue of exposition and explanation in the detail of the analysis itself. To take briefly just one example, con-sider the dream, the terrifying dream of the six or seven white wolves sitting in a tree which came to name the case, and the patient, and which Freud from its first introduction into the analysis held to be the most important piece of evidence in discovering the causes of the infantile neurosis. This dream from childhood, restaged near the beginning of the analysis but fully elucidated only toward its end, subtends the whole course of the analysis as the ur-text which all the other verbal structures exist to elucidate. For the manifest text of a dream, of course, both conceals and reveals. It demands a decipherment, an understanding of the latent dream thoughts staged and distorted by the dream work, which is compa-rable to finding the original *fabula* which a displaced and conden-sed *sjužet* "covers" with clues, at once suggestive and misleading, that must be read by the detective interpreter. My use of terms be-longing to the analysis of narrative finds justification here in that the analysis of a dream involves, among other things, unpacking a dense, over-laid, concentrated text and reordering its components as narrative, finding the implications of *story* behind the dream. As in detective narratives – in "The Musgrave Ritual", for instance – the dream's metaphors, and the dream as metaphor, must be plotted out as metonymies. The thematic material suggested by the dream, and the associations that the dreamer is able to articulate in reviewing the dream, can only begin to make sense when narrativized, ordered as a sequence of events. Yet, of course, in the etiology of the Wolf Man's infantile neurosis, the dream itself is an *event*, indeed the decisive traumatic event, in that by deferred action it produces the neurotic reaction to the "primal scene", witnessed two and a half years earlier, and to the "seduction", which occurred several months earlier. The dream is both, as rememoration, the record of past event, and, in the past, a decisive present event in the Wolf Man's story; a *sjužet* that is itself in turn *fabula*, a text that both explains and alters the reality to which it refers.[4]

Undecidability becomes a particularly acute issue in the question of origins. The specification of origins should be of the utmost importance in any etiological explanation: to understand causes, one must get back to the beginning. Indeed, a great part of the nineteenth-century confidence in narrative explanation, and the need for it, reposes on the postulate that a history can be and should be a tracing of origins. We know what we are because we can say where we are, and we know this because we can say where we came from. The authority of narrative derives from its capacity to speak of origins in relation to endpoints. Freud is no exception in his original postulate. He traces the beginning of the childhood neurosis back to the occurrence of the dream, then traces the origin of the dream back to the occurrence of the "primal scene" – the scene of parental intercourse – to which the child, then one and a half years old, was witness. The primal scene thus appears as the origin of all origins, the bedrock of the Wolf Man's case, the inception of his story. Like what is often called the *drame du coucher* in Proust's novel – the drama of the mother's withheld kiss – it is that moment of the buried yet living past on which the Wolf Man's subsequent existence is founded.

And yet: when Freud has uncovered – or more accurately, reconstructed – this primal scene, which would appear to be crucial to his narrative of the Wolf Man's case, he proceeds to erase it. In the two long bracketed passages added to chapters five and eight (added in 1918, whereas the bulk of the case history had been written in 1914–15)[5] he questions whether the primal scene, the observation of parental coitus, ever had any reality as *event*. It might rather be a phantasy concocted from the observation of animals copulating, then referred back to the parents. Thus in the place of a primal scene we would have a primal phantasy, operating *as* event by deferred action. And Freud refers us at this point to his discussion of the problem in the *Introductory Lectures*, where he considers that such primal phantasies may be a phylogenetic inheritance through which the individual reaches back to the history of mankind, to a racial "masterplot".

We have at this crucial moment of the case history an apparent evacuation of the problem of origins, substituting for a founding event a phantasy or fiction on which is conferred all the authority and force of prime mover, and the evocation of a possible infinite regress in the unconscious of the race. This "solution" might appear irresponsible, an abandonment of all distinction between the fictional and the nonfictional, might indeed appear to build into Freud's explanatory account a kind of self-destruct mechanism. Worse still, Freud closes his discussion of primal scenes versus primal phantasies with a *non liquet*, arguing that the case is properly undecidable. And then, returning to the question, he argues further that undecidability is not of importance, since the subsequent history, whether it derives from primal scene or primal phantasy, remains unchanged.

We have here one of the most daring moments of Freud's thought, and one of his most heroic gestures as a writer. He could have achieved a more coherent, finished, enclosed, and authoritative narrative by sticking by his arguments of 1914–15, never adding the bracketed passages. Or, given his second thoughts of 1918, he could have struck out parts of the earlier argument and substituted for them his later reflections. What is remarkable is that, having discovered his point of origin, that which made sense of the dream, the neurosis, and his own account of them, Freud then felt obliged to retrace the story, offering another and much less evidential (and "eventimential") kind of origin, to tell another version of the plot, and then finally leave one juxtaposed to the other, indeed one superimposed on the other as a kind of palimpsest, a layered text that offers differing versions of the same story. A narrative explanation that surely foresaw that much of its celebrity would come from its recovery of so spectacular a moment of origin doubles back on itself to question that origin and indeed to displace the whole question of origins, to suggest another kind of referentiality, in that all tales may lead back not so much to events as to other tales, to man as a structure of the fictions he tells about himself.[6]

A narrative account that allows the inception of its story to be either event or fiction – that in turn opens up the potential for another story, anonymous and prehistoric – perilously destabilizes belief in explanatory histories as exhaustive accounts whose authority derives from the force of closure, from the capacity to say: here is where it began, here is what it became. Like Holmes with the text of the Musgrave ritual, Freud has unpacked dreams, screen memories, obsessional and hysterical symptoms – those bodily metaphors through which unconscious desire inscribes its messages – but here the result is not the neat Holmesian solution but rather a proliferation of narratives with no ultimate points of fixity. Consequently, the shape of the individual and his biography becomes uncontrollable: their etiology and evolution are assigned to an unspecifiable network of event, fiction, and interpretation.

In Freud's early case histories, those of *Studies on Hysteria*, finding the chain of events leading from the initial trauma, usually infantile, to its sexualized repetition, usually during adolescence, on to the present symptoms provided a seamless narrative that was thought to be cathartic and therefore in itself curative. The detective story in the case of the Wolf Man is evidently far more complex than anything in the Holmes canon; it resembles more the tenuous solutions to uncertain problems presented by *Heart of Darkness* or a number of tales by Jorge Luis Borges. Not only does Freud question whether one can, or need, claim that "in the beginning was the deed" – since the imagined can have the full originary force of the deed – he also proposes a radical revision of conventional notions of narrative causality. The logic of his interpretive work moves Freud to an understanding that causation can work backward as well as forward since the effect of event, or of phantasy, often comes only when it takes on meaning, usually when it takes on sexual significance, which may occur with considerable delay. Chronological sequence may not settle the issue of cause: events may gain traumatic significance by deferred action (*Nachträglichkeit*) or retroaction, action working in reverse sequence to create a meaning that did not previously exist. Thus the way a story is ordered does not necessarily correspond to the way it *works*. Indeed, narrative order, sequence as a logical enchainment of actions and outcomes, must be considered less a solution than part of the problem of narrative explanation. How we narrate a life – even our own life to ourselves – is at least a double process, the attempt to incorporate within an orderly narrative the more devious, persistent, and powerful plot whose logic is dictated by desire.

Freud also recognizes that there are elements of cause and signification that can never really be narrativized at all, but must rather be understood through a structural analysis, in a "mapping" of a certain psychic "set" toward neurosis, a network analyzed with extraordinary complexity in the chapter of this case history entitled "Anal Eroticism and the Castration Complex", which demonstrates explicitly what is implicit throughout the case history, that causality must be thought of in a context of probability, complementarity, and uncertainty. And if we return to Freud's preliminary remarks concerning the analysis, we find an acknowledgment that narrative itself, as a mode of discourse and understanding, has only a provisional status. Its understandings work on and in time, while the unconscious remains timeless. The analyst must patiently submit to this timelessness; yet he must also know when and how to impose a time limit on analysis, in order to speed up the overcoming of resistances – an artificial *finis* which creates temporal form. As the analysis of the Wolf Man proceeds, it reveals (as most narratives do) both a drive toward the end and a resistance to ending. Freud would argue, in one of his last essays, that analysis is inherently interminable, since the dynamics of resistance and the transference can always generate new beginnings in relation to any conceivable end. The narrative of the Wolf Man must be given closure and shape, but these are provisional, and could always reopen to take in further circles of meaning and theory. As Henry James wrote in a famous line from the preface to *Roderick Hudson*, "Really, universally, relations stop nowhere, and the exquisite problem of the artist is eternally but to draw, by a geometry of his own, the circle within which they shall happily *appear* to do so" (*Art* 5). The closure demanded by narrative understanding – the closure without which it can have no coherent plot – is always provisional, as-if, a necessary fiction.

The presence of the analyst as narratee and potential narrator "dialogizes" the discourse of the analysand. The analytic transference thus realizes Mikhail Bakhtin's conception of the "dialogic," whereby discourse internalizes the presence of otherness, becomes marked by the alterity inherent in any social use of language.[7] In this medium of the in-between – Freud, we remember, called the transference a *Zwischenreich*[8] – the "true" narrative lies in-between, in the process of exchange; it is the product of two discourses playing against one another, often warring with one another, working toward recognitions mutually acknowledged but internalized in different ways. Analysis hence constitutes itself as inherently dialogic, a perpetually reversing counterpoint of self and other, closure and opening, origin and process. Centreless and never finally terminable, analytic discourse is consubstantial with the complementarity and uncertainty, either/ors, deferred actions and retroactions, to which Freud has narrative recourse when he finds there is no centred and authoritative explanatory history.

As we have said before, the patient comes to the analyst with a story to tell, a story that is not so much false – since it does in some manner signify the truth – as it is incomplete and untherapeutic. Its plot lacks the dynamic necessary to creating sequence and design that integrate and explain. The fuller plot constructed by the analytic work must be more dynamic, thus more useful as a shaping and connective force; above all it must be hermeneutically more forceful. It must carry the power of conviction, for its tellers and its listeners, that is the ultimate goal of storytelling. Truth, then, arises from a dialogue among a number of *fabula* and a number of *sjužet*, stories and their possible organizations, as also between two narrators, analysand and analyst. A centreless and reversible structure, dialogue is an agency of narration that creates as it questions the narrative, and designates the field of force of the necessary fiction.

A case history is the story of an individual presented to the public for didactic purposes: it is a form of exemplary biography. In the course of his use of the genre, Freud encounters all the problems of narrative design and exposition faced by biographers, historians, and novelists, and the issues of fictionality that have haunted literature since Plato. A nonfictional genre concerning a real person, the case history of the Wolf Man is radically allied to the fictional since its causes and connections depend on probabilistic constructions rather than authoritative facts, and on imaginary scenarios of lack and desire, and since the very language that it must work with, as both object and medium of its explanations, takes its form from histories of desire consubstantial with what cannot be. In his narratives – as in all his writings – Freud shares with such other modernists as Conrad or Joyce or Proust a basic pessimism about life stories and their putative plots. His vision of man insists on the limits its to man's self-knowledge and mastery of his own biography. What man can be depends on the uncertain relation of the conscious subject to the unconscious. "Wo Es war soll Ich werden": the famous dictum is traditionally, and optimistically, translated, "Where Id was shall Ego come to be" (*PF* 2: 112) but it may rather signify a never-ending ending struggle of the ego to coincide with and master that otherness within that drives the subject in obscure ways.[9] And the telling of the history of this struggle is always a hypothetical construction.

Like the modernist novel, the case history of the Wolf Man shows up the limits of storytelling while nonetheless insisting that the story must get told. The plots of narrative have become extraordinarily complex, self-subversive, apparently implausible. They have been forced to abandon clear origins and terminations in favour of provisional closures and fictional inceptions; their causes may work by deferred action and retroaction; their connections are probable rather than logical; their individual dramas stand in uncertain tension with transindividual imaginings. But if plot has become an object of suspicion, it remains no less necessary: telling the self's story remains our indispensable thread in the labyrinth of temporality. It is of overwhelming importance to us that life still be narratable, which may mean finding those provisional, tenuous plots that appear to capture the force of desire that cannot speak its name but compels us in a movement – recursive, complex, unclosed – toward meaning. Hence the importance of the issues in narrative that Freud so forcefully poses. Freud's restless thought and his dynamic model of psychic life summon us to think beyond formalist paradigms, to engage the dynamic of memory and desire that can reconnect, however provisionally and tenuously, time lost and time continuing.

NOTES

[Peter Brooks is Sterling Professor of Comparative Literature and French at Yale University. His many articles and books on narrative, psychoanalysis and narrative theory include *Reading for the Plot: Design and Intention in Narrative* (1984), *Body Work: Objects of Desire in Modern Narrative* (1993), and *Psychoanalysis and Storytelling* (1994). He is editor, with Alex Woloch, of *Whose Freud?* (2000), and author of *Troubling Confessions: Speaking Guilt in Law and Literature* (2000). Ed.]

1. See Gardiner, *The Wolf-Man and Sigmund Freud* (1972). This extraordinary rich, interesting, and well edited volume contains the Wolf Man's memoirs, his "Recollections of Sigmund Freud", as well as further biographical material by Muriel Gardiner and the case histories by Freud and Ruth Mack Brunswick. On the last years of the Wolf Man, see Karin Obholzer, *The Wolf-Man: Conversations with Freud's Patient – Sixty Years Later* (1982). A reinterpretation of the Wolf Man's case has been presented by Nicolas Abraham and Maria Torok

in *The Wolf Man's Magic Word: A Cryptonymy* (1986) [Essay 8], with an important preface by Jacques Derrida [Essay 9].

2. For evidence of the Wolf Man's mental condition in old age, see the conversations recorded by Obholzer in *The Wolf-Man: Conversations with Freud's Patient*. I find Obholzer's own judgements unreliable, since she apparently wants to discredit psychoanalysis, or at least score points against Freud's claims that his patient was "cured". While it is evident that the Wolf Man remained a compulsive personality who was never entirely free from obsessions and delusions, whose erotic life remained marked by his "sister complex" (determining that his choice of women involved the need to degrade), and who never completely resolved the transference relation to Freud, it also seems clear that he managed to negotiate a reasonably normal existence.

3. Diagrammatically – using Freud's analogy of archeological layering – we should have a structure that looks like this: 4/1/3/2, but the construction of the narrative makes the relation of the layers far more complex, and subverts any simple geological model.

4. See *PF* 9: 365 for the final chronology of major events and/or phantasies that Freud constructs and appends as a later footnote (1923) to the case history. This chronology represents the order of the story but not, of course, the way its plot "works".

5. For the additional, bracketed passage in Chapter V see *FR* 423–6; *PF* 9: 335–8 [Editor's note].

6. Freud, of course, faced this problem of originating deed versus originating phantasy in other instances of his thought as well, perhaps most famously in the question of the "the seduction": the large number of recollections [in *Studies on Hysteria*] of attempts at seduction by a parent figure produced by his patients finally led him to suspect that seduction might be a primal phantasy – a turn in his thought which has been criticized by some socially oriented psychoanalysts who want to claim a high frequency of such seductions.

7. See Bakhtin, "Discourse in the Novel".

8. German; literally, "between-world" [Editor's note].

9. Lacan argues convincingly against the optimistic interpretation in "The agency of the letter in the unconscious or reason since Freud" (*Écrits* 146–78).

8

The Wolf Man's Magic Word

NICOLAS ABRAHAM AND MARIA TOROK

INTRODUCTION: FIVE YEARS WITH THE WOLF MAN

Five years ... the average length of an analysis. We have spent them in the company of the Wolf Man. During this entire period, his presence was mediated by Freud, Ruth Mack Brunswick, Muriel Gardiner, and, finally, his own works. He was with us, not in person, like a patient on the couch, but through an immutable collection of documents filling a single volume. This "material", limited in its extent and all of it readily available (except for the memoirs we discovered in midcourse: Muriel Gardiner, *The Wolf-Man and Sigmund Freud*) required, however, many reworkings, a genuine process of maturation on our part, before we could reach the effective close of our work. There is in this something of an experimental proof that the analytic process is not solely the making of the patient: It involves a double evolution – parallel yet complementary – of two partners at the same time. In our unique experiment, the prolonged repetition of sessions was replaced by numerous rereadings, renewed returns to the same documents.

As for the patient, he was not part of the process; only the analyst "worked". In order to attune ourselves to this concrete yet fictitious patient, we needed five years of repeated listening.

136

Nearly two years ago came the beginning of the end. The "Open Sesame" seemed to fall from the sky. In fact, it had been there from the start. But it revealed itself only after many failures at listening in particular to the dreams. The discovery was that English had been the Wolf Man's childhood language. Freud had taken seventeen years to realize this and to draw his decisive yet succinct conclusions.[1]

We only had to think of it to locate the valuable reference in Freud. Why precisely at that moment, not later or earlier or ... never? Why us and not someone else? "Chance" or a "lucky find"? Only a third ear, listening to our listening, could provide an answer. As for us, we have to admit that the subject controlled us more than we controlled it. Insight always came after tense moments and vain fumbling, in moments of grace when suddenly riddles came unraveled, disparity acquired order, absurdity took on sense. The discovery of English as the cryptic language was a crucial step: It allowed us to identify the active and hidden words. But this was in no way sufficient as an instrument of interpretation. All of the source words were known, all the *archeonyms*, or almost, yet there was nothing to weld them into a coherent whole. Until the day when another revelation came: The archeonyms were arranged in the form of a dialogue. From there we took the final step in the construction of a hypothesis: a precocious traumatic scene, removed, sent to a crypt, encrypted. We had the interpretation of the nightmare of the wolves. Better yet, all the dreams and symptoms gradually became accessible. Were we to rest on our laurels?

There followed nearly two years of delight over this "raw material" that had rendered its secrets.

A false Unconscious: the crypt in the Ego – a false "return of the repressed", the action in the Ego of hidden thoughts from the crypt. In sum, a skewed balance emerges if we compare the amplitude of the manifold repetitions of the traumatic scene with its pleasurable counterpart: A simple word becomes the Thing of the Unconscious.[2] All this appeared to us with increasing clarity.

In contrast to the analytic work done between two people – a dialogue that creates new realities – theoretical construction based on documents is merely a translation. It is the translation of an established text into an *invented* text (in both meanings at the same time, "bringing to light" and "creating"). The translator is twice over a traitor: He betrays the other and himself. This would normally void all results. The translator's work is nevertheless tied to an original that, even if tinged with fiction, remains asymptotically the place of convergence for all possible translations and betrayals.

May our "betrayal" have been close enough to our text!

And may readers be endowed with the patience to follow the outlines of our path, so that they may share our hardships and rewards.

CHAPTER 1: "THE WOLF MAN AND HIS INTERNAL WORLD"

Wolf Man, Who Are You? First Hypotheses and Constructions: Who He is Not

In *The History of an Infantile Neurosis*, Freud departed from his habit of showing, revealing, and rendering manifest. This time his aim was to convince. But who would fail to notice the incoherence here, the unlikelihood there, and the overzealous proofs just about everywhere? We felt an urgent duty to overcome such a malaise. Hence this work. In the beginning we had only a vague intuition that gradually grew more specific. It took on an explicit form that we expressed in these terms: The person in despair who, rendered helpless by depression, consulted Freud in 1910 was not quite the same as the one who lay on his couch a few days later. They appeared to be two separate people in one, without either of them representing the basic identity of the Wolf Man. Although often having the same desires as he, they remained nevertheless distinct from him. As a result, a paradox emerged in which the sexual license loudly claimed by one would only reinforce repression in the other. We suspected the existence of a cohabitation, at the core of the same person, involving his elder sister's image and his own. Two people in a third one: Freud's listening may have perceived this only unconsciously.

Such was our first idea. It demanded clarification, in particular concerning the genesis of such an internal constellation. How, indeed, could the initial reality of two children living together in the same home become transformed into an intrapsychic companionship? How could the particular topography implied by such a state of affairs come into being?

Freud devoted a whole chapter to the so-called seduction by the sister and returned to it repeatedly throughout his account. He placed so much emphasis on it, rather more because he sensed the crucial importance of the seduction by the sister on its own terms than because the ideas supported his own theories (Primal Scene, display of passive desire): These theories did not need this elaboration. As for the concrete content of the "seduction", nothing that filtered through was worthy of this name yet Freud seemed to cling to this label. Rather than branding it a misuse of language, we preferred to see in it the sign of a reliable clinical intuition. There remained to be constructed, despite the absence of all information, the entire scene of this seduction. To suggest a version of it, we had to do a lot of guesswork, as when one has to compute two unknown quantities on the basis of a single equation. Only the clinical study of incorporation was of some help in guiding our steps through unknown terrain.

After eliminating quite a few other possibilities, this is how we were able to summarize what was likely to have happened between the two children: First, the sister claimed to repeat with her younger brother a sexual scene that probably took place earlier between her and the father; second, she attached to the resulting pleasure (in the brother) the meaning of castration. Such a situation, however mythical it may appear, illustrates, if nothing else, the starting point and the contradiction inscribed within the libidinal attitude of the Wolf Man. Its contributions are, on the one hand, a reference to the father and, on the other, the castrating jealousy of the young seductress: two unknowns we must assume in order to justify how, at the time of the seduction, *the Stranger could settle in the core of the Ego.*

Such an incorporation of the sister was the only means of loving her in order not to annihilate her, and of annihilating her in order not to love her. Thanks to incorporation, the insoluble conflict between aggressivity and the libido could leave the Object and transfer itself into the core of the Ego. And the Wolf Man had to carry its indelible mark in the very structure of his Ego, that is, in the sum of his introjections. An immediate consequence: Seduced by the sister, as she supposedly had seduced the father, he could not escape a second incorporation, that of the father, and thus his child's penis no longer ceased to coincide in secret with Father's. Hence a double and contradictory exigency: Father's penis must neither perish nor enjoy. Otherwise he, the Wolf Man, would be annihilated. It is conceivable that such an internal situation could have remained unraveled throughout a lifetime.

Our intention here is to retrace the flow of this life, fantastic and pathetic, mediocre and replete with enigmas, along the paths of the

Unconscious. After a long trip backward, we hope to retrieve at the end a hypothetical base point: the moment that must have imprinted on the Wolf Man's life its irresolvable and perpetual contradiction, and that must have initiated his unremitting struggle to safeguard a last refuge for his self.

Yes, picturing the Wolf Man with his incorporations, we begin to understand. What a situation indeed! Whether his desire coincided with that of his "Guest" or whether it is contrary to it, the result would remain identical: the impossibility of ever reaching himself.

He populated his internal world with both benign and malignant characters; these included Father, Mother, Nania, the German tutor, the Doctor, and, finally, the Psychoanalyst as Therapist. The first incorporation attracted others as a magnet draws up iron filings. The Wolf Man identified, conversed, and schemed with each character in turn. His life was made up of maneuverings to avoid hapless meetings and indiscretions. They were all there in him in order to maintain a fundamental repression of a contradiction within the desire itself: that of a death-dealing pleasure. This repression appeared only in two images, each incomplete in its manifest state: first the erogenous image of a woman in the position of a scrubwoman, then the second one, a complement to the first, of a phobia-producing erect wolf. We understand now that the Wolf Man could expose only his various modes of not being himself to analysis. It was the only way he could reveal – without ever being able to use his own name – who in fact he was.

This is our explicit hypothesis of incorporation. It will help us "speak" the unconscious of the case and perhaps the induced unconscious of its analysts as well. It will also guide us in reading between the lines the following biographical notes based on the publications of Muriel Gardiner.

The Symptom of the Nose and the "Group Dynamics" of the Internal Characters

If, following the tragic episode of his wife's suicide, the Wolf Man did not exhibit serious and lasting disorders, as he had twelve to fifteen years earlier upon learning about Freud's illness, and if he was able to recover almost spontaneously, credit must be given to his good analytic relationship with R.M. Brunswick, his former analyst. Unfortunately, the apparently decisive phase of this often interrupted treatment is known to us only through a laconic remark of the analyst alluding, for the first time, to the crucial role of the sister.

"This period of the analysis", she noted, "revealed new material of great import, hitherto forgotten memories, all relating to the complicated attachment of the preschizophrenic girl to her small brother" ("A Supplement to Freud's *History of an Infantile Neurosis* [1928]," Gardiner 263).

Here again, as often elsewhere, Brunswick's formulation bears witness to deep intuition and says more by its form than by its content: "preschizophrenic girl" and "small brother" state clearly that she sensed the presence of these characters in the Wolf Man. It is obvious by now how much we agree with the direction of such an intuition. A good deal of our work aims to expound and illustrate it. We will go quite far on this road and will not hesitate to hypostasize the internal characters by endowing them, for the sake of this presentation, with proper names. These will be the sign of their alien and parasitic nature and will avoid confusion with a self become clandestine. Thus, Brother and Sister have been baptized, respectively, Stanko and Tierka; the other characters will keep the name of their function, emphasized by capitals: Father, Mother, Therapist.

Equipped with this tool, let us once more retrace our steps. The Wolf Man's first encounter with Brunswick was in 1926, that is, twelve years after the termination of his analysis with Freud. It took place, as we know, in rather special circumstances. The Russian ex-nabob, now an ordinary wage earner in Vienna, profited from the collective charity of analysts who enhanced his meagre income; these sums were given to him every spring from 1919 on by Freud himself. Initially, these donations were intended to pay hospital bills for the Wolf Man's wife. Such an intention had all the ingredients to be beneficial for his internal world. Setting up Stanko as relay between Father and Tierka, it created new and harmonious relationships among the characters. It recognized implicitly the mutual belonging of the children, as well as Father's love for his son – this motivated the gifts. But an external event modified this beneficent state of affairs. The Wolf Man recovered some family jewels (1922) and, on his wife's advice, said nothing to Freud about the existence of this supposed treasure. He did not know that this lie by omission would become the source of unresolvable torture. What had happened within him? The answer is simple: Stanko and Tierka again shared a secret. There followed – seen from the outside – a genuine alteration of his character. A man until then unconcerned with material advantage and scrupulously honest suddenly became greedy about his savings, a spendthrift (he lost his money in speculations), and in the end doubly secretive, both with his benefactor, whom he kept unaware of his (supposed) wealth, and with his wife, whom he left in the dark about his extravagance.

Seen from the inside, all these changes are comprehensible once it is appreciated that the introduction of the first secret compromised the *modus vivendi* of the internal characters. It revived by induction a host of other secrets and tended to reestablish the occlusion among the characters that, earlier, analysis had tempered. What was the effect of the new connivance with Tierka? It meant, as regards Father (represented outwardly by Freud), first of all that his place was being usurped (he must not find out at any price), and second, that he had been betrayed by Tierka (he would die of sorrow and the son along with him, *ipso facto*), and that, consequently, the unlivable contradiction of the starting point would revive for both Father and Son. Then again, by using the money received from Father for his own purposes, he surreptitiously put himself in the place of Tierka, the favourite. Were she to learn about this, her jealousy would be boundless, and she would be forever lost as Object. There again secrecy was vital. As for Stanko, he had to remain innocent in the face of death wishes entertained by the Wolf Man concerning Father and Sister because of their relationship. Were they not, both, the privileged objects of his desire?

His dissimulation helped to maintain, surely at the cost of internal dislocation, a precarious balance. But when he learned about the seriousness of Freud's illness in the fall of 1923, the Wolf Man's struggle against his aggressive wishes proved ineffectual. For fear that Father might take their common penis into the grave, it became urgently necessary to denounce the very cause of this situation and thereby liberate his own virility. On the other hand, it was inconceivable that he could deal such a blow to someone being struck by fate, someone who was moreover the brace of his internal world.

His only recourse was to rescue Father by rescuing Tierka from suicide. It was for the purpose of finding a compromise between two opposite wishes – make Father die and revive him – that he invented a symptom: *the language of the nose*, the language of his deep and secret desire. He discovered the vocabulary of this symptom in the guise of a wandering wart on his mother's nose. He endowed his own nose, however, with an undecipherable sign. The child's nose is the place, is it not, where adults can read a lie like an open book? A pimple suddenly discovered in the middle of his nose will have to bear witness to the alteration of his identity: that he is no longer Stanko, but Tierka, worse yet, the Tierka who, ill before her suicide, blamed the pimples on her face for her misfortune. Her loss would bring with it Father's … What would be left then to S. P. [Sergei Pankeiev]? Fortunately, since his analysis with Freud, he was not altogether without recourse in such misery. He had placed within himself an additional character: the Therapist. He would reveal the lie to him, and he would cure his sister. Then everything would be as before. But, for the moment, this wish was expressed only in his nasal symptom. He carried his lying nose with Tierka's pimple on it from one doctor to the next. Treatment, scar. A new treatment, a new scar. Would Tierka ever recover? "No, never! Tierka will be marked forever", someone told him. Then the utmost despair seized him. Could it be he who had pushed her into suicide? Dare he appear before the ill Father with such a conjecture? Could he bear it if Father died of sorrow?

On June 15, 1926, anxiety overcame him. The next day he had to go to Freud for the allowance. But to Father he would say not a word of his symptom. He had better conceal from the ill man this forerunner of a disaster. As for Tierka, her confidence in Stanko – Therapist remained limited. For a long time she had wanted his suggestions checked by a second therapist. But now feeling pushed to suicide, she had had enough. She announced plainly to Stanko the ill will, be it conscious or unconscious, of Dr. X.[3] And for S. P. all escape was blocked.

The Dramaturgy of the Unconscious on Ruth Mack Brunswick's Couch

So it was that in 1926, on Professor Freud's counsel, consulted in *extremis*, the Wolf Man proceeded to lay Tierka on R.M. Brunswick's couch. He was reassured seeing her in the hands of a female therapist, safe from any form of seduction or fraternal rivalry. His hope of rescuing Tierka revived. When the Wolf Man would let Stanko speak, Stanko showed himself to be a good little boy and accorded the therapist a showy confidence. During this time, the symptomatic nose was not an issue. It was out of the question for the Wolf Man to let himself be recognized as himself with his persistent anxiety, or to allow this to attract attention to the true reason for the psychoanalytic treatment that concerned his "nose".

For the moment, much more important things had to be handled, he would say. It was, no doubt, more helpful to return to his happy relationship with Freud and to lavishly produce lots of wolf dreams, a token of his valuable contribution to psychoanalysis.

The Wolf Man's desire must remain silent. The following night-mare explains this characteristic:

> In a wide street is a wall with a closed door. To the left of the door is a large, empty wardrobe ... Near the other end of the wall stands a large, heavy-set woman ... But behind the wall is a pack of gray wolves, crowding toward the door and pacing impatiently back and forth. Their eyes gleam ... I am terrified, fearing that they will succeed in breaking through the wall.   (Gardiner 288)

Here is the paradox: The "wardrobe", if it is emptied, is emptied – according to the Wolf Man's associations to the dream – by the "Bolsheviks"; it stands to the "left", by which we understand: Were S. P. to unburden himself by telling, he would commit an illegitimate act. On the other hand, if he keeps the lie (the scar on his nose), then he stands on the right, he is on the right side. Unable to state his unutterable desire, represented here by the rushing back and forth of the wolves, the Wolf Man takes a backseat to his Guests. The "wolves" of his desire, however, crowd to his lips (like a diarrhea that comes "wolfing" out); the words are ready to cross the limiting wall. They gleam at what the eyes had seen, they throng in a rush to break the obstacle, the anal hymen that can hardly contain them. To say all would be orgasm: Tierka consenting, a "wolf" in hand! This is a nightmare of the end of the world.

No, neither lust nor cataclysm will break out this time. But in the Wolf Man, backed up against his desire, not knowing which way to turn, rage rankles. He would kill them all – Father, Tierka, Therapist – and this time it is not just melodrama. The director has fired the actors. He himself acts. A persecutor-persecuted. He exacts, threatens. He would do anything, and seriously ... rather than ... *tell*! After a long period of disorderly agitation a solution finally emerges: the Mother. He dreams:

> My mother takes the icons down and throws them on the floor. The pictures fall and break into pieces. I am astonished that my pious mother should do such a thing.   (291)

Thus he makes the Mother accomplish the gesture required by his own wrath, his own desire. She, not he, removes the saints of the family. She, not Tierka, will take hold of, break up – shine – his penis. An ingenious subterfuge to achieve climax while avoiding telling. Incest for incest. And this thought will have the virtue of putting everything back in order. His system of contradictions and insulations will be not broached but, for a while, buried. At most, according to the next day's dream, the mommy hand of the masturbator joins with the gaze of the warm Sun he has become, to contemplate in aesthetic admiration the gambols of Father and Daughter (not of the parents as Brunswick claims). His lust, altogether aesthetic, dapples the meadow with lovely spots. "Stones of a strange mauve" placed here and there retain their secret, however, and like the Rosetta stone, await their Champollion.[4] Such an idyll can only be, alas, the wish of a dream. Tomorrow, the violent desire to betray, along with its impasse, will revive.

The next dream already – a nightmare again – shows him cornered with his erection.

> I am with you in a skyscraper where the only way out is a window ..., he awakens in great anxiety, looking desperately for an escape route.   (292)

The escape of telling would be too dangerous. Another must be found at all costs.

CHAPTER 2: "BEHIND THE INNER WORLD"

The Wolf Man's drama remains incomplete for its hero. But once set in motion, its action cannot be stopped; it must proceed in us inevitably to its final outcome. And here our dissatisfaction, spurred on by a providential *deus ex machina*, expounds, imagines, dreams. An irresistible force pulls us: to save the analysis of the Wolf-Man, to save ourselves. With time the fourth act opens within us, stretches before us, and in us comes to fulfillment, bringing salvation.[5]

An Impromptu Walk Through a Verbarium:[6] Cryptonyms and What They Hide

The authors arrived at this very juncture in the process of their writing, and planned to take up Freud's text again with their point of view – incorporation – in mind, when it occurred to them to consult a Russian dictionary. This gesture, performed out of conscientiousness, brought an extra load of unforeseen work, but also a host of altogether unexpected insights. First, it enabled the authors to refine their hypotheses about the genesis and working of incorporation in general and about the specific incorporation of which the Wolf Man was both actor and victim. But even more, it brought home the fact that someone could be driven to take on the same attitude toward words as toward things, namely, objects of love, and that such word-objects could upset a topography to the point where incorporation would seem a self-therapeutic measure.

Initially, the authors had wanted to be certain there was no hidden ambiguity behind the repeated retraction of the number that first appeared in the principal dream.[7] The original number given is six, immediately corrected to seven, whereas on the well-known drawing the number is reduced to five. Six in Russian, SHIEST, also means perch, mast, and probably genitals, at least symbolically. This could have satisfied an ill-formed psychoanalytic mind. Fortunately, the authors' eyes fell on the neighboring words: SHIESTIERO and SHIESTORKA, meaning six or a lot of six people. Contaminated by the German *Schwester* (sister), they could not help checking the word sister as well, and there they discovered, to their amusement and confirming their suspicion, the words SIESTRA and its diminutive SIESTORKA. It became clear that the "pack of six wolves" did not contain the idea of multiplicity, but of the sister instead. Were we not justified from then on to look for the same association of ideas elsewhere? It was likely, in fact, that in the nightmares and the Wolf Man's phobic moments, wolf and sister would occur together. We simply had to survey the Russian vocabulary of the dreams and phobias and, where needed, fill in the gaps with his second language, German.

Here is a brief review of what we found. The nightmare about the "wolves" analyzed earlier enabled us to establish rather easily that the "pack of wolves" crowding behind the door in the wall corresponded, insofar as it was a "pack," to a "pack of six," to a "sixter" of wolves so to speak, though the number is not stated this time. We nevertheless potentially have SIESTORKABUKA (siswolf). The nightmare [related to Ruth Mack Brunswick of being trapped in a] skyscraper gave us more trouble. NIEBOSKREB (skyscraper in Russian) did not seem to have anything to do with either wolf or sister. Conversely, the German word for skyscraper (*Wolkenkratzer*)

– we had to think of it – does indeed contain the "wolf" we were seeking; the other Russian name for wolf, BUKA, being precisely VOLK. As for the "sister," we could only find disagreeable words in the places we had expected her: SKREB, the root of SKREBOK = scraper; SKROIT = to sharpen; SKRIP = scraping sound, and here we came close to giving up Russian altogether. But by tinkering with these words, we gained some new terms for our vocabulary: scrape, scratch, cut, bruise, scar, and, through German, cancer (*skreb* = *Krebs*) – all meanings we will encounter again, under various guises, in the clinical material.

Then we ventured a final hypothesis, and this turned out to be our lifesaver. If all these words – we advanced – in some way allude to the sister, this time they do so otherwise than through a veiled evocation of the word: sister. Why restrict our attention to the nightmares and phobias when the hypochondriac fears concerning the nose speak explicitly about scratch, scar, and cancer? Obviously, behind this was lurking the association, undoubtedly left nonverbalized, of a *lupus*, namely a *lupus seborrheus*.[8] The hypochondriac ideas would appear to rest on the same verbal support as the nightmare of the "skyscraper." The same support, no doubt, but what on earth was it? We pursued our inquiry. What was striking – we used to tell each other – was a certain unity of meaning among all these rather different-sounding words whose list could be lengthened at will by a whole series of analogies. This profusion of terms, carrying the idea of *wound* and stated in such diverse forms, did it really refer to the idea of castration? On the basis of the word couple just reconstituted, *siestorka-buka*, we had no reason to stick with such a hypothesis. Why deviate here from our initial line of thought and not admit – even at the cost of extrapolation – that all these locutions simply cover up another word, this one signaling sexual pleasure and alluding to the so-called seduction scene? Given the abundance of synonyms, we also understood that, in order to reach the sought-after key word, we had to move across the signifieds and search for semantic displacements. The key word, no doubt unutterable for some reason, and unknown for the moment, would have to be polysemic, expressing multiple meanings through a single phonetic structure. One of these would remain shrouded, but the other, or several other meanings now equivalent, would be stated through distinct phonetic structures, that is, through synonyms. To make our conversations about this easier, we would call them *cryptonyms* (words that hide) because of their allusion to a foreign and arcane meaning.

Spurred on by these considerations, we turned to the privileged libidinal moment, Grusha, the floor scrubber with her bucket and broom. A rather problematic scene as to its historical truth but nonetheless significant – we thought – for its erogenous value. How to link it to the seduction by the sister? Would she have touched him in a way that the child could have called "polish" as one also says "polish" a wooden floor? What an incongruous idea! Let's check it out anyway! The French-Russian dictionary gives TIERET, NATIERET. Let's go to the Russian-French dictionary; it will tell us whether the meaning "polish" coexists with others like scratch, scrape, and so forth, a necessary condition for the cryptonymic displacement just conjectured. Conscious of our duty, but not very hopeful, we then turned to the word *tieret* and read: (1) to rub; (2) to grind, to crunch; (3) to wound; (4) to polish. The second word *natieret*, of the same root, did not disappoint us either. It exhibits a comparable semantic variety, going from (1) to rub down, rub; through (2) to rub, scrub, wax; to finally (3) to scrape or wound oneself. We could not have asked for more! Finally we understood the rebus of the skyscraper! With all the necessary substitutions, the solution is simple: It concerns the association of the wolf with sexual pleasure obtained by rubbing.

By the same token, a whole area of the Wolf Man's enigmatic material was opened to our understanding. Lingering for the moment on the nose symptom, it became precise and concrete. The symptom had been produced, it was clear now, through the association of two words: one omitted and the other transformed into a cryptonym. The first pointed to the object of the hypochondriac fear, *lupus* (wolf); the second, scar, referred to the name of the action through which the dreaded pleasure would be accomplished: *tieret, natieret*. The hypochondriac *lupus*, coupled with the cryptonym "scar", did nothing more than show/hide the desire of a pleasurable rubbing applied to the "wolf" in order to make it stand up. "Sis, come and rub my penis." This was the key sentence. These were the unsayable words that he posted in the form of a rebus, making sure to add at the bottom: "You will never guess." It became obvious that this hidden sentence would be found everywhere in the Wolf Man's material.

We could fill pages and pages drawing up the catalogue of its various guises. We could also, in light of this new approach, take up again, point by point, our earlier psychodramatic reinterpretation of

Brunswick's text. In many places we could simplify or even rectify it. If we have left this up to our readers, by printing our initial version intact, we did so wanting to include them all the more in our fumbling around. They will much better appreciate the ground covered.

Among the applications of our discovery concerning the use of cryptonyms, we found most striking our realization that certain words suffered an extraordinary exclusion and that this same exclusion seemed to confer on them a genuinely magic power. The verbs *tieret* and *natieret* had to be entirely banished from the active vocabulary and not only in the sense of rubbing, but also in the sense of waxing or scraping. What if these parallel meanings, these allosemes,[9] had to be stated? Each time they were, by means of synonyms, they obviously implied a constant reference, even if a negative one, to the *taboo word*. It was, we thought, because a given word was unutterable that the obligation arose to introduce synonyms even for its lateral meanings, and that the synonyms acquired the status of substitutes. Thus they became *cryptonyms*, apparently not having any phonetic or semantic relationship to the prohibited word: *tzarapat* (scratch, scrape) bears no apparent relation to *tieret* (to rub). In sum, no simple metonymic displacement is at work here, referring to one element of a concrete situation instead of another element actually intended (as when we say pen to mean style or writer), but a displacement on a second level: The word itself as a lexical entity constitutes the global situation from which one particular meaning is sectioned out of the sum total of meanings. This characteristic could be expressed by saying that what is at stake here is not a *metonymy of things* but a *metonymy of words*. The contiguity that presides over this procedure is by nature not a representation of things, not even a representation of words, but arises from the lexical contiguity of the various meanings of the same words, that is, from the *allosemes*, as they are catalogued in a dictionary. For TZARAPINA (scar), to evoke *tieret* (to rub), a form of lexical contiguity has to be inserted. Having understood the real originality of this procedure, which lies in replacing a word by the synonym of its alloseme, we felt the need of applying to it a distinctive name, *cryptonymy*.

Behind the Scenes: Internal Hysteria – Setting Up and Working a Machinery

With this added clarification and the necessary verification done in the material, the question emerged of how one is led to invent such a procedure considering that it does not provide, either phonetically or semantically, the hallucinatory satisfaction we might reasonably expect. The only pertinent answer seemed as follows: It is not a situation *including* words that becomes repressed; the words are not dragged into repression by a situation. Rather, *the words themselves, expressing desire, are deemed to be generators of a situation that must be avoided and voided retroactively.* In this case, and only in this case, can we understand that repression may be carried out on the word, as if it were the representation of a thing, and that the return of the repressed cannot have at its disposal even the tortuous paths of metonymic displacement. For this to occur, a catastrophic situation must have been created precisely by words. We understand then why they would be excluded, responsible as they are for a situation; why they would be repressed from the Preconscious, dragging with them their lateral and allosemic meanings. In short: It is the idea that words can be excluded from the Preconscious – thus also from the dream texts – and replaced, in the name and capacity of the return of the repressed, by cryptonyms or their visual representation that is required for a general preliminary conclusion to our inquiry.

Let us now try to fill this formal frame with more concrete content. For such a construction, two elements have to be taken into account: First, the words in question must signify an erotic pleasure received from the sister; and second, they are responsible, because stated inauspiciously, for the castration, that is, the demolition of the father. Based on this double hypothesis, various possibilities can be imagined, and among them we settled on the idea that the traumatic catastrophe could not have taken place at one definite moment, but would have unfolded in four stages.

1. *The "seduction" of the younger brother by the older sister.* The term "seduction" might seem somewhat excessive to describe, as Freud did, sexual play among little children. For such games to take on the magnitude we know they can, an adult must be implicated. That is why we have suggested from the very beginning a stage –

2. *The alleged seduction of the daughter by the father.* The sister would have boasted about the privilege she had over her little brother, and in the process would have threatened him with castration at the moment of pleasure. Now, in light of the cryptonymic procedure, we abandon the idea stated at the beginning of this work of such a threat of castration. We now in fact know that the

terms that in the material seemed to evoke castration are simply the cryptonyms of repressed pleasure-words. Nevertheless, the hypothesis of two further stages forces itself on us, stage –

3. *The boy's verification with adults of the allegations made by his sister*, at first perhaps with Nania or the English governess, then with his mother back from a trip, finally with his father – then stage

4. *The outbreak of a scandal*, with an investigation as regards the meaning of the words *tieret, natieret* indicting the father.

This fourth stage is postulated as having the mark of a real experience and can in no way be merged with fantasy. This is what explains, to our mind, the uniqueness of the Wolf Man's case: the radical exclusion of the words of desire. The excluded *words* work as if they were representations of repressed *things*. They seem to have migrated from the Preconscious to the Unconscious. They have taken with them the very possibility of remembering the trauma. Their absence in the Preconscious signifies: The trauma never took place. What distinguishes a verbal exclusion of this kind from neurotic repression is precisely the fact that it renders verbalization impossible. The return of the deeply repressed, if it happens at all, cannot come about within a relation, in the form of symptoms or symbols. It will occur within the psychic apparatus through a kind of *internal hysteria* and will be directed toward the internal Objects incorporated for this purpose.

For the Wolf-Man – we understand why – a return of the repressed in the waking state through symbolization, for example, is out of the question. The single exception concerns the expression of *the very act of the retention of telling*, well expressed hysterically by tenacious constipation. But whatever might be the *object* of telling is so deeply buried behind words never to be uttered that its emergence, when it does take place, occurs not in the form of a symbol or a symptom but of a delirium such as that of the nose or finally of the erogenous fantasy itself. In this last instance, the appearances seem safe: What would be delirious about imagining a coitus performed a tergo and the suitable position of the partners (a tiergo[10] the analyst would say with well-taken mischief)? Apparently nothing, were it not for its incredible verbal origin: *tieret* visualized into a floor scrubber. We see here a genuine dream process in full wakefulness. In order to tell himself his desire, he has to have recourse to dream distortion. The erogenous fantasy, Grusha the floor scrubber, the washer-woman at the fountain as well as the parents' supposed coitus a tergo, were nothing but a word, translated into an image. The face, the person of the woman are of no importance, provided she illustrates, she embodies the taboo word. It is in this sense that we are going to call this erogenous image, this good-luck-charm fantasy, this magical taboo dodger: *a fetish*. Beneath the fetish, the occult love for a word-object remains concealed, beneath this love, the taboo-forming experience of a catastrophe, and finally beneath the catastrophe, the perennial memory of a hoarded pleasure with the ineducable wish that one day it shall return.

The Wolf Man's hope was deposited in the word whose secret lover he was. This word, his Object, he kept in his possession for an entire lifetime. Initially and by vocation, the word was addressed to someone. As an Object of love, it had to be removed from every-one's reach so that it would not be lost. Saying it without saying it. To show/hide. Walk around with a rebus and pretend it is undeci-pherable. Repeat tirelessly to one and all, especially to his analyst: "Here is nothing, hold it tight." Inaccessible, wending his way alongside the unattainable. To love without knowing, to love des-perately, to love loving the analyst endlessly.

The Fourth Act: On Freud's Couch – The Wolf Man as unto Himself

It was – we now know – for never having been able to utter certain words that, sixteen years earlier, the Wolf Man went to consult the famous Professor Freud. Following a bout of gonorrhea (curbed, however, by rather drastic means five years earlier), he remained in a state of near-total impotence. He dragged himself from doctors to health care centres without finding a remedy for what ailed him. The Professor was his last resort. Freud did not consider him a "maniac" for his loves at first sight as psychiatrists had done. He listened, he tried to understand, he requested his collaboration. Together they would find the cause of so much suffering. The Professor inspired confidence in particular by his subdued style of dressing, and the furniture of his office suggested praiseworthy occupations. The austere and sympathetic man of science was per-fectly suitable. S. P. was more than reassured. What got into him then when, hardly having lowered himself on to the couch, he re-quested from his respectable therapist the favour of performing anal coitus and invited him to defecate while standing on his head?[11] Had he been the Tierka he knew at four years of age, he could not have done better. Without a doubt, his "wolf" was surfacing. The

same one that had been so cruelly treated at the time of his gonorrhea. Since then, almost five years earlier, his depression had not
left him. This was evidence that one does not make "wolf" without
risking one's tail, even if it was only a father's tail. Could he ever
recover his *buka* standing up, could he finally protect it from
danger? He placed all his hopes in the Professor. He would tell him
everything. Everything, yes, except ... one thing: the unsayable.
They would launch their investigation together, they would study
the facts, their chronology. Together they would draw conclusions
about the causes and the consequences. He could sleep with peace
of mind, nothing will escape the sagacity of the Professor. Yet,
hardly reclined on the couch, this strange thing happens. What a
coup de théâtre for the analyst! And for him! Has anyone seen
a well-bred young man, not suspected of homosexuality, make such
a request of an eminent specialist of fifty? No, really, he was no
longer himself.

But who, in fact, was he? Before and now? Freud in truth could
never establish it. Are we, at the end of this study, in a position to
put forth a hypothesis on this score? It seems fairly certain that
no affective recollection took place during the transference and
that nothing occurred that could have identified him: "Yes, here
he is, this is definitely S. P., seduced at three years of age by his
sister, desiring his father at five, his mother at eight." S. P. in
person was not present. His official identity only served to cover
up the other characters he clandestinely sheltered within himself:
his father, his sister. A depressed and castrated father for having
rubbed up against Tierka, Matrona, that is who he was during
his depression. But once on the couch everything changed: The
man in the chair was now named Father and the man on the
couch automatically took on the complementary role, Tierka's
role. This was the unexpected but inescapable effect of the analytic situation. His depression vanished, and with his extravagant
request began a flirtation between Father and Sister that was to
last four and a half years. This unusual first session was simply
Tierka dallying with Papa. As the years went by, the coquetry
took on forms more suited to the norms of the analytic dialogue
and to the widely publicized desiderata of the father of psychoanalysis. Throughout more than one thousand sessions, Tierka
unflinchingly recounted Stanko's memories, dreams, nightmares.
She added some of her own invention. Father and Daughter could
live happily.

As for Freud, he must have been thrilled and disconcerted all at the same time. Soon he thought he could identify the "wolf" in the nightmare, the "wolf" in the infantile phobia: It represented some terrifying image in relation to the father. It must have been the father himself. He still needed to understand how this kind and loving father could have instilled fright in the child when all the memories of "castration" were linked to female images. Should one incriminate a phrase such as the unfortunate one used to tease children: "I'm going to eat you," or should one appeal to the phylogenetic fear of being castrated by the father? Such answers hardly convinced anyone, including their author. Freud was just as baffled when faced with the allegation of a Primal Scene supposedly observed at the age of eighteen months. Still, the parents' coitus a tergo seen at this tender age could – theoretically – have caused a neurosis and subsequent sexual behavior. The case seemed too good not to be used in the polemic against Jung. Let us admit though that, removed from its context of heated controversy, such an example was altogether untenable. Moreover, Freud needed no such arguments to defend his ideas. In any case, this matter remains a prime example of theoretical and clinical errors occasioned by a heated controversy.

The Wolf Man himself felt reassured. Tierka and Father united, they spoke of Stanko, and for all of them everything turned out for the best. Of course the "wolf" was Father, of course Father had to castrate Stanko, of course Stanko feared him with good reason. So long as Father is not castrated again, never ever, through inopportune words, through the explosion of outraged anger. To void what had taken place once upon a time, the catastrophic words had to be contained at all costs: Squeeze the sphincter tighter and tighter! Constipate the fatal word! And above all, the "window" must never open by itself! Otherwise there would be the horrifying nightmare of the wolves of long ago: a fossilized phrase in a fossilized picture. "*Siestorka* makes *buka* to Father." "Sis, come and make Stanko's 'wolf' stand up." No! Such words will forever remain in his throat. Let the two of them be happy and S. P. can live!

Yes, S. P. is entirely a gift of himself in the strictest sense. Did he keep to himself some desire that he had not offered? This will remain unknown to all including himself. No one on earth must know who he is. No one on earth must know that one day he *became* his father or that he carried him within himself along with his castrated desire. This father has to be restored, such is his most fervent desire; otherwise he, Stanko, could never pronounce, in his own name, the sentence of his own desire, say it to Tierka without disaster: "Come Sis, rub me, do Buka to me!" Alas, these words, these diabolical words, he will never give voice to them, for they – yes, we have to admit it – castrated the father, castrated the son. They are the ones that threw the mother into despondency. They are the ones that, through their belated effects, led to the sister's suicide, to the father's premature death. A few innocent words, and all of a sudden the whole family is destroyed.

This sentence, however, always the same one, the Wolf Man will never tire of repeating in riddles. Tieret, to rub, wax, wash. Sissy, "get on all fours" to "brush", Grusha, to "wax", Matrona,[12] yes, do *tronut*, do touch, touch me! I'll go crazy ("become touched"). Oh, Matrona! Matrona, a cherished word: Russian doll, you hold my Jack-in-the-box, *vanka, vstanka*, let's put it on its head, you'll see how it *makes out*! It was enough for me to *act* a word: "scrape," "cut" into a tree and I was already in heaven, I had my little finger "cut". Come, Professor, do these words to me. "Cut", oh! "cut me", "pull me", "rip me", oh, confounded words, un-sayable words, oh! yes, rub, rub my genitals for me so they stand up on two paws like a wolf disguised as a grandmother with a white bonnet on its head. Oh, yes "rip off (*tierebit*) the wings of this wasp, of this S. P." (*Wespe*), rub, rub it for he cannot stand it – but… .

All this, S. P. does not say clearly. But fast, very fast, in hardly three months, since that was the nonnegotiable deadline Freud had set in order to finish it off, he laid it out in cryptonyms and cryptomyths.

And with his time up, the Wolf Man left, relieved, for his native Russia. He felt relieved since he had spoken and invented disguises for his desire. Relieved also not to have to speak it in disaster words, relieved finally, since he could take back the memory of a new kind of father, of a father whose seductive practices were re-stricted to harmless words, rather amusing by the way, like the word "castration," so often on the lips of the Professor, and which happily joined the list of cryptonyms.

And in all likelihood everything would have been fine for him after that had the incidents of the Revolution not forced him into exile five years later. In 1919, upon his arrival in Vienna, Freud's famous case study had just been published. He was so happy reading it! The illustrious father had become involved with his case, and more than that, he released his appreciative judgment to the public: "... pleasant and likeable personality"; he had spoken of his "sharp intelligence" and of "his refinement of thought."

Yet, deep down in the Wolf Man, there was disappointment and revolt. He went to see the Master once more. He let him know that he had not been cured, and especially not of this constipation that Freud so proudly claimed to have alleviated. Moreover, being financially ruined as he was, he could not afford another analysis. That should not stand in the way! the Professor said with sympathy. And then came free analysis, donations. Wages for not being himself. For the Wolf Man, the apparently happy situation revived a latent despair: Stanko misunderstood, castrated, disposed of. Father giving money to Tierka. ... When in October 1923, the seriousness of Freud's illness became common knowledge, the horizon blackened even more. If Father disappeared, who would ever free S. P.'s desire? We know the rest.

> Forever he will keep his love in his own possession, his Objects which are words. Unable to convert these word-objects into words for the object, his life-remains, for himself and for us all, an enigma. Yet, in all this life, unfurling the flag of enigma, the Wolf Man has never left us. He remains with us analysts, to quicken our desire to know. Ever bent on offering a new element in order to clear up his mystery, he further obscures it. Our companion of misfortune in no-knowledge, he has become the symbol of a mirage – haunting every analyst – the mirage of understanding. After so many others, we too have succumbed to it.
> Let him be thanked for it!
> And let us be forgiven for it!
>
> September 27, 1970

Postscript. It should be clear that the preceding considerations relate to the Wolf Man only as a mythical person. Their wholly fictitious – though not gratuitous – nature illustrates an approach that can be of clinical use. What we termed *internal hysteria*, and considered as the consequence of *incorporation*, often implies unconscious procedures motivated by a particular topographical structure involving the *cryptonymic displacement of a taboo word*. Rightly or wrongly, we discovered such a taboo word in the Wolf Man: *tieret* and its derivatives. The reader may be interested in some additional information that has come to us through the kind generosity of Muriel Gardiner. We refer here to the Wolf Man's *Memoirs*, which began appearing in serial form in 1961 in the

Bulletin of the Philadelphia Association for Psycho-analysis. These memoirs are of great psychoanalytic interest and deserve an extended study. We mention only two details because they relate directly to our findings. The first is this: Following the suicide of his sister Anna (this was her real name), who ingested a bottle of mercury during a trip to the Caucasus, the Wolf Man went on a trip to these same mountains, without realizing, however, that there might be a geographic connection between these facts. On close reading of his recollections it becomes apparent that the unconscious goal of this trip was to climb to the head of a mountain stream named Tierek. Upon arriving after a long and anxious ascent, he could not keep from taking out his paintbox and brushes to "paint" (*tieret*) a view of the landscape. He also recalls that he was served *trout* caught in the *Tierek* River. The second point we want to make concerns the love at first sight he conceived for his future wife, a pretty nurse in a Kraepelin clinic (in Munich) where he had come to stay in the throes of a depression. He did not exchange a word with her, but an elderly Russian lady, also a resident there, furnished, with the appropriate Russian accent no doubt, one crucial piece of information: the name of the young woman. Her name was Sister Theresa (homophone of the Russian verb TIRETSIA, to rub oneself) and the diminutive was Terka, pronounced in Russian fashion: Tierka. We might have guessed it. In any case, our choice of the same name to designate the incorporated sister predates this information and – though inspired by the verb *tieret* – must be considered the work of some lucky coincidence.

NOTES

[Nicholas Abraham (1919–1975) and Maria Torok (1925–1998) emigrated from Hungary to France in the 1930s and 40s and trained as psychoanalysts; from 1956 on they developed techniques of analysis that, departing from the generalizing aspects of Freud, took the subject's singular or individualized experience as the foundation for psychoanalysis. Formulating distinctive procedures for the analysis of psychic "secrets", "crypts" and "phantoms", their work offered new ways of understanding the relationships between language and psychoanalysis (see Essay 3 and Introductory Note to this section). English translations of their numerous works include Abraham's "The Phantom of Hamlet *or* The Sixth Act, *preceded by* The Intermission of 'Truth'" (1975), *Rhythms: On the Work, Translation, and Psychoanalysis* (1985), and the co-authored *The Wolf Man's Magic Word: A Cryptonymy* (1976) and *The Shell and the Kernel: Renewals of*

Psychoanalysis (1978). Maria Torok published, with Nicholas Rand, *Questions for Freud: The Secret History of Psychoanalysis* (1997). Ed.]

1. Abraham and Torok are alluding to the Wolf Man's brief appearance in Freud's 1927 essay "On Fetishism"; see the "Introductory Note" to this section [Editor's note].

2. Abraham and Torok suggest here that in the Wolf Man's unconscious a (magic) "word" becomes the "Thing", or the lost, impossible *object*, of his desire [Editor's note].

3. "Dr X." is a physician consulted by the Wolf Man for his nasal problems, a history given in Brunswick's "A Supplement to Freud's 'History of an Infantile Neurosis'" (1928; Gardiner 263–307) [Editor's note].

4. Jean-François Champollion (1790–1832), the French Egyptologist who deciphered the hieroglyphics of the Rosetta Stone [Editor's note].

5. The "fourth act" of the Wolf Man's drama, to which Abraham and Torok now turn, succeeds the "drama in three acts" they have traced up to this point in their analysis. The "first act" stages the Wolf Man's hostility to his Sister insofar as she is the object of the Father's desire, and involves him "killing" the image of "Father's Tierka"; the "second act" involves the "psychodramatic personification of Tierka by the analyst", Ruth Mack Brunswick, in the sense that the Wolf Man speaks his "encrypted" desire to her; the "third act" involves the Wolf Man "tak[ing] on Father's role" in relation to his internal "Tierka" by putting *Freud* in the place of "Stanko", and rejecting him (*WMMW* 14–15) [Editor's note].

6. Abraham and Torok argue that the Wolf Man's unconscious composes a "verbarium"; literally, a *place for words* [Editor's note].

7. That is, the dream of the white wolves in Chapter IV of the Freud case (*FR* 404–16; *PF* 9: 259–80) [Editor's note].

8. The Latin word *lupus* means "wolf"; it also means an ulcerous disease of the skin, especially the nose. *Lupus seborrheus* denotes a diseased discharge [Editor's note].

9. "Alloseme": the word combines the Greek *allos* ("other") with *seme* ("unit of meaning") [Editor's note].

10. Even in *a tergo*, the term that denotes the primal scene of parental copulation in Freud's case history, Abraham and Torok hear the Wolf Man's "magic word", "*tier*-et" [Editor's note].

11. According to Ernest Jones, who quotes an unpublished letter written by Freud to Ferenczi on 13 February 1910: "... [the Wolf Man] initiated the first hour of treatment with the offer to have rectal intercourse with Freud ..." (*The Life and Work of Sigmund Freud* 274). This first

session is not recounted in Freud's case study. In view of our hypothesis, the Wolf Man must have requested from Freud to stand "on all fours" (rectal = from behind = *a tergo: tieret* = to rub) and to let his "Jack-in-the-box" reach orgasm.

12. In Chapter VIII of *The Wolf Man*, Freud recounts the Wolf Man's memories of his nursery-maid, "Grusha", and a peasant girl, "Matrona", with whom he falls in love at the age of 18 (*PF* 9: 330–33). For Freud, it is Grusha's and Matrona's *position on all fours* that charges these encounters erotically; for Abraham and Torok, it is the women's action of *scrubbing* or *rubbing* [Editor's note].

9

Fors: The Anglish Words of Nicolas Abraham and Maria Torok*

JACQUES DERRIDA

> From then on, that particular pleasure, jealously preserved in his *inner safe*, could only be subject to total disavowal. In addition, not having himself been included in the scene ...

> The intervention of the mother, with her Russian words, and then of the nurse with her English words, closed two doors for him at the same time.
>
> *The Wolf Man's Magic Word*

TOPOI

What is a crypt?[1] No crypt presents itself. The grounds are so disposed as to disguise and to hide: something, always a body in some way. But also to disguise the act of hiding and to hide the disguise: the crypt hides as it holds. Carved out of nature, sometimes making use of probability or facts, these grounds are not natural.

The crypt is thus not a natural place [*lieu*], but the striking history of an artifice, an *architecture*, an artifact: of a place *comprehended* within another but rigorously separate from it, isolated from general space by partitions, an enclosure, an enclave. So as to purloin *the thing* from the rest. Constructing a system of partitions,

---

* Translated by Barbara Johnson

160

with their inner and outer surfaces, the cryptic enclave produces a cleft in space, in the assembled system of various places, in the architectonics of the open square within space, itself delimited by a generalized closure, in the *forum*. Within this forum, a place where the free circulation and exchange of objects and speeches can occur, the crypt constructs another, more inward forum like a closed rostrum or speaker's box, a *safe*: sealed, and thus internal to itself, a secret interior within the public square, but, by the same token, outside it, external to the interior. Whatever one might write upon them, the crypt's parietal surfaces do not simply separate an inner forum from an outer forum. The inner forum is (a) safe, an outcast outside inside the inside. That is the condition, and the stratagem, of the cryptic enclave's ability to isolate, to protect, to shelter from any penetration, from anything that can filter in from outside along with air, light, or sounds, along with the eye or the ear, the gesture or the spoken word.

Caulked or padded along its inner partition, with cement or concrete on the other side, the cryptic safe protects from the outside the very secret of its clandestine inclusion or its internal exclusion. Is this strange space *hermetically* sealed? The fact that one must always answer *yes* and *no* to this question that I am deferring here will have already been apparent from the topographical structure of the crypt, on its highest level of generality: The crypt can constitute its secret only by means of its division, its fracture. "I" can *save* an inner safe only by putting it inside "myself", *beside(s)* myself, outside.

What is at stake here is what takes place secretly, or takes a secret place, in order to keep itself *safe* somewhere in a self.

Before turning our minds to the break-in technique that will allow us to penetrate into a crypt (it consists of locating the crack or the lock, choosing the angle of a partition, and forcing entry), we have to know that the crypt itself is *built* by violence. In one or several blows, but whose marks are at first soundless. The first hypothesis of *The Magic Word* posits a preverbal traumatic scene that would have been "encrypted" with all its libidinal forces, which, through their contradiction, through their very opposition, support the internal resistance of the vault like pillars, beams, studs, and retaining walls, leaning the powers of intolerable pain against an ineffable, forbidden pleasure, whose locus [*lieu*] is not simply the Unconscious but the Self.

That supposes a redefinition of the Self (the system of *introjections*) and of the fantasy of *incorporation*. The Wolf Man would have had to have incorporated within him, in his Self, his older sister: his sister as seduced by the father and trying to repeat the same scene with her brother. And by the same token, the Wolf Man, the brother, would also have had to have incorporated the father's place, the paternal penis confused with his own. The violence of the mute forces that would thus be setting up the crypt does not end with the trauma of a single unbearable and condemned seduction scene.

The seduction scene alone is not sufficient. What is needed, still mute, is the contradiction springing from the incorporation itself. It ceaselessly opposes two stiff, incompatible forces, erect against each other: "deadly pleasure" ... "two contradictory demands: that the Father's penis should neither *come* [*ne jouisse*] ... nor go [*ni ne périsse*]." Without this contradiction within desire, nothing would be comprehensible: neither the relative solidity of the crypt – what architects call "the resistance of the materials" that balances the pressures, repels intrusions, foresees collapse, or in any case delays it, tries to compute, like miners, the moment a shaft should be allowed to cave in – nor the hermeticism and the indefatigable effort to maintain it, nor the failure of that effort, the permeation from within or from without, seeping through the crypt's partitions, passing from one part of the divided Self to the other, engraving itself upon several surfaces along the angular lines that we will identify later and that always follow the division of a "fantasmatic double(ness)", each fantasy being "double and opposed."

The "indelible mark" (a mark that is at first prelinguistic) left by the incorporation of the seductress sister forms a contradiction, enclosed, entombed, encysted inside the Self. This is not a solution, rather the opposite of one, but it allows for the easing of the conflict (by feigning its internalization) between the aggressiveness and the libido that are directed toward the Object. The crypt is always an internalization, an inclusion intended as a compromise, but since it is a parasitic inclusion, an inside heterogeneous to the inside of the Self, an out-cast in the domain of general introjection within which it violently takes its place, the cryptic safe can only maintain in a state of repetition the mortal conflict it is impotent to resolve.

Introjection/incorporation: Everything is played out on the borderline that divides and opposes the two terms. Before ever deciding to take a new look at the case of the Wolf Man, Nicolas Abraham and Maria Torok had submitted the concept of introjection to a rigorous reelaboration. First introduced by Ferenczi in 1909, and later seen tracing its problematic way through the works of Freud, K. Abraham, and Klein, introjection, as defined by Ferenczi, is the process by which autoerotic cathexes are extended. By including the object – whence the name introjection – the process expands the self. It does not retreat; it advances, propagates itself, assimilates, takes over. "I emphasized the idea of 'inclusion' in order to say that I conceive of all object-love (or all transference), both in a normal subject and in a neurotic ..., as an enlargement of the Self, that is, an introjection. Basically, a person's love can be directed only toward himself. Insofar as he loves an object, he adopts it as a part of his Self" (Ferenczi). Referring to this definition, Maria Torok goes on to point out that introjection includes not only the object but also the instincts and desires attached to it. In contrast to the widespread tendency to confuse the terms introjection and incorporation, she traces a rigorous demarcation between them. That boundary is indispensable to the localization of the crypt, for it surrounds, within the Self (the set of introjections), the cryptic enclave as an extraneous or foreign area of incorporation. According to Freud's *Mourning and Melancholia* (which was written between the Wolf Man's first analysis and the publication of *The History of an Infantile Neurosis*, the two texts being more or less contemporaneous), the process of incorporation into the Self provides an economic answer to the loss of the object. The Self tries to identify with the object it has "incorporated."

Sealing the loss of the object, but also marking the refusal to mourn, such a manoeuvre is foreign to and actually opposed to the process of introjection. I pretend to keep the dead alive, intact, *safe* (*save*) *inside me*, but it is only in order to refuse, in a necessarily equivocal way, to love the dead as a *living* part of me, dead *save in me*, through the process of introjection, as happens in so-called normal mourning. The question could of course be raised as to whether or not "normal" mourning preserves the object *as other* (a living person dead) inside me. This question – of the general appropriation and safekeeping of the other *as other* – can always be raised as the deciding factor, but does it not at the same time blur the very line it draws between introjection and incorporation through an essential and irreducible ambiguity?[2] Let us give this question a chance to be reposed. For Maria Torok, "incorporation, properly speaking", in its "rightful semantic specificity", intervenes at the limits of introjection itself, when introjection, for some

reason, fails. Faced with the impotence of the process of introjection (gradual, slow, laborious, mediated, effective), incorporation is the only choice: fantasmatic, unmediated, instantaneous,
magical, sometimes hallucinatory. Magic (the Wolf Man himself
will resort to a "magic word" to silently commemorate – his word
is also a "word-thing" and a "mute word" – the act of incorporation) – magic is recognized as the very element of incorporation.

With the real loss of the object having been rejected and the
desire having been maintained but at the same time excluded from
introjection (simultaneous conservation and suppression, between
which no synthesis is possible), incorporation is a kind of theft to
reappropriate the pleasure object. But that reappropriation is simultaneously rejected: which leads to the paradox of a foreign body
preserved as foreign but by the same token excluded from a
self that thenceforth deals not with the other, but only with itself.
The more the self keeps the foreign element as a foreigner inside
itself, the more it excludes it. The self *mimes* introjection. But this
mimicry with its redoubtable logic depends on clandestinity. Incorporation negotiates clandestinely with a prohibition it neither
accepts nor transgresses. "Secrecy is essential", whence the crypt, a
hidden place, a disguise hiding the traces of the act of disguising, a
place of silence. Introjection speaks; "denomination" is its "privileged" medium. Incorporation keeps still, speaks only to silence or
to ward off intruders from its secret place. What the crypt com-
memorates, as the incorporated object's "monument" or "tomb", is
not the object itself, but its exclusion, the exclusion of a specific
desire from the introjection process: A door is silently sealed off like
a condemned passageway inside the Self, becoming the outcast safe:
"*a* commemorative monument, the incorporated object betokens
the place, the date, and the circumstances in which desires were
banished from introjection: they stand like tombs in the life of the
ego." (*SK* 114). The crypt is the vault of a desire.

The most inward safe (the crypt as an artificial unconscious, as
the Self's artifact) becomes the outcast (*Hormis*: except for, save,
fors), the outside (*foris*) with respect to the outer safe (the Self) that
includes it without comprehending it, in order to comprehend
nothing in it.[3] The inner safe (the Self) has placed itself outside the
crypt, or, if one prefers, has constituted "within itself" the crypt as
an outer safe. One might go on indefinitely switching the place
names around in this dizzying topology (the inside as the outside of
the outside, or of the inside; the outside as the inside of the inside,

or of the outside, etc.), but total con-fusion is not possible. The parietal partitions are *very* solid. Maintained by "conservative re-pression", the dividing wall is *real*. So is the inclusion. Doubtless the Self *does* identify, in order to resist introjection, but in an "imaginary, occult" way, with the lost object, with its "life beyond the grave." Doubtless this "endocryptic identification" designed to keep the topography intact and the place safe, remains fantasmatic, cryptofantasmatic. But the *inclusion* itself is real; it is not of the order of fantasies. The same can be said of the partitions set up for that purpose, and thus of all the divisions in the topographical structure.

When one part of the self that is split by the crypt speaks to the other in order to say, *like* an unconscious, in the manner of the un-conscious, Wo *Ich war soll Es werden*,[4] it is a stratagem for keeping *safe* a place or rather a no-place in the place, a "manoeuvre to pre-serve this no-place in the spot where the most extreme pleasure can no longer occur, but due to which that pleasure can occur else-where." This place, the place of the excluded word-thing, of the nonsymbolizable, is subject to a "true repression" that thrusts it into the Unconscious, from out of which we will see it act, live, return.

DEATH

The cryptic place is also a sepulchre. The topography has taught us to take a certain nonplace into consideration. The sepulchral func-tion in turn can signify something other than simply death. A crypt, people believe, always hides something dead. But to guard it from what? Against what does one keep a corpse intact, safe both from life and from death, which could both come in from the outside to touch it? And to allow death to take no place in life?

When the word-thing *tieret* is buried (in the unconscious, in fact, as the cryptic Unconscious's Thing), it is "interred with the falla-cious fiction that it is no longer alive." The inhabitant of a crypt is always a living dead, a dead entity we are perfectly willing to keep alive, but *as* dead, one we are willing to keep, as long as we keep it, within us, intact in any way save as living.

The fact that the cryptic incorporation always marks an effect of impossible or refused mourning (melancholy *or* mourning) is cease-lessly confirmed by *The Magic Word*. But at the same time the incorporation is never finished.

It always remains contradictory in its structure: By resisting intro-jection, it prevents the loving, appropriating assimilation of the other, and thus seems to preserve the other *as* other (foreign), but it also does the opposite. It is not the *other* that the process of incor-poration preserves, but a certain topography it keeps safe, intact, untouched by the very relationship with the other to which, para-doxically enough, introjection is more open. Nevertheless, it remains that the otherness of the other installs within any process of appropriation (even before any opposition between introjecting and incorporating) a "contradiction".

The incorporation that gives rise to the Wolf Man's crypt is con-tradictory in the very singularity of its libidinal content: "a contra-diction within the very desire" of the man who wanted his father and sister dead. Once he had incorporated his sister – "the only way to love her in order to keep from killing her and to kill her in order to keep from loving her" – he had to incorporate the person who seduced her: the father. The identification between the two penises both internalizes the contradiction and makes it insoluble. The incorporated object (Father-Sister) must be both killed and kept safe.

The couple: a dead man and a live girl, a living man and a dead girl – a living death outside him inside him, within his most outcast inner safe. His force and his fortress are made of their death as much as of their life. This tireless compulsion is shown, in *The Magic Word, working*, always the same, throughout all the clinical material, the verbal or preverbal marks, the symptoms, the dreams, the representations of words or things. In constructing the crypt, in letting the crypt construct and consolidate itself, the Wolf Man wants to save the living death he has walled up inside him. That is, *himself* – the lodging, the haunt of a host of ghosts, and the *dra-matic* contradiction of a desire, a desire that is, however, no longer even his.

The Magic Word is a singular tale, the tale of the *drama* of the Wolf Man, but also the pulsing, rhythmic, step-by-step tale of the act of deciphering, decrypting, itself dramatic, the tale of a tale, of its progress, its obstacles, its delays, its interruptions, its discoveries all along a labyrinth; of its entrance hall, its corridors, its angles. The analysts' desire (there are two analysts and the question of desire becomes less simple than ever) is fully engaged in the tale; it is never left obscure. That desire invests the entire space, is part of the operation, and even gives it its first push.

At regular intervals, a narrator or a speaker steps forward on the stage and says "we" (the couple who signed *The Magic Word*), as in a Poe story or a Brecht play: to sum up, to measure the step reached, to present the hero of the action, that is, of a *drama*. For example, the italicized paragraph, as the curtain rises upon what is "Behind the inner world."

The desire of the two "authors", of their double unit, is assumed in the first person plural, even if, outside the italics, that double unit uses the third person. The assumed desire is indeed that of *saving* not the Wolf Man but his analysis and "ourselves", the two, or the three, of them finding themselves here bound beneath the seal of a contract to be deciphered.

> The Wolf Man's *drama* remains incomplete for its *hero*. But once set in motion, its *action* cannot be stopped; it must proceed *in us* inevitably to its *final outcome*. And here *our* dissatisfaction, spurred on by a providential *deus ex machina*, expounds, imagines, dreams. An irresistible force pulls *us*: to *save* the analysis of the Wolf Man, to *save ourselves*. With time the fourth act opens within us, stretches before us, and *in us* comes to fulfillment, bringing *salvation*.

1. An Impromptu Walk through a Verbarium: Cryptonyms and What They Hide

> The authors arrived at this very juncture in the process of their writing, and planned to take up Freud's text again with their point of view – incorporation – in mind, when it occurred to them to consult a Russian dictionary.   (emphasis mine)

In unfolding the "drama" of the Wolf Man, in deciphering the monumental record of his history, in reconstituting the hieroglyphic code (which he had to invent in order to say without saying the interdict) (they allude at one point to Champollion and the Rosetta stone), the two analysts constructed: the analysis of a crypt, of course, of a cryptography, with its language and its method; but also, inseparably, the crypt of an analysis, its "decrypted" (deciphered) crypt, its crypt in the act of decrypting, the commemorative monument of what must be kept alive and seminally active.

The Wolf Man's Magic Word reads like a novel, a poem, a myth, a drama, the whole thing in a plural translation, productive and simultaneous. I am not here defining the forms or genres that would *lend themselves* (let themselves be borrowed) to a psychoanalytic exposition. I am pointing out, in the invisible intersection of these apparently formal necessities, what is unique about a procedure that has to invent its own language. And certain readers (the quick-witted type) will perhaps be surprised not to find in the style of *The Magic Word* any of the prevalent mannerisms of this or that French discourse today: within the psychoanalytic agora, outside it, or in that intermediary zone that expands so rapidly.

A certain foreign body is here working over our household words. The feeling of foreignness does not come from the authors' mother tongue or their polyglotism, nor from the most active, insistent "references" (Freud, Ferenczi, K. Abraham, Hermann, Klein, poets from France, England, Hungary, etc.). It is attached to the Thing they are occupied with.

And *The Magic Word* calls us in turn with a tale: the tale of a novel, a poem, a myth, a drama, the whole thing translating into French what was first the analytic translation (the active hollowing-out that produces a crypt that is simultaneously attacked in the three languages that are building it), the analytic translation, that is, of a text (the Wolf Man's real "drama") that itself already constituted a cryptic translation.

The tale recounts, besides the genesis of the "case", its own *history as a story*, staging its speakers and marking all the genres employed in this double articulation: the *novel* (family saga, the adventures of one or more subjects in a modern European society traversed by several wars or revolutions), the *drama* (a "hero" who is legion, an "action" in four acts, and even a "dramaturgy of the Unconscious on Ruth Mack Brunswick's couch", several theatrical scenes, a "recognition scene" and even a "denouement", but only, it is true, for the speakers), or the *poem* (the production of a work as language, "a single poem for several voices", as it is called, a "poem of life" in which, in addition to the Wolf Man himself, all the analysts known or unknown to him will have participated) or the *myth* (reconstruction of an immemorial origin, *in illo tempore*), or *translation* (circulation among types of writing, corporeal marks, whether verbal or not, which form a more or less [as always] idiomatic corpus and which call for the production of *another* kind of writing to translate them). But if this description is still insufficient, it is because it does not explain the necessity of this recourse to all these "forms". That necessity, it seems to me, springs in the final analysis from the *cryptic* structure of the ultimate "referent". The referent is constructed in such a way as never to present itself "in person", not even as the object of a theoretical discourse within the traditional norms. The Thing is encrypted. Not *within* the crypt (the Self's safe) but *by* the crypt and *in* the Unconscious. The "narrated" event, reconstituted by a novelistic, mythodramatico-poetic genesis, never appears.

The postscript to the first part emphasizes the "entirely fictional"[5] character of the preceding reconstitution. That reconstitution was about a "mythical person". We should not take this type of remark as merely the rhetoric of a prudent, modest self-irony. But neither should we hasten to oppose "science", "truth", or the "real" to this fiction. "Fictive" does not mean "gratuitous", adds the postscript. To be constrained by a certain internal logic in the original still remains the rule of translation, even if that original is itself constructed, by the structure of the "original" event, as a "cryptomythic" system. A certain type of verification is constantly at work, whose procedures can depend only on new anasemic and metapsychological stipulations, notably the new topographical definitions of the Thing, Reality, Fantasy, etc. These stipulations are both produced and tested by this type of work. By their very nature they exclude gratuitousness, they leave no freedom for re-ordering the story or for tampering with the internal necessity of the translations.

To track down the path to the tomb, then to violate a sepulchre: that is what the analysis of a cryptic incorporation is like. The idea of violation might imply some kind of transgression of a right, the forced entry of a penetrating, digging force, but the violated sepulchre *itself* was never "legal". It is the very tombstone of the illicit, and marks the spot of an extreme pleasure [*jouissance*], a pleasure entirely *real* though walled up, buried alive in its own prohibition. When the process of introjection is thwarted, a contradiction sets in, as we have seen, and with it that opposition of forces that constructs the crypt, props up the partitions, organizes a system of transactions, a kind of market, inside it, evaluates the *rates* of pleasure or pain (this is by definition the *forum* or *for*, the *market*place where jurisdiction, laws, rates and proportions are determined).

The Self: a cemetery guard. The crypt is enclosed within the self, but as a foreign place, prohibited, excluded. The self is not the proprietor of what he is guarding. He makes the rounds like a proprietor, but only the rounds. He turns around and around, and in particular he uses all his knowledge of the grounds to turn visitors away. "It stands fast there, keeping an eye on the comings and goings of the members of its immediate Family who – for various reasons – might claim access to the tomb. When the ego lets in some curious or injured parties, or detectives, it carefully provides them with false leads and fake graves" (*SK* 159).

As for language, it inhabits the crypt in the form of "words buried alive", defunct words, that is, words "relieved of their communicative function". They no longer point to the desire via the prohibition, as in hysterical repression, which they therefore threaten to the extent that they no longer carry on the effect of prohibition. They mark, on the very spot where they are buried alive, "preserved", the fact that the desire was in a way satisfied, that the pleasurable fulfillment *did take place*.

THE CIPHER (MORTGAGE)

The first part of this book, "The Magic Word", provides the general matrix of the analysis. It is subdivided into two chapters corresponding to two phases of the research, the positioning of the investigatory apparatus and data, then the discovery.[6] The first chapter reconstructs a traumatic scenography and the incorporation that accompanies it. It appears not to resort to any fact of language or any verbal material. All we learn in it is why the Wolf Man's desire had to remain "mute". A certain "nose language" *is* analyzed, but this is still (provisionally) a symptom in which no word can yet be read, a symptom made to be illegible in a lexical framework: a sort of writing without language, a "billboard" or "open book" covered with unpronounceable signs. The proposed translation is thus not yet that of a *rebus*: Another allusion to a mute hieroglyphic: the "mauve-colored stones" of a certain dream that "like the Rosetta stone, are awaiting their Champollion". The following chapter does not contradict the schema thus mapped out. But without hiding a certain rearrangement of the investigatory apparatus and a noticeable modification in the procedure, this time it does bring in verbal material. That material unfurls in a proliferating mass, but it is always contained, oriented, *comprehended*, at the most determinate moments of the interpretation, by the general structure of the previously recognized organization of the investigation. Why does this happen, and how?

Why: in order to explain that certain words, as a means of autotherapy, were both able and obliged to be treated as things, or even as Objects. That was indispensable to the fantasy of incorporation and to the topographical requirements already defined. If indeed the Wolf Man went on to a cryptic incorporation (the hypothesis of the first chapter), he had to have behaved in *just such a way* with words.

How: The analysts begin, at both ends of the first verbal chain to be reconstituted, with two silent scenes, two visible (visualized) "tableaux" that had to have as their end the transformation of words into things and that thus, inversely, must be read as *rebuses*. Two "images", one phobogenic, the other erogenic. We cannot yet know whether they are complementary. On the one hand, we have the original dream. Schematically: The *six* in the six wolves (the number is maintained even though it had been corrected as seven and sketched as five), is translated into Russian (*shiest*, perch, mast and perhaps sex, close to *shiestiero* and *shiestorka*, "the six", the "lot of six people", close to *siestra*, sister, and its diminutive *siestorka*, sissy, toward which the influence of the German *Schwester* had oriented the decipherment). Thus, within the mother tongue, through an essentially verbal relay this time, the sister is associated with the phobic image of the wolf. But the relay is nevertheless not semantic: It comes from lexical contiguity or a formal consonance.

But the sister-wolf association seems to break down in the nightmare about the skyscraper. The sister, it seems, is no longer there. The wolf *is* there, at least in the German word for skyscraper *Wolk*enkratzer, or in the other Russian word for wolf (not *buka* this time but *Volk*). However, if it is thus attested, the presence of the wolf is no longer associated with that of the sister, but only (as in the French name *Grateloup* [literally, Scrapewolf], which I propose as a substitute for skyscraper) with the semantic family that certain languages group under the initial sounds *gr, kr, skr*, (the mechanism that interests us here in this "case" is that of these "motivations", whatever one may think about linguistic motivation in general): the Russian *skreb*, which is the root of *skrebok*, scraper-eraser, *skroït*, to sharpen, *skrip*, scraping sound, the German *Krebs*, cancer, which is like *skreb* backward, etc. The *Grateloup* family, apparently having no connection with the sister, is less unrelated, *in its name*, to her hypochondriac fears concerning the nose (scratches, scars, cancer) no doubt associated, along both semantic and phonic paths *at the same time* – quasi-homonyms *and* quasi-synonyms (the *play* between the two, without any absolute privilege of *either* the signifier or the signified, is an indispensable part of the mechanism) – with lupus seborrheus. The hypothesis according to which the sister (the seduced seductress) was replaced in her absence by this lexical abundance around the focus *Grateloup* (scrape, scratch, scar) excluded, because of the very abundance and mobility of the substitutive vocabulary, the possibility that any single word with one single meaning could have been replaced by another, according to some simple metonymic displacement. The rich, orderly polysemia of an unspeakable (hidden, crypted) word had to be lurking behind a regular – in spite of a certain amount of play – series of *cryptonyms*. But what was that unspeakable word?

At this point we take up the chain from the other end. We follow it in the direction of a second mute scene, a second visualized tableau. Grusha, the floor scrubber, with her bucket and broom, seen from the rear, and the compulsive return to this erogenic image. It is a *rebus* of a particular kind. As soon as, in contrast with Freud, we focus on the act of *rubbing*, and turn our attention to the Russian words for that act (*tieret, natieret*), we will see that the catalogue of uses (allosemes) of these two words provides us with the whole range of associations and dissociations among the ideas of rubbing and/or wounding = scratching (*tieret*: 1. to rub, 2. to grind, 3. to wound, 4. to polish; *natieret*: 1. to rub down, 2. to rub, scrub, wax, 3. to scrape or wound oneself). The sky-scraper as *Grateloup* could thus relate the wolf to the pleasure obtained by rubbing. The word *tieret*, forbidden because it would betray the scene of the encrypted desire, would be replaced not by a single other word, nor by a thing, but by translations, into words or into rebus symptoms, of one of its allosemes. Cryptonymy would thus not consist in representing-hiding one word by another, one thing by another, a thing by a word or a word by a thing, but in picking out from the extended series of allosemes, a term that then (in a second-degree distancing) is translated into a synonym. The scar, for example, (real in the symptom) is the bodily, visible, theatrical representation of a synonym of one of the magic word's allosemes (to scratch or wound oneself).

It is as though the cryptonymic translation, playing with the allosemes and their synonyms (always more numerous in their open series than is indicated by a dictionary), swerves off at an angle in order to throw the reader off the track and make its itinerary unreadable. An art of chicanery: judicial pettifogging or sophistic ratiocination, but also [*chicane* = maze] a topographical stratagem multiplying simulated barriers, hidden doors, obligatory detours, abrupt changes of direction [*sens*], all the trials and errors of a game of solitaire meant both to seduce and to discourage, to fascinate, and fatigue.

It is because of the angular, zigzagging procedure of this cryptonymy, and especially because the allosemic pathways in this strange relay race pass through nonsemantic associations, purely phonetic contaminations, it is because these associations in themselves constitute words or parts of words that act like visible and/or audible bodies or things, that the authors of *The Magic Word* are hesitant to speak of metonymic displacement here, or even to trust themselves to a catalogue of rhetorical figures.

That supposes that each lexical element, whether or not it is repressed (in the strict sense of the word) as (a) thing, has an angular, if not crystalline, structure, like a cut gem, and maintains, with its allosemes or other words, contact – a contiguity sometimes semantic, sometimes formal – according to the most *economical* line or surface. One of the first consequences of this placement is the recognition of the cryptonymic character of certain meanings that had hitherto been interpreted uncircuitously and inflexibly: for example, the threat of castration. The terms in which that threat is evoked would themselves be but "cryptonyms of repressed pleasure words". The type of repression that chases the pleasure word toward the Unconscious where it functions like a thing (rather than like the representation of a thing) is different from neurotic repression: No verbalization is possible as such.

Chronic constipation at most symbolizes this "retention of saying", this impossibility of expressing, of placing words on the market. In place of verbal symbolization, the floor scrubber scene makes *tieret* visible, the erogenic fantasy translates the taboo word as a rebus, and from then on functions as an undecipherable fetish.

The "word" *tieret*, subjected to a "true repression" that banishes it into the Unconscious, can thus only have the status of a word-thing. From out of the Unconscious, the *tieret*, as a Thing of the cryptic unconscious, can return along two routes that attest to its *double density*: the route of the alloseme that crosses the border of the Unconscious directly in order to fix itself in a tableau or a symptom (for example, in an erogenic tableau: the woman scrubbing the floor), or the route of the alloseme's synonym in the case where, as a *word* (conscious or unconscious, illuminated by the lucid reflecting agency of the crypt), it crosses the intrasymbolic crack, the partition of the crypt, without passing through the

Unconscious. It is then disguised as a cryptonym in the strict sense, that is, in the form of the word.

A single example. I lift it, out of so many others, from the middle of that prodigious interpretation of dreams that *The Magic Word* deploys into an immense polyphonic poem. This interpretation of dreams, it should not be forgotten, draws its cryptonymic (in the strict sense, intrasymbolic and lexical) inferences from the hypothetical matrix: the crypt in the Self and the repression of a single word-thing *tieret* into the Unconscious. Here is the example: In order that, in the sentence *Ich stehe vor dem Kasten*, the phrase "I am standing" should mean "I am telling a lie", at least *three* combined operations are necessary: (1) A system of reversals proper to this dream. The mainspring of these reversals cannot be linguistic (neither semantic nor formal) and in another dream, *I am standing up* will indeed mean *I am not lying down* whereas here it "means" *ich liege, I am lying down*. (2) A translation from one language [German] into another [English] in the ordinary sense. Here the same *meaning* is maintained in another discourse: synonymy: *ich liege = I am lying down*. (3) A formal equivalence (a homonymic contamination, if you like) within the English language: *I am lying*, I am in a supine position; *I am lying*, I am telling an untruth. These operations belong to three essentially different systems. The passage from one technique to another is part of a particular stratagem but its possibility belongs to the hieroglyphic's polyhedral structure.

In some ways *The Magic Word* seems to implicate and develop certain Freudian propositions: less those concerning the Wolf Man himself than those touching on the splitting of the ego or the topographical distribution of the representations of words (the preconscious-conscious system) and the representation of things (the unconscious system). In fact, the very possibility of the cryptic structure within the divided self, as well as the analysis of the partitions in the intrasymbolic surface, proposes a total rethinking of the concept of *Ichspaltung*.[7] Especially when, given that *tieret* is not simply the representation of a word in the Unconscious, that it is not even a representation nourishing a mnemic trace, but, in the new sense of the unconscious cosymbol, the Thing, we recognize it neither as a word nor as a thing. In the Unconscious, this "word" is a "mute word", absolutely heterogeneous to the functioning of other words in other systems. How would one be able to contain, within the opposition between words and things, the trace this "word" constitutes of an event that has never been present? The Thing does not speak and it is not a thing. Its testamentary structure organizes all the funereal pomp and circumstance of the cryptic functioning.

The Thing (*tieret*) would perhaps be the Wolf Man's name if there were any such thing here as a name or a proper name. He *gave* himself no name. *Beneath* the patronymic he received from civil society without having been present to the certification of his birth, *beneath* the second name he pretended to adopt from the international psychoanalytic society and with which he signs his memoirs and his will, another cryptonym, he seems to call himself by the name of the Thing. When in secret he dares, barely aware of it, to *call himself*, when he wishes to call himself and to call his wish by its (his) name, he calls himself by the unspeakable name of the Thing. He, but who? The Thing is part of a symbol. It no longer calls itself. The entire body of a proper name is always shattered by the *topoi*. As for the "word" that says the Thing in the word-thing, it is not even a noun but a verb, a whole collapsed sentence, the operation of a sentence and the sentence of an operation engaging several subjects, several instances, several name bearers, several places, a desire excluded precisely by that which inhabits it like a voluble contradiction, forbidding him to call himself simply, identically, by a single glorious word. And to sign one single time with only one hand, in a single continuous stroke, without breaking the seal.

In spite of its exclusive privilege, *tieret* is not the only word. The edifice of the name is supported by at least three columns:

"The Wolf Man created a magic word that, without betraying anyone, allowed him to obtain actual or sublimated sexual satisfaction; that would be the word *tieret*. But he also had a lot of other secrets ... *goulfik*, 'fly' [of a pair of pants], the father's occult attribute, the real name of his ideal, transformed into *Wolf*, his cryptic family name. In the same fashion, he carries inside him a third disguised word, the name of his vocation as a witness: *vidietz*. ... These three words ... seem to constitute the three invisible but solid columns that the Wolf Man edified upon his impossible desire to occupy one place or the other in the scene he witnessed, his true 'primal scene'. These three columns have supported, for some eight decades, a booby-trapped life still struggling under the influence of the inaugural infantile hypnosis." (*WMMW* 40).

NOTES

[A leading contemporary thinker and founder of "deconstruction", Jacques Derrida (1930–2004) published texts on an extraordinary range of topics and writers. His work intervenes in and interrogates (among others) the fields of philosophy, autobiography, anthropology, linguistics, politics, religion, literature – and psychoanalysis. His many writings on psychoanalysis and interpretation include "Freud and the Scene of Writing" (1978), "Me – Psychoanalysis: An Introduction to the Translation of 'The Shell and the Kernel' by Nicolas Abraham" (1979), "The Purveyor of Truth" (1987), "*Fors*: The Anglish Words of Nicolas Abraham and Maria Torok" (1986), "To Speculate – on 'Freud'" (1987), "Let Us Not Forget – Psychoanalysis" (1990), *Archive Fever: a Freudian Impression*(1996) and *Resistances of Psychoanalysis* (1988). Ed.]

1. Derrida's long meditation on Abraham's and Torok's book is excerpted here to foreground his account of the strange and elusive *topography* of the Wolf Man's "crypt" [Editor's note].

2. In Abraham's and Torok's work, to "introject" something is to internalize it in the self mentally and emotionally through language, thought and memory; "introjection" is the everyday embrace of desires, events, objects, feelings and losses in our world. By contrast, "incorporation" is the repudiation of certain desires, events, objects, feelings or losses that are for some reason unbearable or traumatic – a repudiation that crucially bypasses language, thought and memory, and throws what is incorporated into an inaccessible "crypt" in the psyche, outside language, speech, thought, consciousness.

    Derrida wonders here whether, if "incorporation" is an inclusion of the lost object in the self as *other to* rather than as *belonging in* the self, is this not the case at some level with "introjection", too? In other words, doesn't the "introjected" object *retain* its otherness to the self, haunting the self with something that it cannot really make its own? [Editor's note].

3. This is not mere wordplay, or syntax twisting, not a gratuitous contamination of meanings; only the constraints of this strange topography. This topography has already produced the *necessity* of this kind of language, even before being described through its bizarre turns of phrase, its syntactical ambiguities, its outward resemblances.

4. This is a reversal of Freud's expression "Wo *Es* war soll *Ich* werden": "Where it (Id) was, there shall I (Ego) come to be" [Translator's note]. In terms of Abraham's and Torok's topography of the crypt, Derrida's reversal indicates that the crypt evacuates the self of itself and installs an "it" or "thing" where the "I" should be [Editor's note].

5. It is precisely in his *The History of an Infantile Neurosis* that Freud articulates together the problems of "deferred action", reconstruction,

the real or fantasmatic character of certain traumatic scenes, and the analytic narration (relation) itself. To account for the *unbelievable* as such was the object *The Magic Word*'s authors were seeking. Freud had warned us: The Wolf Man is "incredible". ("But certain details seemed to me so extraordinary and incredible that I feel some hesitation in asking others to believe in them". The Wolf Man, who gave rise to a whole tradition of the unbelievable, here expands the range of the incredible even further, far beyond the boundaries Freud had determined. Faced with a demonstration of this, the unbeliever can always resort, if he does not end up enjoying the demonstration, to rubbing his eyes.

6. The "two chapters" that Derrida refers to appear as Essay 8 in this book [Editor's note].

7. *Ichspaltung* (German): splitting of the "I" [Editor's note].

Part IV
Hélène Cixous, *Portrait of Dora*; Sigmund Freud, *Dora*

Introductory Note

DORA IN FREUD AND FEMINISM

"Please try and bring her to reason ..." (*FR* 183; *PF* 8: 57).

These words are spoken by Ida Bauer's father when, in 1900, he brings his reluctant daughter to Freud for treatment and sets in motion what will become *Fragment of an Analysis of a Case of Hysteria* (1905): the *Dora* case history.

Freud is told that "Dora" is being difficult. She has been intermittently unwell for some time, but is brought to Freud at 18 because of fits of depression, alterations in her character and, most dramatically, accusations she is consistently levelling at family members and friends, along with threats of suicide and what Freud (apparently with some irony) calls "hysterical unsociability" (*FR* 181; *PF* 8: 54).

Dora's father brings her to Freud as a last resort; according to him, she needs to be sorted out, to be brought to "reason".

Her ideas and imagination are, says Herr B., running wild. Most alarmingly, she has accused a close family friend, Herr K., of making sexual advances to her during a walk by a lake two years before; she has refused to withdraw the accusation, and is pressing her mother and father to break off their relationship with the K.'s. Herr B. thinks that Dora "fancied" (*FR* 182; *PF* 8: 56) the whole scene by the lake; he also thinks the scene is the result of her overexcited imagination, fired by her reading of books about sexual matters (this latter piece of information is supplied to Herr B. by Frau K.). Dora's supposed sexual waywardness is, for Herr B., the cause of her disturbance and depression; he believes she is suffering from a condition that intolerably combines sexual disturbance with daughterly deviance. She is being badly behaved; she is disturbed, hysterical.

To his credit, Freud believes Dora not her father. Freud thinks the scene by the lake happened; and he sees that Dora's insistent accusations against and demands to her father are a problem for Herr B. because they are putting in jeopardy the adulterous affair that he is clearly having with Frau K. Freud, then, sees through the bourgeois domestic lie that is being built around Dora, namely, the dance of middle-class hypocrisy in which married friendship masks sexual infidelity in a self-deluding, "respectable" Viennese social world. Despite the fact that Freud believes Dora's story – and recognizes the game the adults are playing, that Herr B., Frau K. and Herr K. are all conspiring to deny the seedy adulterous comedy that governs their relationships – he effectively *joins* their game by siding with the logic of the adults' version of events.

How does this happen?

Herr K. denies making advances to Dora, Herr B. trusts him and Frau K. underwrites the denial by saying Dora takes "no interest in anything but sexual matters" (*FR* 182; *PF* 8: 56): thus Dora is isolated as a sexual fantasist, a liar, making it all up, an hysteric. She is a bad girl. Freud believes Dora, but instead of seeing her outrage at Herr K.'s advances as a sign that she *does not desire* the older man, he interprets it as a sign of the opposite: that she *wants* Herr K., but is denying that desire. Freud sees Dora, then, as sexually or hysterically *repressed*; Dora, for him, is denying the desire that she "should" naturally have as a sexually developing young woman for a man who, Freud remarks tellingly, was "still quite young and of prepossessing appearance" (*FR* 184; *PF* 8: 60). Dora should desire Herr K., Freud thinks; more than that, he thinks she *does* desire him, it's just that she is repressing the desire. Dora, Freud tells us, thinks she is being used as an "object of barter" (*FR* 188; *PF* 8: 66) between her father and Herr K. – that her father is handing her over to Herr K. as the price of his tolerating the affair going on between Herr B. and his wife. The fact that *Freud too* tells Dora, during the analysis, that she is in love with Herr K. means, for her, that Freud is on her father's and Herr K.'s side: that, like the powerful and self-serving men in her world, he is treating her as an object of sexual exchange. This, arguably, is why she leaves the analysis with Freud before he has a chance to "complete" it. Dora takes her revenge on the men in her world (and on Freud) by turning down their sexual and psychoanalytic proposals.

As the essays in this section show, Freud constructs the meaning of Dora's desire so as to insert her into an "Oedipal" or patriarchal romance: he thinks that Dora's "hysterically" repressed sexual desire for Herr K. is masked in her unconscious by her old, infantile attachment to her father, a love she has summoned up "in order to protect herself against the feelings of love [for Herr K.] which were constantly pressing forward into consciousness" (*FR* 202; *PF* 8: 93). Freud's implicit (and normalizing) account of Dora's desire is that, to get past her hysteria, she needs to relinquish her Oedipal love for her father, replace him by another man (Herr K.), and embrace instead of avoid her accession to adult (hetero)sexual desire. Dora needs to resolve her Oedipus complex; she must stop loving her father and find a replacement object of affection for him. Dora must grow up; she *needs a man*. That this is Freud's "solution" (*FR* 230; *PF* 8: 149) to the dilemma of Dora's desire is baldly stated when, commenting on her awareness of the K.'s intention to divorce, he claims that Dora knew that "Herr K.'s proposals were serious, and that he would not leave off until [she] had married him" (*FR* 230; *PF* 8: 150). At this point in the analysis Dora leaves: from Freud's point of view, this is one more (hysterical) denial, but from the feminist point of view (represented variously in the following essays) it is Dora's escape from Freud's insistent patriarchism and phallocentrism.

Freud thinks that Dora's Oedipal love for her father should be replaced by her heterosexual love for another man; and this is the classical "Freudian" narrative of feminine sexual development into which he tries to write Dora's desire. Yet this normative movement from Oedipal to genital love is a trajectory that Dora's desire subverts – and that Freud in fact comes to doubt, too. As Ruth Parkin-Gounelas remarks: "under the pressure of persuasive evidence for a *pre*-Oedipal bond between mother and child demonstrated in particular by Klein in the 1920s and '30s, Freud came to admit that the maternal influence had been under-rated in his work and that for girls in particular, there is an 'original exclusive attachment' to the mother" (*Literature and Psychoanalysis: Intertextual* 87). The girl's attachment to the mother and women is overlooked by Freud in *Dora*: he sees only Dora's attachment to men, including himself – until, that is, she abandons the analysis and he is left to reflect on its failure (as we will see).

In *Dora*, there is a striking *absence* of the mother. Freud shows no interest in Dora's mother, and remains intent on reading his patient's longings Oedipally, heterosexually, phallically. Yet, as Jacques Lacan remarks, the problem for Dora, as "is true for all women ... is fundamentally that of accepting herself as an object of desire for the man" ("Intervention on Transference" 99): and Dora *refuses to accept herself as such an object.* The feminist account of Dora's hysteria in the essays that follow is, indeed, that it is a mute (and painful) *resistance* to the patriarchal sexual imperatives of the culture around her: the culture that renders her an object of desire and exchange between men. Dora's hysteria is read, in Elisabeth Bronfen's words, as the "language within which the daughter could articulate her discontent" (*The Knotted Subject* xiv): her discontent with the patriarchal subordination and the heterosexual destination assigned to her. Thus Hélène Cixous in *Portrait of Dora* (1976) – discussed by Erella Brown in Essay 11 – reinserts within the Freudian case history Dora's *missing* scene of maternal attachment: a maternal scene that Cixous symbolically reconfigures in the vivid, clandestine and homosexual relationship between Dora and Frau K.[1]

Dora jilts Freud; and, after she leaves, Freud seeks to explain the fact. He does so through the notion of "transference". In psycho-analysis, transference is the process in which, during analysis, the patient transfers on to "the person of the physician" (FR 234; PF 8: 157) psychical material – memories, anxieties, desires – from his or her unconscious, and unwittingly acts them out. Thus the analyst is put in the "place" of ideas and persons that belong to the patient's unconscious – and the patient replays the theatre of the unconscious in his or her relation to the analyst. Much of the task of psychoanalysis is, says Freud, nothing other than an *analysis of the transference.*

In the case of *Dora*, Freud as analyst (he realizes belatedly) is placed by Dora in the position of both her father and Herr K.: and Dora acts out in the transference her feelings of hostility to the powerful men in her world, resisting and refusing Freud as she re-sisted and refused them. Reflecting on his failure to "master" (FR 236; PF 8: 160) Dora's transference in sufficient time to analyze it, Freud adds in a footnote: "The longer the interval of time that sepa-rates me from the end of this analysis, the more probable it seems to me that the fault in my technique lay in this omission: I failed to discover in time and to inform the patient that her homosexual (gy-naecophilic) love for Frau K. was the strongest unconscious current in her mental life" (FR 237; PF 8: 162). Failing to interpret Dora's transference (or resistance) to him in time, Freud failed too to open up Dora's unconscious love for Frau K. – he ended, that is, in pushing heterosexual, "Oedipal", phallic conformity on her in a way that replayed the patriarchal libidinal imperatives governing her social and familial world. However, resisting the destiny of (hetero)sexuality and marriage, Dora escapes into the mute body language of hysteria – just as she escapes from Freud's consulting rooms into the silence that she preserves about her longings and her loves. Along with Dora's resistant transference in the case there is also, Lacan says, Freud's "countertransference" on to her – that sense in which he "put himself rather too much in the place of Herr K." ("Intervention on Transference" 99) in the analysis. As a result, Freud causes Dora to flee him just as she flees patriarchy.

Elaine Showalter argues that Freud constructs his case histories of male patients "like open-ended modernist fictions" ("On Hysterical Narrative" 32) – as narratives without closure, narratives in play. (Showalter offers the *Wolf Man* as an example; see Part III of this collection, particularly Essay 7, for a consideration of the textual form of the Wolf Man's history.) By contrast, Freud's case studies of female patients, says Showalter, are "structured like Victorian novels with the endings of marriage, madness or death" (32); they are closed narratives of confinement within patriarchy or the grave. Yet in this connection the *Dora* case can be seen, as Peter Brooks remarks, as a "failed Victorian novel" (27), for it *lacks* the "happy ending" of marriage and family that Freud himself would have liked to write. And it is Dora herself, of course, who forbids Freud – and herself – that orthodox ending. As Steven Marcus puts it, Dora "refused to be a character in the story that Freud was composing for her" ("Freud and Dora: Story, History, Case History" 88). Thus Dora fractures Freud's Victorian novel into modernist form, fragmenting the coherence of his story and hystericizing the "scientific" voice of his narrative. Breaking past the strictures of Freud's normalizing romance plot, *Dora* articulates what Anne Juranville, speaking of the hysteric's condition, calls a "horizon ... beyond the phallus" (cited by Bronfen, Essay 12) – beyond the desire for the father, or for any man.

Hélène Cixous, in *Portrait of Dora* and "The Untenable" (Essay 10), reads Dora as refusing to be an object of man's desire: instead, Dora preserves in her unconscious "a very beautiful feminine homosexuality, a love for woman that is astounding" – her love for Frau K., the wife of her seducer and lover of her father. But while

Cixous regards Dora as a figure of resistance within patriarchy, Catherine Clément reads her as a figure of subjection, conserving the oppressive social and sexual structures built around her rather than contesting them. For Clément, the hysteric challenges or endangers nothing; rather, both family and patriarchy reclose themselves effortlessly around her voiceless aberrations. If Dora is a "heroine for Cixous", as Jane Gallop says, she "is only a victim for Clément" ("Keys to Dora" 203). This difference, however, points to the ideological ambivalence within hysteria itself; for female hysteria is legible as an ambivalent sign *both* of woman's subjection *and* resistance within patriarchy, a dual mark of containment and contest. In this way, Clément's and Cixous's debate in "The Untenable" acts out the ideological ambiguity of hysteria as a double mark of female sexual subjugation and subversion.

Erella Brown (Essay 11) outlines the dramatic logic of Hélène Cixous's *Portrait of Dora* by arguing that Cixous employs "Brechtian strategies" of performative disruption to foreground the "subversive figures of dissonance and internal confusion that the hysteric body displays"; and this involves a dramatic action in which fixed gender and subject positions are put into play, and opened up to reinvention. According to Brown, Cixous's drama sanctions Kristeva's contention that "woman, like theatre, does not take (a) place, but rather revisions positionality itself". She suggests Cixous's play foregrounds the performativity of Freudian discourse, disclosing how psychoanalysis is an active inscription of hegemonic gender positions. While Freud's *Dora* case study produces an "Oedipal stage", assigning its characters roles within that structure or framework, Cixous's drama, says Brown, produces a "hysteric stage" that deranges normative symbolic, sexual and social identities. Brown points out that Cixous "takes hysteria as a key to both feminine sexuality and performance", for Dora's hysteria *enacts* her silence and suffering within the oppressive patriarchal symbolic and sexual order in which she is contained.

Elisabeth Bronfen takes her title "'You Freud, Me Jane'" (Essay 12) from Alfred Hitchcock's 1964 film, *Marnie*. In Hitchcock's film, the female character Marnie answers the questions of a male character about her dreams with the response, "You Freud, me Jane?" In doing this, says Bronfen, Marnie discloses the questioner's "masculine aggression" as he combines the roles of "hunter" and "analyst" in his approaches to her (*The Knotted Subject* 362). Bronfen's reading of Freud's *Dora*, too, focuses partly on Freud's acts of masculine aggression to Dora; but her analysis also shows the ways in which Freud's mastery is dissolved by Dora's unconscious strategies as both hysteric and as woman. Intriguingly, Bronfen prefaces her discussion with T.S. Eliot's remarkable prose poem, "Hysteria" (1917), in which a male speaker finds himself frighteningly engulfed by the body of a woman,[2] namely, her hysterical laughter; and she points out that Freud in his case study likewise finds himself drawn into "the very texture of the hysterical spectacle" in a way that embroils him in hysteria's aberrations, unnerves him, and shatters his analytic sovereignty. Bronfen's discussion develops Brown's emphasis on hysteria as a condition of semiotic mobility by insisting that Freud's *Dora* "discloses the sexuality of the hysteric as one inscribed with gender slippage". Yet if hysteria can be read as a sign of gender slippage, it is also, Bronfen indicates, a sign of *textual* slippage; and in this way one might argue that the hysteric stage of Cixous's *Portrait of Dora* is strangely prefigured by the hysteric textuality of Freud's *Dora* itself. Bronfen, indeed, hints that a certain hystericization characterizes *Dora* as a text insofar as, like Dora's discourse, it is a "gap-riddled ... affair"; *Dora* becomes a text that, subversively and against his own wishes, feminizes Freud.

NOTES

1. For a sophisticated theoretical account of the missing mother in *Dora* – read through the lens of Julia Kristeva's work – see Mary Jacobus, *Reading Woman*: 137–193.

2. Intriguingly, the frightened response of Eliot's speaker to the spectacle of feminine corporeality in this text echoes his own argument about the way Hamlet is unable to deal with the enigmatic femininity of Gertrude in *Hamlet* (see Rose 1988).

10

The Untenable

CATHERINE CLÉMENT AND HÉLÈNE CIXOUS

> Double history of seduction.
> What woman is not Dora?
> She who makes the others (desire).
> The servant-girl's place. Does the hysteric change
> the Real? Desire, the Imaginary, class struggle –
> how do they relate? What are the yields?

H: I got into the sphere of hysteria because I was drawn – called. I knew absolutely nothing about it. I had read "The Dora Case", but didn't see myself in it. Once into it, though, I made great headway.

First, still rather naively, I produced a text on it. Later, I had a sort of "after-taste", and I started working on the question. I arrived at a whole series of positions; some of these positions, perhaps, are contestable. It is impossible to have a single, rigid point of view about it. If it is only a metaphor – and it's not clear that this is so, it functions well, it has its use. I started with *Dora*; I read that text in a sort of dizziness, exploding over the situation presented, where at heart I found myself siding frenetically with the different characters. I immediately worked out a reading that was probably not centred the way Freud had wanted it to be. I had to bring centre stage obliterated characters, characters repressed in notes, at the bottom of the page, and who were for me in the absolute foreground. I read it like fiction. I didn't worry about an analytic investment at that moment, and besides, I couldn't have.

She identifies herself.

One never reads except by identification. But what kind? What is "identification"? When I say "identification", I do not say "loss of self". I become, I inhabit, I enter. Inhabiting someone, at that moment I can feel myself traversed by that person's initiatives and actions. (Actually, that has always disturbed me. When I was younger I was afraid because I realized I was capable of mimicry. Then I accused myself of thieving flight.) I turned round and round. I found myself caught up in those characters' same state, because they too were identifying. ... Almost all those involved in Dora's scene circulate through the others, which results in a sort of hideous merry-go-round, even more so because, through bourgeois petti-ness, they are ambivalent. All consciously play a double game, plus the games of the unconscious. Each one acts out the little calcula-tions of classic bourgeois comedy – a comedy of clear conscience on the one hand, a comedy of propriety on the other. First of all, "you don't divorce"; then you make a combination of structures with interchangeable elements to get the greatest possible pleasure from an adulterous situation. And that can hold only if there is a social pact that is observed. That pact is, "no one will say what he knows". Everybody knows, but everybody is silent, and everybody profits from it. Therefore, one is in a world that rests on a system of silent contracts, contracts of general hypocrisy. And it is a chain: "*I* won't tell what you are doing and *you* won't tell what I do". As I was reading, I heard voices sighing in the text – voices of people who, in the chain, were finally those on whom weighed heaviest the great weight of silence, those who were crushed, who obtained no satisfaction in the roundabout. In the front line was Dora, who fas-cinated me, because here was an eighteen-year-old girl caught in a world where you say to yourself, she is going to break – a captive, but with such strength! I could not keep from laughing from one end to the other, because, despite her powerlessness and with (thanks to) that powerlessness, here is a kid who successfully jams all the little adulterous wheels that are turning around her and, one after the other, they break down. She manages to say what she doesn't say, so intensely that the men drop like flies. We can very well see how – at what moment, in what scenes, by which meaning – she has cut through. Each time cutting through the marshmallow ribbon that the others are in the process of spieling. A hecatomb.

It is she who is the victim, but the others come out of it in shreds. The father, Mr. K., Freud – everybody passes through. They all drop. Doubtless a symbolic carnage because the men always re-group. Then, afterward, comes a reflux, and you have the party of men who come, reiterating the father, repeating the famous scene of

Dora in bed, Dora lying down, Daddy standing and looking at Dora. In the end *she* makes *them* lie down; they fall: the most beautiful image is the one of Mr. K.'s accident. Before Dora's eyes, he was run over by a cart. All of this was linked with a criticism of society which touches me because I belonged to that lower middle class when I was little: the criticism passing through a secondary figure. In the same way that the woman is the man's repressed in the conjugal couple, there is this little character who is in the process of disappearing from society and on whom rested the family structure: the servant-girl.

Maid in the family.

C: She is everywhere, in all Freud's analyses. The servant-girl is a character who is just beginning to disappear from analyses. And she is always on the side of eroticism.

H: The seductress. She is the hole in the social cell; "it" goes through "that", it goes through her body. In *Dora* what was terrifying was that these archetypical servants were put by Freud himself in "the maid's room" – that is, in the notes. There are two who are identical. Both are called "the servant-girl", "the governess". One succeeds the other in Dora's life, with years in between, but they have exactly the same role. They have the same history: seduced by the boss and then eliminated for having been seduced by the boss. Woman's situation carried to the paroxysm of horror. So, the servant-girl is the repressed of the boss's wife.

C: The boss's wife is the lady: "madame". She spends her days in bed, or she buys smoked salmon. She is a strange, absent face. But certainly servant-girls are there only as fantasy objects, like animals. Grusha, in the analysis of *The Wolf Man*, is both the maid and a pear – the child says it straight out. He links it together out loud: pear striped with yellow, maid, butterfly, sex between a woman's legs. There are the servant-girls, stuck in between fruits and bugs. Elsewhere Freud speaks of a bottle of pineapple liqueur; it is spoiled, this liqueur; it smells bad.

H: That situation – why doesn't it appear in the cases that Freud recounts? Dora's case is archetypical, "the servant-girl is the boss's wife's repressed", but in Dora's case, Dora is in the place of the boss's wife: the mother is set aside. She is dead, she is nothing, and everybody has agreed to bury her. Including Freud. Not for a moment does he analyze the reports given him about the mother.

She is "in the hole". Which is exactly what permits Dora's rising to the fore and this sort of Oedipal idyll that is going to be played out between her and daddy. What does that mean? It means that, for Freud, the mother, once her role is fulfilled, is through. As the Germans say: "Der Mohr hat sein Pflicht getan, er kann gehen." The Moor has done his job, out with him. Now he can go. That is Othello in "The Moor of Venice". You can replace "the Moor" with the mother. She is done making kids, so she is made secondary in the story.

C: There is another reason, which is Freud's blindspot, not only about the Oedipal but also about class attitudes – a banality we must not forget to mention.

H: That is why I say that it is not significant that there is no boss's wife. It is significant that it is Freud who sets the stage, who puts covers on those things that are not important to him, who isn't in the play, and who puts the most important people in the best seats. It is certain that that corresponds socially to something quite real: the servant-girl, the prostitute... .

C: Eroticism happens through what is "clandestine", not through what is "official". Remember the text on sensual love and affectionate love in which Freud opposes them as almost incompatible. But Engels, after all, doesn't say anything different. That is all very coherent, and at the same time, there are sharp contradictions. What is coherent is the opposition of the legal wife and the prostitute and their complementarity in the family. The contradictions would be Freud's silences – the things he couldn't see in his own ideological misunderstanding. The family does not exist in isolation, rather it truly supports and reflects the class struggle running through it. The servant-girl, the prostitute, the mother, the boss's wife, the woman: that is all an ideological scene.

H: Freud didn't give the servant-girl enough recognition. Never do you see her in the body of the text – she is always in the kitchen, in her station: she appears in the notes. When Freud speaks of Dora's sexual initiation, entirely acquired from books, it is automatically attributed to the normal sources of this sort of pernicious education – it is probably the maid's doing, and indeed it is the servant-girl whom we find in a note.

Also, we always say that Freud failed to make the analysis of transference – that he didn't see what was happening. The truth (which he saw only once when he was really put down) is that, in the system of exchange, me in your place, you in my place ... Freud in relation to Dora was in the maid's place. It is Freud who was the servant-girl, and that is what is intolerable for Freud in the Dora case – that he was treated as one treats maids, having been fired the way you fire a servant-girl. There is no failure worse than that. The knot, the crux of the *Dora* case, is that Dora was afraid of being the maid, and, on the other hand, she was afraid of being nothing, like her mother. That "nothing" is stressed in the words the married men are saying. They are the words of comedy. At the same time, they pass on dramatic metaphors: Mr. K. says to Dora, and to the servant-girl whom he tried to seduce, "You know very well that my wife is nothing to me".

Freud as servant-girl.

No woman tolerates hearing (even if it is about the other woman), "My wife, a woman who is my woman, can be nothing". That is murder. So Dora, hearing it, knowing that the servant-girl had already heard it, sees woman, her mother, the maid die; she sees women massacred to make room for her. But she knows that she will have her turn at being massacred. Her terrific reaction is to slap Mr. K. This girl has understood, all her actions in the story Freud tells and is telling blindly show how she has seen each time the ignominy and the enactment of woman's murder. And to that must be added that in Dora there is a very beautiful feminine homo-sexuality, a love for woman that is astounding.

Dora seemed to me to be the one who resists the system, the one who cannot stand that the family and society are founded on the body of women, on bodies despised, rejected, bodies that are humiliating once they have been used. And this girl – like all hysterics, deprived of the possibility of saying directly what she perceived, of speaking face-to-face or on the telephone as father B. or father K. or Freud, et cetera do – still had the strength to make it known. It is the nuclear example of women's power to protest. It happened in 1899; it happens today wherever women have not been able to speak differently from Dora, but have spoken so effectively that it bursts the family into pieces.

Yes, the hysteric, with her way of questioning others (because if she succeeds in bringing down the men who surround her, it is by questioning them, by ceaselessly reflecting to them the image that truly castrates them, to the extent that the power they have wished to impose is an illegitimate power of rape and violence). The hysteric is, to my eyes, the typical woman in all her force. It is a force that was turned back against Dora, but, if the scene changes and if woman begins to speak in other ways, it would be a force capable of demolishing those structures. There is something else in Dora's case that is great – everything in the nature of desire. A desire that is also, often, love – for love. The source of Dora's strength is, in spite of everything, her desire. The hysteric is not just someone who has her words cut off, someone for whom the body speaks. It all starts with her anguish as it relates to desire and to the immensity of her desire – therefore, from her demanding quality. She doesn't let things get by. I see the hysteric saying: "I want everything." The world doesn't give her people who are "everythings"; they are always very little pieces. In what she projects as a demand for totality, for strength, for certainty, she makes demands of the others in a manner that is intolerable to them and that prevents their functioning as they function (without their restricted little economy). She destroys their calculations. The reckoning, for example, that consists of saying, "My wife is nothing, therefore, you can be everything" – because she knows that it isn't true, she knows what "everything" is, she knows what this false-nothing is, et cetera. I also thought the famous scene of the Madonna was terrific. It is the capacity for an adoration that is not empty – it is the belief in the possibility of such a thing.

The ones on the margins and social upheaval.

C: That is certainly why it is somehow also a containment. It is metaphoric, yes – a metaphor of the impossible, of the ideal and dreamed of totality, yes, but when you say "that bursts the family into pieces", no. It mimics, it metaphorizes destruction, but the family reconstitutes itself around it. As when you throw a stone in the water, the water ripples but becomes smooth again. The analysis I make of hysteria comes through my reflection on the place of deviants who are not hysterics but clowns, charlatans, crazies, all sorts of odd people. They all occupy challenging positions foreseen by the social bodies, challenging functions within the scope of all cultures. That doesn't change the structures, however. On the contrary, it makes them comfortable.

H: I am not sure that is where I would put hysterics.

C: But yes – it all comes together. Ethnologists, analysts, or anyone naively able to say this, at the same time recognize in them an exceptional capacity for language and an *exclusion correlative to it*. In that position, they are part of one of the deepest reenforcements of the superstructures, of the Symbolic. It keeps the net of the Imaginary in a tight grip, and the hysterics are inside it. If I am the network between witch and hysteric, passing one on through the other, through the same signifiers, it is certainly because the hysteric seems to me to inscribe herself within that line.

H: I think there are degrees. I imagine hysteria as distributing itself along a scale of the possible intensity of disturbance. Along with, beyond a certain threshold, something that makes a complete victim of the hysteric. She loses all effectiveness, then, because she herself is the place where everything is turned back against her; she is paralyzed by it, physically or otherwise, and thus loses her impact. There are structures characteristic of hysteria that are not neuroses, that work with very strong capacities of identification with the other, that are scouring, that make mirrors fly, that put disturbing images back into circulation; because only if you're not an Iago can you play your little game of hypocrisy, only if you don't say to yourself, "I – am a filthy creature". Because in general the system's functioning is based on blindness, on denial. There is also the fact that there is no place for the hysteric; she cannot be placed or take place. Hysteria is necessarily an element that disturbs arrangements; wherever it is, it shakes up all those who want to install themselves, who want to install something that is going to work, to repeat. It is very difficult to block out this type of person who doesn't leave you in peace, who wages permanent war against you.

C: Yes, it introduces dissension, but it doesn't explode anything at all; it doesn't disperse the bourgeois family, which also exists only through its dissension, which holds together only in the possibility or the reality of its own disturbance, always reclosable, always reclosed. It is when there is a crossing over to the symbolic act that it doesn't shut up again.

But otherwise it doesn't, and Dora doesn't. For me the fact of being passed on to posterity through Freud's account and even Freud's failure is not a symbolic act. That is already more true of Freud and Breuer's hysteric who became the first welfare worker and who made something of her hysteria. The distinction between them, between those who nicely fulfill their function of challenging with all possible violence (but who can enclose themselves afterward) and those who will arrive at symbolic inscription, no matter what act they use to get there, seems essential to me. Raising hell, throwing fits, disturbing family relations can be shut back up.

H: It is that force that works to dismantle structures. There are some who are not effective, and others who are; it is a question of circumstances, of degrees. Dora broke something.

C: I don't think so.

H: The houses that "resided" on her, whose stability was ensured by her... .

C: What she broke was strictly individual and limited.

H: Because at that time it was impossible to go any further.

C: Listen, you love Dora, but to me she never seemed a revolutionary character.

H: I don't give a damn about Dora; I don't fetishize her. She is the name of a certain force, which makes the little circus not work anymore.

C: Let's take that metaphorically: that is true of hysteria, agreed, but why limit that to the hysteric and hence to the feminine? From a certain point of view, the obsessive person does an equally destructive job, in the sense of passing limits in the direction of law, constraint, and conformity, which he transforms into caricature. In adding more to the rigidity of structures, and in adding more to ritual, he works destructively.

H: I'm not sure. When Freud says that what is obsessive, on a cultural level, yields the religious and that what is hysterical yields art, it seems right to me. The religious is something that consolidates, that will reenclose, that will seal and fasten everything that is rigid in the social realm. There is a difference between what makes things move and what stops them; it is what moves things that changes them.

C: Do you know the games like "taquin"? They are games where you move a piece in a system in which you can move only a limited number of pieces to explore the possibilities of permutation without the "taquin's" moving. One shifts an element within a perfectly rigid structure, which is all the better for it. Language only moves one square to the place of another – that's all; the real distribution of elements, the real change cannot happen on that level.

Can one put desire to sleep?

H: I don't think that the revolution is going to happen through language either. But there is no revolution without a conscious grasp – without there being people who get up and begin to yell. I think that what cannot be oppressed, even in the class struggle, is the libido – desire; it is in taking off from desire that you will revive the need for things to really change.

Desire never dies, but it can be stifled for a long time. For example, in peoples who are denied speech and who are on their last gasp. One ceases to move the moment one no longer communicates.

C: Except in taking what you say poetically, I have to admit that these sentences have no reality for me. Take an example. What *is* a people that doesn't communicate?

H: One can very easily smother desire. Let's take France, in fact. From the moment that you no longer circulate discourse, when you circulate only a dead, stereotypical discourse... .

C: But who is "one"? Who circulates? Who are the subjects? Where are they?

H: A certain power. The class that holds power has exercised it for a long time, but it has gotten worse, it is getting worse and worse, it systematically crushes all the places where the imagination is inscribed: the mass media, publishing – everywhere the word and its inventive forms can get through. This deals a heavy blow to political consciousness.

NOTES

[Hélène Cixous is a Professor of English Literature at the University of Paris VIII, Vincennes, where she founded the "Centre d'Études Féminines" in 1974. A prolific feminist writer, she has published many works of literary criticism, philosophy, drama and fiction. Her writings bearing on Freud, femininity, literature and psychoanalysis include "The Laugh of the Medusa" (1975), "Sorties" (1975), "Castration or Decapitation?" (1976), the novel *Portrait du Soleil* (1974) and the drama *Portrait de Dora* (1976; see Essay 11). A selection of her work across the many genres in which she has written appears in *The Hélène Cixous Reader*, edited by Susan Sellers (1994). "The Untenable" is from *The Newly Born Woman* (1975), co-authored by Cixous and feminist essayist and novelist Catherine Clément; Clément's translated works include *The Lives and Legends of Jacques Lacan* (1983), *The Weary Sons of Freud: Questions For Feminism* (1987), "Imaginary, Symbolic and Real" (1993) and, with Julia Kristeva, *The Feminine and the Sacred* (2001). Ed]

11

The Lake of Seduction: Body, Acting, and Voice in Hélène Cixous's *Portrait de Dora*

ERELLA BROWN

> There's no greater sorrow than to
> remember love. And Freud knew that   (32).
> And after that?   (1)
> > (*Portrait of Dora*)

In *Portrait de Dora* (1976), Hélène Cixous explores the possibility of feminine theatre by rewriting Freud's *Dora: An Analysis of a Case of Hysteria* for stage performance. Anticipating her *Nom d' Oedipe* (1978), *Portrait* takes as a pretext the myth of Oedipus, which underlies Freud's analysis of the case history, as central to both psychoanalysis and classical drama.[1] Indeed, *Portrait de Dora* along with her *Nom d'Oedipe* are innovative attempts to define feminist performance by placing psychoanalysis and classical drama under the scrutiny of the theatrical. By locating Freud's case-history within theatre, Cixous underscores the theatricality of psycho-analytical discourse as the "talking cure", using voice, gestures, staging, ritual, and myth, in order to scrutinize the relationship between the semiotics of symptoms as the "acting out" of the hysteric body and the Symbolic order that authorizes its meaning. Moreover, as Sharon Willis observes, Cixous's *Portrait* puts into question the theatrical frame itself, and the body staged within it,

196

thereby becoming "exemplary of the critical operations of certain feminist performance practice[s]" (78). Cixous, who takes hysteria as a key to both feminine sexuality and performance, stages Freud's failure with Dora as a dysfunctional dramatic operation by depicting his insistence on reading his paternal Oedipal model into Dora's hysteria as ineffective in regard to the real performative throbbing of the hysteric stage. By confronting thereupon the symbolic order of the Oedipal stage with the imaginary theatre of pain and seduction that the hysteric's body displays, Cixous challenges the phallocratic origins and prejudices of both classical theatre and psychoanalysis. Indeed, if, as Jacqueline Rose observes, Dora's case opens "a dialogue between psychoanalysis and feminism" ("Dora" 128), then Cixous's *Portrait* not only places this dialogue within a theatrical space, it enlarges the dialogical frame by introducing also the question of the relationship between feminism and theatre.

On this stage, Brechtian strategies and the semiotics of the performance coincide with the subversive figures of dissonance and internal confusion that the hysteric body displays. Cixous thus designs a hysteric performative space which is subversive of inner/outer distinctions, and as such her stage no longer guarantees stability nor production of gender and identity.

Cixous's play is a feminist version of Freud's case-history. It is an attempt to read hysteria as a site where feminine sexuality displays its otherness as rebound to cultural positionality. According to Cixous and Clément, the hysteric occupies an imaginary zone of what her culture excludes. The hysteric, who "unties familiar bonds, introduces disorder into the well-regulated unfolding of everyday life", touches "the roots of a certain symbolic structure". In her role of resistant heroine, the hysteric, "whose body is transformed into a theatre for forgotten scenes, relives the past, bearing witness to a lost childhood that survives in suffering" (*NBW* 5). Following Lacan, Cixous and Clément maintain that "hysterical symptoms, which are metaphorically inscribed on the body, are ephemeral and enigmatic. They constitute a language only by analogy". This analogy, however, differs from Freud's notion of the symptoms as the return of the repressed scene of paternal seduction. For Cixous and Clément, the analogy is read at the level of cultural systems of production and exchange-value, in "the relations between the Imaginary, the Real, and the Symbolic" (9).

Cixous and Clément, therefore, are interested in circumscribing the place that anomaly takes at the heart of cultural activity: "[t]he history of the hysteric ... takes place in half-confinement; the hysteric, dolefully reclining, tended and surrounded by doctors and worried family, is a prisoner inside the family; or else, in crisis, she bears the brunt of producing a medical spectacle. This repressive dimension doubles the mobility of those on the margins, but, at the same time, it is the sign of their integration into the system of the whole" (8).

Cixous's play, then, is an attempt to undermine Freud's pretext of the Oedipal model by emulating the hysteric's symptoms as a theatre of seduction and cruelty. Although Cixous mainly quotes fragments from Freud's narrative, those citations are displaced, condensed, and thus re-framed so as to play the hysteric's symptoms against Freud's overdetermined reading. Modeled on the hysteric's symptoms, the play lacks a linear narrative and ordered temporal continuity. Dora's aphonia and her inability to relate a coherent chronology of her life story are displayed ironically against Freud's authoritative narration. Dora's unstable identity, her ability to identify with everyone and with no one in particular, is staged in an ironic writ against Freud's claim that bodily symptoms imitate, as in a pantomime, the repressed fantasy of the patient's real desires, perverting the original fantasy of paternal seduction. Finally, the pains of the real seduction and of the father's betrayal are also acted out by mocking in exaggerated gestures the symbolic exchanges of gifts so as to reinforce the validity of Dora's subjective position and will against Freud's calculated interests.

Cixous uses the two-hour analytical session as the frame for her two-hour play, thus, marking both as a theatrical event. The actual time the audience spends seated before the stage is analogous to the time Dora spent as Freud's patient. By condensing Dora's life story into a two-hour session Cixous also emphasizes the fact that most of Freud's case records are based on his distant memories, rather than on an immediate account of each of his analytical sessions with his hysteric patient Ida Bauer.[2] To maintain this gap between reality and its distortion by memory and fantasy, Cixous keeps the false name Freud gave his patient. Cixous thus marks the double theatrical frame, the fact that theatrical performance is real although its referentiality and meaning are based on fiction. She renders fragile the relations between presence and representation, because by modeling the stage on the symptoms of hysteria rather than on Freud's interpretation of them, Cixous calculates and destabilizes the gap between theatrical performance and its extra-theatrical referent, between the semiotics of symptoms and the symbolic meaning that Freud attempts to establish in his narrative.[3]

This strategy, which uses the semiotics of symptoms to undermine the symbolic coherency of identity and narration, is in line with Kristeva's theory. According to Freedman, in order to escape the dichotomy of man/woman, Kristeva defines woman as real otherness and offers a strategy which explores "the pulsion between the semiotic and the symbolic": "[t]o work from the semiotic is to adopt 'a negative function; reject everything finite, definite, structured, loaded with meaning, in the existing state of society.' It is to work 'on the side of the explosion of social codes, with revolutionary movements'" (70). Hence, Kristeva maintains that "woman, like theatre, does not take (a) place, but rather revisions positionality itself" (70). Like Kristeva, Cixous and Clément maintain that "[t]he whole evaluation of a cultural revolution is still in play – a revolution that simultaneously anticipates a future utopia and results from an effective transformation in the Real of the relations of production" (*NBW* 9). By tampering with the apparatus of theatrical framing, Cixous's hysteric stage manages to inscribe the Imaginary in the Symbolic, to acknowledge the Symbolic and to disrupt it from within. The realization that the Imaginary cannot act on the Symbolic and on the Real[4] is rendered by the incoherent, erratic, and fragile frame. The dysfunctional hysteric stage contrivance shows that "the anomaly fails," that "it is a quasi production, but it is not production. Since it is a matter only of individual symbolism and not communicable, the culture cannot take it into account and make it the object of transmission." This is even more true of hysteria, "for though paranoiac writing can be situated at the limit of transmissibility, though one can recognize in them 'a margin of human communicability,' ... hysterical symptoms, which are metaphorically inscribed on the body, are ephemeral and enigmatic." (9). Hence, rather than acknowledge and subvert positionality on a conscious basis, as classical theatre has always done through masks and gender-crossings, Cixous's hysteric stage further undermines the difference between unconscious symptoms and conscious discourse, signifier and signified. Cixous lets the bar that separates signifier and signified coincide with the apparatus of framing and re-framing of the *mise-en-scène*: while upholding the analytic session as the play's formal frame, Cixous explodes this frame from within by rendering unstable the frame-of-reference that allows the various characters and events to appear on her stage. In this sense, her hysteric character, like her hysteric stage, "does not take (a) place, but rather revisions positionality itself".

The title of the play underlines the spatial dimension by stressing the portrait rather than the actions of Dora. Indeed, while Freud insists on establishing a coherent narrative he presents the case as a "fragment of analysis". Although Cixous titles her own presentation a "portrait", the double mirroring of Dora and Freud implies a certain chiasmic inversion between what is portrayed and what is fragmented. This reversal of classical perspective is elucidated in Cixous's *Portrait du soleil* (a novel which also deals with the Dora case). Morag Shiach describes Cixous's notion of the portrait as follows:

> The desire to construct a "portrait" with its implications of framing and fixed perspective, seems, thus, bound to fail. Cixous acknowledges the problem in her allusion to Rembrandt's painting of *The Anatomy Lesson of Dr. Tulp*. This painting represents an anatomical demonstration, with a corpse surrounded by willing scholars. The arm of the corpse has already been dissected, showing flesh and blood vessels of a hideous colour, which contrast with the luminous whiteness of the corpse, and the staid clothes of the scholars and the doctor. The narrator of *Portrait du soleil* rejects Rembrandt's representation of the body, saying its geometrical precision renders the corpse doubly dead, by enclosing it, making of it a fixed and passive spectacle. Such practice is contrasted with the aspirations of the narrator, who seeks to understand the body as living, as multiple, as impossible to pin down: any portrait she draws will be transient and unfinished. (82)

Cixous's stage is designed to reflect Dora's hysterical, fragmented, and deformed portrait dissected under the gaze of psychoanalytical authority; under Freud's attempt to penetrate her unconscious and restore the Oedipal stage. Yet, to prevent the portrait of Dora from becoming doubly dead, Cixous depicts the symptoms of hysteria as marked by fragmentation, while simultaneously allowing these symptoms to mirror Freud's own Oedipal biases as the cause of his inability to master his own transference. Thus, he fails both to cure his patient and to master his own fragmented account of Dora's case history.

The first half of the play is framed by two projections of the seduction scene by the lake, thus by two mirroring lakes. The first projection follows the event as it occurred according to Freud's account of Dora's story. This account is, therefore, accompanied by

Freud's voice-over as "The Voice of the Play". The play opens with the following stage directions:

> Projected on the scrim is "the incident by the lake". Slow flickering of an incessant mourning.
>   Freud's voice (seated, seen from behind)
>   "... *These events project themselves like a shadow in dreams, they often become so clear that we feel we can grasp them, but yet they escape our final interpretation, and if we proceed without skill and special caution, we cannot know if such a scene really took place*" (2).

The second projection is distorted because here, Freud takes the perspective of Herr K. (who sees himself as seduced by Dora), but the projection is presented as Freud's own dream (19). Thus, the two projections of seduction by the lake are framed within Freud's perspective. Freud's vision mediates the seduction of Dora by Herr K. and Herr K. by Dora – the seduction of the masculine and the feminine, one by the other. This mirroring of perspectives creates a chiasmic correspondence between them: while the first scene is labelled by Freud a "dream"; the second, distorted version of Freud's dream of the seduction by the lake is recounted by him in a "very cold and monotonous voice" as if it was an objective scientific account of the original event.

Since Freud's voice is not the stable and authoritative voice of the piece, the accompanying voice of the initial projection does not support the dreamlike projection on the scrim. It also does not support the alibi that the seduction scene is based on fantasy. Instead, the chiasmic reversals of voice and sight, the use of a dreamy voice to treat the real and of a cold scientific voice to treat the dream, show that Freud treated the traumatic effects of the real seduction as if Dora's reaction derived from an earlier Oedipal fantasy of seduction by the father.

Beyond this destabilizing double mirroring, Cixous's position is rendered clear through the separation between voice and sight. While the second projection of the seduction by the lake is modelled on Dora's second dream, it is not only presented as Freud's own dream, it is also narrated by Freud who speaks of himself in the third person:

> Doctor Freud could have dreamt this, at the end of December 1899. Dora is an exuberant girl, eighteen or nineteen years old. She has something contradictory and strange about her which is attractive. A

healthy complexion but a rigid mouth, a girl's forehead, fixed icy eyes. She looks like those hidden cupids, vengeful and dangerous. Doctor Freud cannot take his eyes off her. Dora, holding him by the hand tightly, like an irritated governess, led him to the edge of the mountain lake which she pointed out to him with one finger. She does not throw him into the water; but she insists that he go pick up a bouquet of the brilliant white flowers growing on the other side of the lake whose scent he can smell despite their distance. Even though Freud is hesitant, he is curious, because he senses that this is a test or maybe a trap. He wonders why they didn't get off the train one station earlier which would have left them on the other side of the lake. But not for long, because Dora suddenly eyes him up and down, casts him a scornful look and turns her back on him, moving her neck in a way that overwhelms him: freely, haughtily, relentlessly. Then, without any warning, she raises her dress in a purposely seductive gesture which slightly reveals her ankle, and she walks across the lake, stepping on hundreds of bones. Something prevents Freud from doing the same. (19)

By alluding to the alluring *trompe l'oeil* effects of "now you see it now you don't", Cixous does not merely provoke here a titillating fetishist gaze at the sight of Dora's exposed ankle and neck. Cixous places a mirror against Freud's interpretation of Dora's second dream as a dream about (bi)sexual intercourse (with either Herr K. or Frau K.), by constructing the scene as a reflection of Freud's own infantile fantasy of being seduced by Dora, who realizes the name Freud gave her by taking here the place of his governess. Thus, while in his narration Freud takes the position of voyeur, doctor, and judge, Cixous uses the mirror of the Imaginary to presents Freud at the same time as the other half of the couple, as the seduced pervert who repeat a scene they have in common for the audience's gaze.[5]

This second projection is still framed by the initial projection of the seduction by the lake. The first projection of the seduction scene ends with Dora's hysteric reaction toward Herr K. (and Freud): "if you dare kiss me, I'll slap you" (2). At the end of the second projection, Herr B., Dora's father, comments on Dora's seductive role as follows: "With her white hand, she was fiddling awkwardly with the pearls around her neck. Without thinking about it. Her eyes elsewhere". Ironically, now it is the seduced Freud who reacts hysterically to Herr B.'s comment (and thereby to Dora's seductiveness) by saying: "Annoyed, Freud suddenly slaps her to stop this". Dora herself wonders in response "if she weren't Herr K. herself. In his place, how would she have loved her!" The ironic thrust of this second projection is pronounced by Freud who then asks Dora: "But who is replacing whom in this story?" and Dora answers: "Yes. Everyone. Except me" (20).

Indeed, Herr B. here repeats his initial position of betraying Dora while identifying with both Herr K. and Freud as the seduced males. The paralyzed Freud at the end of the second projection thus emerges not as the subject who is able to proceed with caution, but rather as the anesthetized dissected patient, as the object of his own "treatment".[6] Like the hysteric, he plays both the masculine and the feminine roles, the seduction of one by the other. Beyond the destabilization of sexual identities and subjective positions, Cixous here uses the mirror to reflect the circulation of sexual energy and the emergence of positionality thereof in order to underline the political thrust of the symbolic system of exchange and to undermine the domination of women through patriarchal exogamy rites.

Cixous's play constructs a doubly seductive space. Cixous stages Dora's portrait before our fascinated gaze, but the mirror turned toward the back of the stage is rendered analogous to the mirror of transference turned on the hysteric's unconscious circus: "Freud will go to the other side of the couch, henceforth a figure from behind, an invisible presence. And he will formulate the fundamental rule – say what comes into your head, don't hide anything anymore – which makes extraordinary things come out during the too ordinary exchange of repetitive words. Transference, now possible, will be carried out in a mirror; and we move on to psychoanalysis" (*NBW* 13–14). At the very beginning of the play Freud is not seen as seated behind the patient, rather his back is presented to the audience, as he watches along with us the projection of the original seduction scene by the lake on a scrim, he exposes his own unconscious behind to the audience's gaze. When Freud says "if we proceed without skill and special caution, we cannot know if such a scene really took place" (2), Cixous exposes the mirror of Freud's transference by displaying his narcissistic investment in the countertransference. Since Freud admits only at the very end that he failed to master the transference in time, this warning for caution at the beginning is doubly ironic.

The split between the visual and the auditory dimensions of the play marks the political space of seduction. While Freud's Oedipal obsession is marked by loss of sight, Dora's hysterical aphonia marks the missing centre of both stage and subject. The more Freud insists on being the seer who can penetrate Dora's secret by breaking her silence open, the clearer it becomes that his means, his Oedipal perspective of the space of representation, are inadequate for his goal since the hysteric's condition is defined by her permanent aphonia. Thus, Dora's silence also marks her feminine resistance to becoming spectacle, or a transparent subject under the masculine voyeuristic gaze of both the clinical and the theatrical authority. The portrait of Dora thus emerges indirectly, as an inverted ghostly reflection of her seductive image in Freud's eyes.

Originally written for radio, the typography of the stage directions clearly indicate that the play was meant to be read as much as to be heard and seen. The reader, however, is expected to calculate this gap between the written, the heard, and the seen, as well as the gap between the theatrical, the radiophonic, and the filmic representations. This problem is most significant, and all the more acute, in the representation of Dora's aphonia. To achieve this Cixous divides the text (as she splits her entire stage) between italicized utterances spoken by Dora and lines which are not heard.

While *Oedipus Rex* opens with the riddle of the Sphinx raising the question "what is a man?" and ends with the oracular message "know thyself," Cixous's play opens with the riddle of Dora's silence, which is the key to Cixous's notion of feminine sexuality. Three times, in three different ways, Dora poses the question "Pourquoi me suis-je tue?" to Freud, thus: "Why did I keep silent the first days after the incident by the lake?" Freud answers the question with a question: "To whom do you think you should ask that question?" Then Dora again: "Why did I then, suddenly, tell my parents about it?" And Freud again: "Do you know why?" Then, Dora: "does not answer but tells this story in a dreamlike voice: As father prepared to leave, I said that I would not stay there without him. Why did I tell my mother about the incident so that she would repeat it to my father?" (2–3).

The transition here from third to first person is remarkable: Dora stages her own refusal to answer, thus marking her speech in the first person as an act of disavowal, as if saying "I" is not "me". Cixous here mocks Freud by alluding to Lacan's notion of the echoing silence of the analyst, the silence of the subject who is supposed to know. Rather than silently letting the patient resound the echoes of her own story and thus come to her truth through the reflective transference as Freud and Lacan had envisioned, Cixous exploits Freud's misunderstanding of Dora's sexuality by placing throughout the play Dora's silence against his leading questions. Here this mockery begins with the oracular echoes of the repeated psychoanalytic "why" of the analyst's Oedipal and Oedipus-like search for origins and truth as Logos, as Word and Reason. By ignoring Freud's guiding questions, by turning them into rhetorical questions, and by repeating the same question, Dora acts as Echo to an invisible Narcissus, that is, as the seductress *par excellence*. While addressing Freud as an all-knowing oracle who can divine her true name, can tell her who she is, Dora, in fact, lets us know only who Freud thinks he is. At once ironic and tragic, she later asks Herr K. to tell her what her real name is. She thus lures him (as well as Freud) into her trap, and he, blinded by his desire, is oblivious to the fact that all he will find there is the meaning of his own name and death.

Dora addresses both Freud and Herr K. seductively, behind a veil of appearances, rather than truthfully acknowledging Freud's presumed transference. She is, in fact, teasing Freud's narcissistic countertransference, his illusion that he is the father-figure, the subject who knows and can solve her riddle thorough his guiding questions. She is constantly mocking his presumption that he as analyst replaces both the real father and Herr K. as a potential lover. Freud thus appears as a drowned Narcissus or as a wounded Oedipus: a blind subject who does not know how to solve the Sphinx's riddle because he does not know his feminine side and does not recognize himself as the seduced rather than the seducing man in the riddled silence of the hysteric-sphinx.

By posing the question of her silence to Freud and to the audience alike, Dora at the same time breaks her Sphinx-like silence. Paradoxically, her symptomatic refusal to speak directly, in sequence, and in a self-reflective manner about herself, is at once revealed and "cured" in her repetitious insistence on the echoing "why". For Dora emerges here as an oracle whose echoing voice fatefully determines the future. Cixous uses the rhyming expression "faire taire", the conjugated *tue*, as a homonym which echoes the verb *tuer*, to kill. Thus, the initial question "why I kept silent?" also carries the oracular prediction of "why I attempted to kill myself/you?" Indeed, later in the play, Dora will indeed attempt to kill herself by asking Herr K. to kill her,[8] and in the end she will "kill" Herr K. by her sudden appearance in the street which causes his injury in a carriage accident. Thus, Dora's initial "why" predicts the final meaning of her "killing" silence. She is the oracle that predicts Freud's identification with the wounded Herr K. at the end of the play, his recognition of the analogy between Herr K.'s physical and emotional injury and his own wounded ego as a result of Dora's termination of the treatment. Thus, Dora's echoing question "why did I keep silent?" evokes both the riddles of the silent Sphinx and the Oracle's revealing echoing voice in *Oedipus Rex* so that Cixous can link Oedipus' insistence on *hearing* the silent Sphinx and setting himself *to see* the truth of his identity in the voice of the Oracle.

Moreover, Oedipus' act of blinding himself at the end of the classical play parallels Freud's lack of insight. For while he keeps telling Dora that she will tell him everything in detail, Dora asks like an echo "and after that?" foreseeing from the very beginning what Freud will not see until the play's end, namely, the termination of the treatment. In the English version Freud's mourning over his wounded ego resonates through his final reaction to Dora's report about Herr K.'s accident months after her therapy ended. The closure of the play rests on this belated recognition, whose resonance is heard as an echo to Dora's initial oracular "that" ("And after that?") in Freud's last words at the end of the play: "There is no greater sorrow than to remember love. And Freud knew that."[9]

The closest realization of the origin of [Dora's] lack as reference to the missing mother is [her] fascination with the picture of the Sistine Madonna that she saw in the Dresden Gallery. In this scene, Cixous finally presents a real mirror on stage. Along with the reflection of the two framing lake scenes, this third mirror is turned towards the backstage of Dora's unconscious. Through the reflected images in this mirror the audience is invited to speculate about Dora's aphonia and about the possibility of her cure. As Dora describes her fascination with the Madonna picture, Cixous introduces the following scene: "filmed sequence of three stills. The Sistine Madonna, substitution of the Madonna, and Frau K. Dora behind the Madonna, seen through a mirror. (The audience does not know who is speaking, Mary or Frau K.)". The lay-out of the stage directions indicate that almost simultaneously, as if on another screen, the following also takes place: "Suddenly, the evidence, unnoticed perhaps by everyone: the infant Jesus held by the Madonna is none other than a baby Dora" (11).

The dialogue between Dora and Frau K. that follows this projection culminates in Dora's pleadings with Frau K. to return her love and to nourish her like a mother. The stage is further split by the simultaneous dialogues between Dora, Herr K., and Freud. As Dora reveals her pain and disappointment at Frau K.'s betrayal, Herr K.'s voice is heard asking: "But what did she want, finally?" (13). As Dora answers "Nothing, now. Nothing ever again", there appears once again a still shot of the Madonna. Dora stands in front and says sadly: "I beg you, give to me. Do something for me. Tell me the words that give birth. Nourish me. I'm dead, dead! I don't even desire anymore. Make something happen to me" (13).

Here lies Cixous's interpretation of Dora's silence. Dora's attempt to break her silence and tell her mother about the seduction ended with another disappointment, a last blow by her father and Frau K. After that, there was nothing she could say or want, for it is the nothing of her dead desire that her silence expresses. Her silence is, thus, the mark of her fixation in the pre-Oedipal and pre-linguistic infant's relations to the mother's image in the primal narcissistic stage (as opposed to the Oedipal stage that marks the intervention of the symbolic and the acquisition of language). Cixous thus shows that while the Imaginary stage is not real, the reality of hysteria consists in the "memory of the flesh," of what Lacan calls the Real, like the marks of maternity care on the body.

Just as the plague brought about by Oedipus's sexual sin harbours the secret of his identity, Dora's hysteria masks her own sexual "sin": her own unrealized sexual identity.

On this flickering translucent stage of specular representation, Cixous also establishes an analogy between Dora's silence about the incident by the lake, her silence about her father's relationship with Frau K., as well as her silence about her own homosexual love for Frau K. In this other delusive drama, on that other side of the Oedipal stage, the meaning of the "flickering of incessant mourning" emerges as well, the meaning that replaces the Father in the Oedipal drama with the myth of the pre-Oedipal mother. This is the stage on which Dora's desire is hypothetically realized: close to the end, at a moment equivalent to the tragic revelation or the anagnorisis in *Oedipus Rex*. And, as in *Oedipus Rex*, the mark of identity is a swollen foot, a "*faux pas*," which Freud interprets as a false pregnancy, a sign of Dora's "fall" after the seduction by the lake.[10] Toward the end of the play Dora imagines herself being treated for her swollen foot by Frau K., much as Frau K. nursed her father when he had a loose retina and had to lie in a dark room. The father's symbolic blindness of course alludes to Oedipus's blindness. Placing the daughter-mother relationship on the Oedipal stage of the father, reverses and parodies Freud's theory of castration and underscores his own fetishist bias.

NOTES

[Erella Brown teaches in the Department of Theatre and Drama Studies at the University of Haifa. Her writings on literature and psychoanalysis include "The Lake of Seduction: Silence, Hysteria, and the Space of Feminist Theatre" (1996) and "A Pompeiian Fancy under Jaffa's Sea: Agnon's *Betrothed* and Jensen's *Gradiva*" (1996). Her work on drama and postmodernism includes "Cruelty and Affirmation in the Postmodern Theatre: Antonin Artaud and Hanoch Levin" (1992) and "Between Literature and Theatre: Hanoch Levin and the Author's Function" (1999–2000).   Ed.]

1. Hélène Cixous, *Portrait de Dora* (1976; references in the text are to *Portrait of Dora*, trans. Sarah Burd [1983]). Although originally written for radio, Cixous's play was extensively reworked for the Théâtre d'Orsay and was directed by Simone Benmussa in 1976. (Translations of *Portrait of Dora* also appear in *Benmussa Directs* [1979]; and *The Selected Plays of Hélène Cixous* [2003] [Editor's note]).

2. Freud named Ida Bauer, "Dora", not merely in order to protect her identity, as he claimed. The actual analysis took place in the last three months of 1900 while the first "Fragment of an Analysis" appeared only in 1905, and the final version only in 1923. Feminist critics argue that Ida Bauer's identity hardly could be exposed by 1923. Moreover, the name Dora, Freud explains, was the name his mother forced their maid to adopt because his sister had the same name as the maid. Thus, Freud takes his revenge on Dora for deserting his treatment and for giving him "a fortnight's warning" (*FR* 229; *PF* 8: 148) as required of maids and governesses.

3. The paradox of the semiotic and the symbolic is discussed by Julia Kristeva in "Women's Time" (*The Kristeva Reader* 187–213).

4. The "Real", "Imaginary" and "Symbolic" are terms derived from the work of Lacan which are appropriated and revalued in the writings of Cixous, Kristeva and others. Broadly, the "Imaginary" is the realm of psychic fantasy within which we project images of our completion and fulfilment; the "Symbolic" is the social order of linguistic signs within which we are inscribed through the acquisition of language; and the "Real" is an unrepresentable substratum which eludes both the fantasy projections of the Imaginary and the social significations of the Symbolic [Editor's note].

5. Cixous here uses another hysteric model described by Freud: that of the woman who during a hysteric attack was holding a dress close to

her body with one hand while with the other she was tearing off her own dress and thus acting as both seducer and seduced. Freud also observed that this double role is typical of the hysteric, who is bisexual. According to Freud, hysterics perform both male and female roles, because the symptoms, which are "detached fragments of the act of copulation", have replaced the inclination to masturbation (*PF* 8: 117).

6. Moreover, as we shall see, the white pearls on Dora's neck carry a double symbolic meaning, linking desire with the rites of exchanging gifts and women in an endless circulation. Here in particular the pearls also refer to the money Freud received from Herr B. for "treating" Dora.

7. Translates as: "Why did I silence/kill myself?" [Editor's note].

8. Cixous stages Herr K.'s invasion of Dora's privacy while she was sleeping in his house. In that scene, Dora is acting out a conjugal/murderous writ, by imagining herself and Herr K. pushing against each other on either side of an invisible door: "*Soon I would like him to kill me. Who'll kill me? Whoever kills me, I want it*. I want to be killed. You can stand still for just so long without moving, but eventually you must. *Kill me! Kill me! Kill me!*" (8). Here too, the text is divided between Dora's speech and aphonia. The play on the *Tue-moi* [Kill me], at once kill-me/you-me, is invoked already in her initial response to Freud's demand to tell him everything. Her words "Si tu veux" also echoes her words from the door-scene where Dora says: "*tue, je le veux*" (kill/you, I want it/him).

9. In the French version "that" is the "ça", which also alludes to the id [it]. The echoing oracular effects are also achieved through the resonance of the sounds "vous" (the formal "you"), "veux" (want) and "voix" (voice). During the projection of the scene by the lake, Dora addresses the absent Herr K., while talking to Freud: "If you [*vous*] dare kiss me, I'll slap you [*vous*]!" and "Dare kiss me, I'll slap you!" Freud interferes with, "Yes, you [*vous*] will tell me. In full [*tous les*] detail". And Dora responds, "If you want [*tu veux*]" and "If you want [*vous voulez*]. And after?" (2). The change from the formal "vous" to the informal "tu" (informal "you") also echoes the "tous" (all) and the "tue" (silence) in Dora's question, "pourquoi me suis-je *tue*" (emphasis mine). This wordplay on voice and silence (voix/tue), subject and desire (tu/vous/veux), is amplified by the stage directions which focus on the changing tones of Dora's voice (voix). The ironic echoes undermine Freud's control over the situation. Throughout the play Dora's acting out echoes and mocks Freud's authority and knowledge. The final words of the play in the French version, "Et cela Freud le savait" ["And Freud knew that"] carry a similar ironic resonance by stressing the "savait", the limitation of Freud's knowledge.

10. Nine months after the incident by the lake and shortly after her aunt's death, Ida Bauer had a false appendicitis attack that left her with a limp that returned periodically. Freud interprets the limp as symbolizing a "false step" (*FR* 226; *PF* 8: 143).

12

"You Freud, Me Jane"

ELISABETH BRONFEN

> As she laughed I was aware of becoming involved in her laughter and being part of it, until her teeth were only accidental stars with a talent for squaddrill. I was drawn in by short gasps, inhaled at each momentary recovery, lost finally in the dark caverns of her throat, bruised by the ripple of unseen muscles. An elderly waiter with trembling hands was hurriedly spreading a pink and white checked cloth over the rusty green iron table, saying: "If the lady and gentleman wish to take their tea in the garden. ..." I decided that if the shaking of her breast could be stopped, some of the fragments of the afternoon might be collected, and I concentrated my attention with careful subtlety to this end.
>
> *– T.S. Eliot*

In her comment on T.S. Eliot's prose poem "Hysteria," which appeared in his first book *Prufrock and Other Observations* (1917), Claire Kahane suggests that it "announces in its very title its intention to appropriate a pathological dislocation as a poetic subject. Erasing the line that distinguishes poetic form from prose, 'Hysteria' technically performs the obliteration of boundaries that threaten its speaker" (128), drawing the male spectator into the very texture of the hysterical spectacle. Indeed, as Juliet Mitchell claims, one could fruitfully see the hysteric as a creative artist of sorts, telling tales and fabricating stories, "particularly for doctors who will listen" (299). Furthermore, because these stories are about psychic reality, seduction, and phantasy, psychoanalysis came to use the language of hysteria to ground both a theory and a therapy of subjectivity on the question of who tells the story and to whom it is directed.

Yet the hysteric is fully aware that the scenario she enacts involves not only playing games but also employing deceptions. Her desire, Anne Juranville argues, not only presents itself as profoundly enigmatic. Rather, the hysteric is also a master in laying false traces, never forgetting that she is herself implicated in the deception of her interpellator. Even though she may define the rules of this game of desire and may shine in the role she has cast for herself, she also hides herself in the course of this game. As Juranville explains, on the one hand she evokes the desire of the Other by offering to him her performance of a scene revolving around nothing, staging sentences that declare her lack: I do not know ..., I do not have ..., I can not ..., I am not ...[1] Yet even though the desire of the Other fascinates her, the hysteric's discourse is ultimately aimed at avoidance. So as not to disappear in the lack she represents to her interpellator, she constitutes her desire as being unsatisfiable, preventing her desire from ever reaching its destination. Juranville formulates the aporia staged by the hysteric: "By pitting desire against desire she supports the desire of her masculine interpellator, which she uses to support herself. She finds her enjoyment in this nonsatisfaction of desire. Not, however, by acting as the object causing the Other's desire, but rather as the subject of her symptoms" (76). In other words, the hysteric's subjectivity is, in the course of her phantasy work, that she identifies with the symbolic father. She represents herself through a performance of paternal seduction, but to trick the representative of paternal authority her game addresses she dons the guise of femininity. As Juranville puts it, "When addressing a man, she plays the woman, when addressing someone in the maternal position, she 'acts the man'" (77).

In the course of this complex game of self-effacement, however, the hysteric self-consciously remains within the realm of dissimulation, betraying the very premise of deception her self-enactment is based on by performing her disbelief or mistrust in paternal truth. She paradoxically rejects what is mere appearance, since her negation of so-called normal femininity is aimed at interrogating precisely the discursive formations of gender within which she finds herself. Turning this self-dismantling masquerade of femininity and filiality into her symptom, the hysteric believes neither in the femininity nor the daughterdom she nevertheless awkwardly assumes. At the same time she also appropriates masculinity, so as to undermine the paternal authority she plays to, not least of all because amid all her doubt she holds onto the conviction that, as Juranville concludes, there is a "horizon of absolute femininity, beyond the phallus" (79), that plays itself out without any reference to phallic economy, but which still confirms her belief in the Other.

Because she was such an adept performer of what Regula Schindler calls the hysteric's "misappropriation of the paternal master narratives",[2] no other hysteric appearing in Freud's writings has fascinated critics quite as much as Ida Bauer. Indeed, there appears to be nothing that has not been said about this case history.[3] This eighteen-year-old woman had been brought to Freud by her father in the winter of 1900 but decided to break off her analysis after only three sessions. In response to the wound she inflicted on his analytic authority, when she so staunchly refused to accept the interpretive solution he had come to offer her, and seeking to fill the gaps left by her sudden departure, Freud published his account of this case history five years later under the title *Fragment of an Analysis of a Case of Hysteria* (1905), giving her the name Dora. As he explains in the first part of his narrative, Dora suffered from difficulty in breathing, migrainelike headaches and a nervous cough, fatigue, lack of concentration, and an intermittent loss of voice. The year she went into analysis she had shown severe depressions, which had culminated first in a fainting attack after a moderately serious argument with her father and then a letter addressed to him, in which she threatened to take her life. Without great difficulty Freud recognizes her symptoms as being typical articulations of a minor case in hysteria, whose manifest cause appears to reside in her *"taedium vitae"*.

Yet what intrigues him is that, for several reasons, Dora's speech is enigmatically fragmentary. Many neurotic patients leave "gaps unfilled, and riddles unanswered", with the connections, for the most part, incoherent and the sequence of different events, uncertain (*PF* 8:45). In this particular case, however, he is acutely aware that Dora does not want to tell everything, that she knows more than she is willing to admit. Thus Freud's own reconstruction revolves around a point of indeterminacy, which cannot be solved because we have only his narration of the case yet which has inspired a host of critical rereadings. For when he records that Dora would often respond to his questions by saying "I do not know", what the reader cannot know for certain is whether Freud is right in claiming that her utterance signifies a lack in knowledge owing to repression or whether she is merely playing a game with her analyst, tricking him into believing she lacks knowledge, seducing him by offering a fragmented story to support his hermeneutic desire to uncover latent meaning.

Using his narrative to prove his theory that there is a sexually traumatic etiology for every case of hysteria, Freud believes that the key to her enigmatic behaviour – her symptoms and her reticence – must lie in the solution to two riddles: First, "What is her desire and, concomitant with that, why does she reject the position of femininity ascribed to her by her father?" and second, "Where does her sexual knowledge come from?" What is manifestly clear in the analysis he puts down on paper is that, regardless of whether he is interpreting Dora's symptoms – her coughing, aphonia, melancholy – or the two dreams she offers him, in either case he assumes a rivalry between Dora and Frau K.: on the one hand in relation to her unacknowledged erotic fascination for Herr K., on the other hand in relation to her father, where Dora's jealousy stands in for the mother, who is so strikingly absent from the entire intrigue except as the addressee of her daughter's complaint. As Lacan suggests, one wonders why Freud insists on reading aphonia, brought on during the absences of Herr K., as a symptom for the fact that when the prospective lover is absent, the daughter need not speak, but fails to see this as "an expression of the violent appeal of the oral erotic drive when Dora was left face to face with Frau K., without there being any need for Freud to invoke her awareness of the fellatio undergone by the father when everyone knows that cunnilingus is the artifice most commonly adopted by 'men of means' whose powers begin to abandon them" ("Intervention on Transference" 98). Indeed, one could just as easily speculate that Dora's aphonia was a response not to an absence but rather to an abundant presence that called forth a transgressive desire and thus recast the Oedipal configuration in a manner Freud was not willing to entertain for his *petite hystérique*. Only after the event did he come to recognize that Dora had actually harboured a desire for the woman who had taken her mother's place in the love life of her father, in the gesture of a psychic compromise, which had allowed her to abandon yet also adore the maternal body. Perhaps the fact that she withdrew from the masculine lover (whom the players in her family's intrigue had sought to offer her, even though her father openly admitted that he had no high opinion of this man) was less at issue than her hysteria's allowing her to articulate obliquely the masculinity forbidden to her. Aimed at rebuking her father's command, but uncannily also refuting Freud's dictum of the daughter's Oedipal trajectory, Dora's transgression seems to have revolved around the gender of those she chose to address: presenting her complaint about Herr K. to her mother, falling silent before her desire for the feminine body offered to her in the figure of her mother's surrogate and in the image of the Madonna she talks about in her second dream.

The hysteric's gaps in consciousness and memory seem to have infected not only the analytic scenario between Freud and Dora but also his belated transcript, forcing him to produce an equally gap-riddled text. Still, Freud's professional integrity becomes nowhere more evident than in the fact that even while he seeks to establish the validity of his solution, he admits that Dora usually responded to the interpretation he was offering her with a flat No. Subsuming her resistance into his theory, he takes recourse in the psycho-analytic dictum that declares, "The 'No' uttered by a patient after a repressed thought has been presented to his conscious perception for the first time does no more than register the existence of a re-pression. ... 'No' signifies the desired 'Yes'" (FR 203; PF 8: 93). One of the exchanges between Freud and his resistant patient is particularly striking because it not only registers the way he seeks to turn interpretive fallibility into a strength, but unwittingly also dis-closes that Dora might perhaps have been playing cat and mouse with him, offering Freud precisely the images she knew he desired and enjoying the fact that he duly fell prey to this bait. When he suggested that the mother's jewel box in the first dream should be read as a symbol for the female genitalia, Dora responds, "I knew *you* would say that", with Freud adroitly recasting her rebuke to fit the narrative he seeks to confirm, "That is to say, *you* knew it [was so]", and adding in a footnote, "A very common way of putting aside a piece of knowledge that emerges from the repressed" (FR 210; PF 8: 105).

If then, in one sense, such a rhetorical sleight of hand can be seen as typical for Freud's phallic violence toward Ida Bauer, it neverthe-less also illustrates his impotence, for all his efforts at proving to his readers that he had the knowledge she lacked resonate against his patient's adamant refusal to accept his solution, her silence and abrupt departure once her contradictions and negations no longer seemed in place. Thus this text, which discloses the sexuality of the hysteric as one inscribed with gender slippage, is itself a slippery affair. In the same gesture that Dora rejects Freud's interpretive authority, the gaps and negations she uses to respond allow a very different story to emerge from the midst of his text than he purports to transcribe. The other story Dora may well have given such duplicitous articulation to would be that the failure in interpellation played through in their exchange resulted from the fact that she will not recognize herself in the Other's construction and, more, from Freud's misunderstanding the source of her self-image. Rather than the realm of the erect penis, so crucial to his theory-romance, her distress addressed the realm of adored femininity, recalling how during her visit to a famous picture gallery in Dresden she had "remained two hours in front of the Sistine Madonna, rapt in silent admiration" (FR 222; PF 8: 135–6). Once again we find hysteria demarcating the limit of a representational system, interrogating the position of authority it also supports. Whereas Freud's investigation questions Dora's desire and the source of her sexual knowledge, Dora, by her negations and her sudden silence, turns the text back on the narrator, forcing it to also question Freud's desire and the source he is willing to ascribe to his knowledge of hysteria.

In his postscript Freud directly addresses the failure of his analysis, which, significantly, he does not attribute to any incorrect reading of her symptoms on his part, but rather to his being unable at the time to deal with the transference at work in their analytic scene. Lacan astutely attributes Freud's inability to face Dora's homosexual tendency to the fact that he had "put himself rather too much in the place of Herr K.", to fully untangle his countertransference ("Intervention on Transference" 101). Indeed, in contrast to the opinion of Dora's father, Freud had explained in a footnote, "I happen to know Herr K., for he was the same person who had visited me with the patient's father, and he was still quite young and of prepossessing appearance" (FR 184; PF 8:60). In other words, part of the failure in interpellation played through in Dora's case can be attributed to Freud's inappropriate presupposition that there could be a heterosexual solution to this case of hysteria by identifying with the position of the male lover.

However, part of Freud's blindness could equally be attributed to his inability or unwillingness to identify with Dora in their mutual enterprise. More crucially, Freud may also have been unable or unwilling to imagine that the transference at stake was not merely that Dora had recast him in her phantasy as the repetition of her father and her rejected suitor, but rather that the love relation she found herself repeating in the analytic scene was that he had come to represent Frau K. Again, Freud self-consciously addresses this blindness in a footnote, explaining that "The longer the interval of time that separates me from the end of this analysis, the more probable it seems to me that the fault in my technique lay in this omission: I failed to discover in time and to inform the patient that her homosexual (gynecophilic) love for Frau K. was the strongest unconscious current in her mental life. I ought to have guessed that the main source of her knowledge of sexual matters could have been no one but Frau K., the very person who later on charged her with being interested in those same subjects. Her knowing all about such things and, at the same time, her always pretending not to know where her knowledge came from was really too remarkable. I ought to have attacked this riddle and looked for the motive of such an extraordinary piece of repression" (*FR* 237; *PF* 8: 162).

Taking a different route than the one Freud privileges, one might speculate that Dora was fully aware that the object of her desire and the source of her sexual knowledge were one and the same person and that she was not repressing but quite willfully withholding this information. Adept at laying false traces, she could just as easily have been in control of their analytic scenario, all along fully possessing the knowledge Freud belatedly thought he might have helped her discover. Read in this way the deception performed in these fragments is that even while Freud sought to convince Dora that her hysteria was a symptom, broadcasting a message about her repressed desire for Herr K. – which she staunchly resisted to the end – she seems to have functioned as *his* symptom, broadcasting to him a message about his identification with the feminine position, which he in turn resisted by proclaiming that when she said no she meant yes.

Reading Freud's own negation against the grain, I would speculate that Dora's homosexuality causes him to falter [*steckengeblieben*] and leaves him completely confused [*in völlige Verwirrung geraten*] (as he notes in his footnote) precisely because it broadcasts to him a message about the hysteria in himself he seeks to disavow. For Dora seems to perform an analytic phantasy scenario in which she asks him to alternate between the paternal authority with which the hysteric daughter takes issue (her father and his surrogate, Herr K.) and the maternal position, which is both the source and the addressee of her sexual knowledge. In other words, even as Freud sought to replace a dialogue between a maternal surrogate and a daughter (the gynecophilic currents of love she felt for Frau K.) with the heterosexual couple he needs to privilege (the confession

Dora refuses – her unconscious desire for Herr K.), he is belatedly forced to recognize that Dora had been using him all along as a figure in a very different scenario. While he thought he was masterminding an analytic scenario that replicated the heterosexual family romance, the marriage between Herr K. and Dora that he fancied would be the "only possible solution for all parties concerned" (FR 230; PF 8: 149), the transference at work was that he was actually repeating the enigmatic and clandestine scenario of a duplicitious orality between two women, which as Appignanesi and Forrester suggest, was sensual and discursive in one and the same gesture. This other scenario, existing in tandem with the phallic reenactment Freud sought to privilege, shows him implicated in the very realm whose enigma he seeks to solve (so that it might be abandoned once and for all) namely, the magical fascination eminating from the maternal body. Although Freud can discover the origin of Dora's secret – the clandestinely shared orality with Frau K. – only in the belated and intermittent rhetoric of his own hystérikè, Appignanesi and Forrester insist that he could not or would not imagine that in the course of countertransference he was actually taking on the roles of the governess and Frau Zellenka (Frau K.): "He did not want to have his latinate language of psychoanalysis defiled by proximity with the oral exchanges between these women." However, as Appignanesi and Forrester add, Freud was perfectly willing to play another female part, "this a traditionally Jewish one that came naturally to his active analytic stance" (Freud's Women 162). Phantasizing how the case could have found a happy ending if only the participants had accepted his proposal of a double wedding, Freud proves himself to be a thwarted matchmaker.

Yet Dora does not vanish after she leaves Freud's office on 31 December 1900. Appignanesi and Forrester sight her again in the Vienna of the 1930s, when bridge playing had become popular among female members of the Jewish bourgeoisie. Ida Bauer had turned into a highly successful teacher and player of this social game – with Frau Zellenka as her partner. Having resisted both her father's and her analyst's heterosexual family romance as the "only possible solution" to the hysteric daughter's discontent, she seems to have constructed for herself a more viable scenario of alliance. As they note "it was as if, across the years, they had finally dispensed with the superfluous men who had previously been their partners in their complex social games and contracts, yet they had retained their love of those games whose skill lies in the secret of mutual understanding of open yet coded communications within and across a foursome. Ida, adept at keeping her hand secret, also knew when and how to play it". And, as if to exonerate the analyst they had accused of rhetorical violence, they quickly add, "Freud might also have thought Ida's choice of occupation as a bridge master as an example of that rarest of all skills, successful sublimation" (167). At this point in her life at least, Dora seems to have been successful at juggling the contradictions in her hysteria – playing a game with her female partner that she had learned from identifying with her analyst.

NOTES

[Elisabeth Bronfen is Professor of English and American Studies at the University of Zurich. Her many essays and books on gender, literature and psychoanalysis include *Over Her Dead Body: Death, Femininity and the Aesthetic* (Manchester: Manchester University Press, 1992), *Sylvia Plath* (London: Northcote House/British Council, 1998), *The Knotted Subject: Hysteria and its Discontents* (Princeton: Princeton University Press, 1998), "Hysteric and Obsessional Discourse: Responding to Death in *Dracula*" (1999), "The Language of Hysteria: A Misappropriation of the Master Narratives" (2000), and *Feminist Consequences: Theory for the New Century*, edited with Misha Kavja (Columbia: Columbia University Press, 2001). Ed.]

1. In a footnote to the first dream Dora offers him, Freud notes that her I do not know "was the regular formula with which she confessed to anything that had been repressed" (*FR* 210; *PF* 8: 104).

2. Unpublished response read at a conference entitled "One Hundred Years of Hysteria" at the art academy in Zurich, 27 October 1995.

3. See Bernheimer and Kahane (1985), as well as the special volume of *Diacritics* (1983).

Bibliography

Abraham, N., "The Phantom of Hamlet or The Sixth Act, *preceded by* The Intermission of 'Truth'", (trans.) N.T. Rand, *Diacritics*, 18.4 (1988), 2–19; also in *SK* pp. 187–205.

——. *Rhythms: On the Work, Translation, and Psychoanalysis*, (trans.) B. Thigpen (Stanford: Stanford University Press, 1995).

Abraham, N. and Torok, M., *The Wolf Man's Magic Word: A Cryptonymy*, (trans.) N.T. Rand (Minneapolis: University of Minnesota Press, 1987 [Abbreviated as *WMMW*]).

——. "Introduction: Five Years with the Wolf Man", in N. Abraham and M. Torok, *The Wolf Man's Magic Word: A Cryptonymy*, (trans.) N.T. Rand (Minneapolis: University of Minnesota Press, 1987 [Abbreviated as *WMMW*]), pp. lxx–lxxii.

——. "The Wolf Man and His Internal World", in N. Abraham and M. Torok, *The Wolf Man's Magic Word: A Cryptonymy*, (trans.) N.T. Rand (Minneapolis: University of Minnesota Press, 1987 [Abbreviated as *WMMW*]), pp. 3–15.

——. "Behind the Inner World", in N. Abraham and M. Torok, *The Wolf Man's Magic Word: A Cryptonymy*, (trans.) N.T. Rand (Minneapolis: University of Minnesota Press, 1987 [Abbreviated as *WMMW*]), pp. 16–26.

——. *The Shell and the Kernel: Renewals of Psychoanalysis*, (trans.) N.T. Rand (Chicago: University of Chicago Press, 1994 [Abbreviated as *SK*]).

Appignanesi, L. and Forrester, J., *Freud's Women* (New York: Basic Books, 1992).

Armstrong, P., *Shakespeare in Psychoanalysis* (London: Routledge, 2001).

Bakhtin, M., "Discourse in the Novel", in *The Dialogic Imagination* (ed.) M. Holquist, (Austin: University of Texas Press, 1981).

Barthes, R., "Diderot, Brecht, Eisenstein", in R. Barthes, *Image-Music-Text*, (trans.) S. Heath (Glasgow: Fontana, 1977).

Baudrillard, J., *Seduction*, (trans.) B. Singer (New York, 1990).

Bernheimer, C. and Kahane, C. (eds) *In Dora's Case: Freud – Hysteria – Feminism* (New York: Columbia University Press, 1985).

Bowers, F.T., *Elizabethan Revenge Tragedy 1587–1642* (1940; reprinted Gloucester, MA: Peter Smith, 1959).

Bowie, M., *Lacan* (London: Fontana, 1991).

Bronfen, E., *Over Her Dead Body: Death, Femininity and the Aesthetic* (Manchester: Manchester University Press, 1992).

——. "Freud's Hysterics, Jaspers' Nostalgics", *Parallax*, 3 (1996), pp. 49–64.

——. *Sylvia Plath* (London: Northcote House/British Council, 1998).

——. *The Knotted Subject: Hysteria and its Discontents* (Princeton: Princeton University Press, 1998).

——. "'You Freud, Me Jane': Alfred Hitchcock's *Marnie*, the Case History Revisited", in E. Bronfen, *The Knotted Subject: Hysteria and its Discontents* (Princeton: Princeton University Press, 1998), pp. 332–377.

——. "Hysteric and Obsessional Discourse: Responding to Death in *Dracula*", in G. Byron (ed.), *Dracula* (Basingstoke: Palgrave, 1999), pp. 55–67.

——. "The Language of Hysteria: A Misappropriation of the Master Narratives", *Women: A Cultural Review*, 11.1-2 (2000), pp. 8–18.

Bronfen, E. and Kavja, M. (eds) *Feminist Consequences: Theory for the New Century* (Columbia: Columbia University Press, 2001).

Bronson, B.H. (ed.), *Selections from Johnson on Shakespeare* (New Haven: Yale University Press, 1986).

Brooks, P., *Reading for the Plot: Design and Intention in Narrative* (Oxford: Clarendon Press, 1984).

——. "Fictions of the Wolf Man: Freud and Narrative Understanding", in P. Brooks, *Reading for the Plot: Design and Intention in Narrative* (Oxford: Clarendon Press, 1984), pp. 264–85.

——. *Body Work: Objects of Desire in Modern Narrative* (Cambridge, Massachussetts: Harvard University Press, 1993).

——. *Psychoanalysis and Storytelling* (Oxford: Blackwell, 1994).

——. *Troubling Confessions: Speaking Guilt in Law and Literature* (Chicago: University of Chicago Press, 2000).

Brooks, P. and Woloch, A. (eds), *Whose Freud?* (Yale: Yale University Press, 2000).

Brown, E., "Cruelty and Affirmation in the Postmodern Theatre: Antonin Artaud and Hanoch Levin", *Modern Drama*, 35.4 (1992), pp. 585–606.

——. "The Lake of Seduction: Body, Acting, and Voice in Hélène Cixous's *Portrait de Dora*", *Modern Drama*, 39.4 (1996), pp. 626–49.

——. "The Lake of Seduction: Silence, Hysteria, and the Space of Feminist Theatre", *Journal of Theatre and Drama*, 2 (1996), pp. 175–200.

——. "A Pompeiian Fancy under Jaffa's Sea: Agnon's *Betrothed* and Jensen's *Gradiva*", *Prooftexts: A Journal of Jewish Literary History*, 16.3 (1996), pp. 245–70.

——. "Between Literature and Theatre: Hanoch Levin and the Author's Function", *Journal of Theatre and Drama*, 5–6 (1999–2000), pp. 23–57.

Case, S.-E. (ed.), *Performing Feminisms: Feminist Critical Theory and Theater* (Baltimore, MD, 1990).

Charnes, L., *Notorious Identity: Materializing the Subject in Shakespeare* (Cambridge, MA: Harvard University Press, 1993).
——. "Dismember Me: Shakespeare, Paranoia and the Logic of Mass Culture", *Shakespeare Quarterly*, 48.1 (1997), pp. 1–16.
——. "The Hamlet formerly Known as Prince", in H. Grady (ed.), *Shakespeare and Modernity: Early Modern to Millennium* (London: Routledge, 2000), pp. 189–210.
——. "We Were Never Early Modern", in J. Joughin (ed.), *Philosophical Shakespeares* (London: Routledge, 2000), pp. 51–67.
——. "The 2% Solution: What Harold Bloom Forgot", in C. Desmet and R. Sawyer (eds), *Harold Bloom's Shakespeare* (New York: Palgrave, 2001), pp. 259–68.
——. *Hamlet's Heirs: Essays on Inheriting Shakespeare* (London: Routledge, 2005).
Chase, C., "Oedipal Textuality: Reading Freud's Reading of *Oedipus*", in M. Ellmann (ed.), *Psychoanalytic Literary Criticism* (London: Longman, 1994), pp. 56–75.
Cixous, H., *Portrait du Soleil* (Denoël, 1974).
——. "The Laugh of the Medusa", [1975], in E. Marks and I. de Courtivron (eds), *New French Feminisms* (Brighton: Harvester, 1980), pp. 245–64.
——. "Sorties", [1975], in *The Newly Born Woman*, (trans.) B. Wing (Minneapolis: University of Minnesota Press, 1986), pp. 63–132.
——. "Fiction and its Phantoms: A Reading of Freud's *Das Unheimliche* ("The 'Uncanny'")", *New Literary History*, 7.3 (1976), pp. 526–48.
——. "Castration or Decapitation?" [1976], *Signs*, 7.1 (1981), pp. 41–55.
——. *Portrait de Dora* (Paris: Édition des femmes, 1976). [Translated as: *Portrait of Dora*, (trans.) A. Barrows, in *Benmussa Directs* (London: John Calder, Dallas: Riverrun Press, 1979), pp. 9–67; *Portrait of Dora*, (trans.) S. Burd, *Diacritics*, 13.1 (1983), pp. 32–45; *Portrait of Dora*, (trans.) A. Liddle, in E. Prenowitz (ed.), *The Selected Plays of Hélène Cixous* (London: Routledge, 2003), pp. 35–58].
Cixous, H. and Clément, C., *The Newly Born Woman*, [1975], (trans.) B. Wing (Minneapolis: University of Minnesota Press, 1986 [Abbreviated as *NBW*]).
——. "The Untenable", [1975], in *The Newly Born Woman*, pp. 147–160.
——. *Chant du corps interdit / Le Nom d'Oedipe* (Paris: Des Femmes, 1978).
——. *The Hélène Cixous Reader*, S. Sellers (ed.), (London: Routledge, 1994).
Clément, C., *The Lives and Legends of Jacques Lacan*, (trans.) A. Goldhammer (New York: Columbia University Press, 1983).
——. *The Weary Sons of Freud: Questions for Feminism* (London: Verso, 1987).
——. "Imaginary, Symbolic and Real", *Journal of the School of Languages*, 3 (1993), pp. 692–99.
Clément, C. and Kristeva, J., *The Feminine and the Sacred* (Columbia: Columbia University Press, 2001).
Coleridge, S.T., *Lectures on Shakespeare* (New York: Dutton, 1951).

Conan Doyle, A., "The Adventure of the Cardboard Box", in *The Complete Sherlock Holmes*, vol. 2 (Garden City, N.Y.: Doubleday, 1953).

Copjec, J., *Read My Desire: Lacan Against the Historicists* (Cambridge, MA: MIT Press, 1994).

Crews, F., *Out of My System: Psychoanalysis, Ideology, and Critical Method* (New York: Oxford University Press, 1975).

Culler, J., *The Pursuit of Signs: Semiotics, Literature, Deconstruction* (London: RKP, 1981).

Derrida, J., "Freud and the Scene of Writing", in J. Derrida, *Writing and Difference*, (trans.) A. Bass (London: Routledge and Kegan Paul, 1978), pp. 196–231.

——. "Me – Psychoanalysis: an Introduction to the Translation of 'The Shell and the Kernel' by Nicolas Abraham", (trans.) R. Klein, *Diacritics* 9.1 (1979): pp. 4–12.

——. "*Fors*: The Anglish Words of Nicolas Abraham and Maria Torok", in N. Abraham and M. Torok, *The Wolf Man's Magic Word: A Cryptonymy*, (trans.) N.T. Rand (Minneapolis: University of Minnesota Press, 1987), pp. xi–xlviii.

——. "To Speculate – on 'Freud'", in J. Derrida, *The Postcard: From Socrates to Freud and Beyond*, (trans.) A. Bass (Chicago: University of Chicago Press, 1987), pp. 257–409.

——. "The Purveyor of Truth", in J. Derrida, *The Postcard: From Socrates to Freud and Beyond*, (trans.) A. Bass (Chicago: University of Chicago Press, 1987), pp. 411–96.

——. "Let Us Not Forget – Psychoanalysis", (trans.) G. Bennington and R. Bowlby, *Oxford Literary Review*, 12 (1990): pp. 3–7.

——. *Acts of Literature*, (ed.) D. Attridge (London: Routledge, 1992).

——. *Dissemination*, (trans.) B. Johnson (London: Athlone, 1993).

——. *Specters of Marx: The State of the Debt, the Work of Mourning, and the New International* (trans.) P. Kamuf (New York, London: Routledge, 1994).

——. *Resistances of Psychoanalysis*, (trans.) P. Kamuf, P.-A. Brault and M. Naas (Stanford: Stanford University Press, 1998).

Dolar, M., "'I Shall Be with You on Your Wedding-Night': Lacan and the Uncanny", *October*, 58 (1991), pp. 5–23.

Eliot, T.S., "Hamlet", in F. Kermode (ed.), *Selected Prose of T.S. Eliot* (London: Faber & Faber, 1976), pp. 45–9.

Ellmann, M., "Blanche", in *Criticism and Critical Theory*, (ed.) J. Hawthorn (London: Edward Arnold, 1984), pp. 99–112.

——. "The Ghosts of *Ulysses*", in *James Joyce: The Artist and the Labyrinth*, (ed.) A. Martin (London: Ryan, 1990), pp. 193–227.

——. (ed.), *Psychoanalytic Literary Criticism* (London: Longman, 1994).

Felman, S., (ed.), *Literature and Psychoanalysis: the Question of Reading Otherwise* (Baltimore: John Hopkins University Press, 1982).

——. "To Open the Question", in *Literature and Psychoanalysis: the Question of Reading Otherwise* (Baltimore: John Hopkins University Press, 1982), pp. 5–10.

——. *Jacques Lacan and the Adventure of Insight: Psychoanalysis in Contemporary Culture* (London, Mass.: Harvard University Press, 1987).

——. "Women and Madness: the Critical Phallacy", in C. Belsey and J. Moore (eds), *The Feminist Reader: Essays in Gender and the Politics of Literary Criticism* (Basingstoke: Macmillan, 1989), pp. 133–53.

——. *What Does a Woman Want?: Reading and Sexual Difference* (Baltimore: John Hopkins University Press, 1993).

Fink, B., "Reading Hamlet with Lacan", in *Lacan, Politics, Aesthetics*, (ed.) W. Apollon and R. Feldstein (Albany: State University of New York Press, 1996), pp. 181–198.

Freedman, B., "Frame-Up: Feminism, Psychoanalysis, Theatre", in *Performing Feminisms: Feminist Critical Theory and Theater*, (ed.) S.-E. Case (Baltimore, MD, 1990), pp. 54–76.

Freud, S., *The Penguin Freud Library*, vols. 1–15 (trans.) J. Strachey (London: Penguin, 1990–93 [Abbreviated as *PF*]).

——. *The Freud Reader*, (ed.) P. Gay (London: Vintage, 1995 [Abbreviated as *FR*]).

——. *The Standard Edition of the Complete Psychological Works of Sigmund Freud*, vols. 1–23 (trans.) J. Strachey (London: Hogarth Press, 1953–74) [Abbreviated as *SE*].

Gallop, J., "Keys to Dora", in *In Dora's Case: Freud–Hysteria–Feminism*, (eds) C. Bernheimer and C. Kahane (New York: Columbia University Press, 1985), pp. 200–220.

Garber, M., *Shakespeare's Ghost Writers: Literature as Uncanny Causality* (New York, London: Routledge, 1987).

Gardiner, M. (ed.), *The Wolf-Man and Sigmund Freud* (London: the Hogarth Press, 1972).

Green, A., *The Tragic Effect: The Oedipus Complex in Tragedy* (Cambridge: Cambridge University Press, 1979).

——. "On Hamlet's Madnesses and the Unsaid", in P.L. Rudnytsky and E.H. Spitz, *Freud and Forbidden Knowledge* (New York, London: New York University Press, 1994), pp. 164–182.

Griffiths, H. (ed.), *Shakespeare – "Hamlet"* (Basingstoke: Palgrave, 2004).

Grosz, E., *Jacques Lacan: A Feminist Introduction* (London: Routledge, 1990).

Hawkes, T., "*Telmah*", in *Shakespeare and the Question of Theory*, (eds) P. Parker and G. Hartman (New York, London: Methuen, 1985), pp. 310–32.

Hazlitt, W., *Characters of Shakespeare's Plays* (London: Reynell, 1817).

Hertz, N., (special ed.) "A Fine Romance: Freud and Dora", *Diacritics* 13.1 (1983).

——. "Freud and the Sandman", in J. Harari, (ed.) *Textual Strategies* (Ithaca, N.Y.: Cornell University Press, 1979).

——. *The End of the Line: Essays on Psychoanalysis and the Sublime* (New York: Columbia University Press, 1985).

Hoffmann, E.T.A., "The Sandman" in *Tales of Hoffmann*, (trans.) R.J. Hollingdale (Harmondsworth: Penguin, 1982), pp. 85–125.

———. "The Sandman" in *Tales from Hoffmann*, (ed.) J.M. Cohen (New York: Conard-Mc.Cann Inc., 1951), pp. 109–45.

Jacobus, M., *Reading Woman: Essays in Feminist Criticism* (London: Methuen, 1986).

———. *First Things: The Maternal Imaginary in Literature, Art and Psychoanalysis* (London: Routledge, 1995).

———. *Psychoanalysis and the Scene of Reading* (Oxford: Oxford University Press, 1999).

James, H., *The Art of the Novel* (New York: Scribner's, 1934).

Jones, E., *Hamlet and Oedipus* [1949], (New York: Norton, 1976).

———. *The Life and Work of Sigmund Freud*, 2 vols. (New York: Basic Books, 1953).

Juranville, A., "Hysterie und Melancholie bei der Frau", *Riss: Zeitschrift für Psychanalyse*, 4. 11 (1989), pp. 53–80.

Kahane, C., *Passions of the Voice: Hysteria, Narrative, and the Figure of the Speaking Woman, 1850–1915* (Baltimore, Md.: John Hopkins University Press, 1995).

Kamuf, P., "Abraham's Wake", *Diacritics*, 9.1 (1979), pp. 32–45.

Kerrigan, J., *Revenge Tragedy: Aeschylus to Armageddon* (Oxford: Clarendon Press, 1996).

Kofman, S., *The Childhood of Art: An Interpretation of Freud's Aesthetics* [1970], (trans.) W. Woodhull (New York: Columbia University Press, 1988).

———. *Freud and Fiction* [1974], (trans.) S. Wykes (Oxford: Polity Press, 1991).

———. "The Double is/and the Devil: The Uncanniness of *The Sandman*", in S. Kofman, *Freud and Fiction* [1974], (trans.) S. Wykes (Oxford: Polity Press, 1991), pp. 121–162.

———. *The Enigma of Woman: Woman in Freud's Writings* [1980], (trans.) C. Porter (Ithaca, London: Cornell University Press, 1985).

———. "Conversions: *The Merchant of Venice* under the Sign of Saturn" [1988], (trans.) S. Whitside, in P. Collier and H. Geyer-Ryan (eds), *Literary Theory Today* (Ithaca: Cornell University Press, 1990).

Kristeva, J., *The Kristeva Reader*, (ed.) T. Moi (Oxford: Blackwell, 1986).

———. *Strangers to Ourselves*, (trans.) L.S. Roudiez (New York: Columbia University Press, 1991).

Lacan, J., "Le Séminaire, Livre Xx: L'angoisse, 1962–63", 2 vols, Unpublished.

———. *Speech and Language in Psychoanalysis*, (ed.) Anthony Wilden (Baltimore, London: John Hopkins University Press, 1981).

———. "Desire and the Interpretation of Desire in *Hamlet*", in *Literature and Psychoanalysis: the Question of Reading Otherwise*, (ed.) S. Felman (Baltimore: John Hopkins University Press, 1982), pp. 11–52.

———. "Hamlet, par Lacan", *Ornicar?*, 26–27 (1983), pp. 7–44.

———. "Intervention on Transference", in *In Dora's Case: Freud – Hysteria – Feminism*, (eds) C. Bernheimer and C. Kahane (New York: Columbia University Press, 1985), pp. 92–104.

——. *Écrits: A Selection*, (trans.) A. Sheridan (London: Tavistock, 1985).

——. *The Ego in Freud's Theory and in the Technique of Psychoanalysis 1954–1955*, Book II, *The Seminar of Jacques Lacan*, (ed.) J.-A. Miller, (trans.) S. Tomaselli (New York, London: W.W. Norton, 1988).

——. *The Four Fundamental Concepts of Psycho-Analysis*, (ed.) J.-A. Miller, (trans.) A. Sheridan (Harmondsworth: Penguin, 1991).

Laplanche, J., *Life and Death in Psychoanalysis* (Baltimore: John Hopkins University Press, 1976).

——. *Jean Laplanche: Seduction, Translation and the Drives*, (eds) J. Fletcher and M. Stanton (London: ICA, 1992), pp. 217–223.

Lechte, J. (ed.), *Writing and Psychoanalysis: A Reader* (London: Edward Arnold, 1996).

Lukacher, N., *Primal Scenes: Literature, Philosophy, Psychoanalysis* (Ithaca and London: Cornell University Press, 1986).

Lupton, J.R., *Afterlives of the Saints: Hagiography, Typology, and Renaissance Literature* (Stanford, CA: Stanford University Press, 1996).

——. "Othello Circumcised: Shakespeare and the Pauline Discourse of Nations", *Representations*, 57 (1997), pp. 73–89.

——. "Creature Caliban", *Shakespeare Quarterly* 51 (2000), pp. 1–23.

——. "The Gertrude Barometer: Teaching Shakespeare with Freud, Eliot, and Lacan", in B.W. Kliman (ed.), *Approaches to Teaching Shakespeare's "Hamlet"* (New York, NY: Modern Language Association of America, 2001).

Lupton, J.R. and Reinhard, K., "Shapes of Grief: Freud, Hamlet, and Mourning", *Genders*, 4 (1989), pp. 50–67.

——. *After Oedipus: Shakespeare in Psychoanalysis* (Ithaca and London: Cornell University Press, 1993).

——. "*Hamlet*'s Flesh: Lacan and the Desire of the Mother", in J.R. Lupton and K. Reinhard, *After Oedipus: Shakespeare in Psychoanalysis* (Ithaca and London: Cornell University Press, 1993), pp. 60–88.

MacCannell, J.F., "The Semiotics of *Fatal Attraction*: Preliminary Remarks", *The American Journal of Semiotics*, 7. 3 (1990), pp. 5–12.

Malcolm, J., *The Purloined Clinic: Selected Writings* (New York: Alfred A. Knopf., 1992).

Marcus, S., "Freud and Dora: Story, History, Case History", in C. Bernheimer and C. Kahane (eds), *In Dora's Case: Freud – Hysteria – Feminism* (London: Virago, 1985), pp. 56–91.

——. *Freud and the Culture of Psychoanalysis: Studies in the Transition from Victorian Humanism to Modernity* (Boston: Allen & Unwin, 1984).

Mehlman, J., "Poe Pourri: Lacan's Purloined Letter", *Semiotext(e)*, 1 (1975), pp. 51–68.

Meltzer, F., "The Uncanny Rendered Canny: Freud's Blind Spot in Reading Hoffmann's 'Sandman'", in *Introducing Psychoanalytic Theory*, (ed.) S.L. Gilman (New York: Brunner/Mazel, 1982), pp. 218–239.

Mentzos, S., *Sigmund Freud: Bruchstäck einer Hysterie-Analyse* (Frankfurt am Main: S. Fischer, 1993).

Miller, J-A., "To Interpret the Cause: From Freud to Lacan", *Newsletter of the Freudian Field*, 3 (1989), pp. 30–50.

Miller, J. Hillis, "Derrida's Topographies", *South Atlantic Review*, 59.1 (1994), pp. 1–25.

Mitchell, J., *Women: the Longest Revolution: Essays in Feminism, Literature and Psychoanalysis* (London: Penguin, 1984).

Møller, L., *The Freudian Reading: Analytical and Fictional Constructions* (Philadelphia: University of Pennsylvania Press, 1991).

——. "*The Sandman*: The Uncanny as Problem of Reading", in L. Møller, *The Freudian Reading: Analytical and Fictional Constructions* (Philadelphia: University of Pennsylvania Press, 1991), pp. 111–139.

——. "Repetition, Return, and Doubling in Henrik Ibsen's Major Prose Plays", *Ibsen Studies*, 2 (2001), pp. 7–31.

——. "Thomas De Quincey's Arabesque Confessions", *Arbejdspapirer: Department of Comparative Literature*, 35 (Aarhus: University of Aarhus Press, 2002), pp. 1–25.

Møller, L. and M.-L. Svane (eds), *Romanticism in Theory* (Aarhus University Press, 2001).

Morrissey, K., *Dora: A Case of Hysteria* (London: Nick Hern Books, 1994).

Obholzer, K., *The Wolf-Man: Conversations with Freud's Patient – Sixty Years Later*, (trans.) M. Shaw (New York: Continuum, 1982).

Parkin-Gounelas, R., *Literature and Psychoanalysis: Intertextual Readings* (Basingstoke: Palgrave, 2001).

Rabaté, J.-M., *Jacques Lacan: Psychoanalysis and the Subject of Literature* (Basingstoke: Palgrave, 2001).

Rand, N., "Family Romance or Family History? Psychoanalysis and Dramatic Invention in Nicolas Abraham's 'The Phantom of Hamlet'", *Diacritics*, 18.4 (1988), pp. 20–30.

——. "Psychoanalysis with Literature: An Abstract of Nicolas Abraham and Maria Torok's *The Shell and the Kernel*", *The Oxford Literary Review*, 12.1-2 (1990), pp. 63–68.

——. "The Talking Cure: Origins of Psychoanalysis", in *Talk, Talk, Talk: The Cultural Life of Everyday Conversation*, (ed.) S.I. Salamensky (New York: Routledge, 2001).

——. *Psychoanalysis and Literature* (Basingstoke: Palgrave, 2004).

Rand, N. and Torok, M., "'The Sandman' looks at 'The "Uncanny"'", in *Speculations After Freud: Psychoanalysis, Philosophy and Culture*, (eds) S. Shamdasani and M. Münchow (London, New York: Routledge, 1994).

——. *Questions for Freud: The Secret History of Psychoanalysis* (Cambridge, MA: Harvard University Press, 1997).

Rashkin, E., "Tools for a New Psychoanalytic Literary Criticism", *Diacritics*, 18. 4 (1988), pp. 31–52.

——. *Family Secrets and the Psychoanalysis of Narrative* (Princeton: Princeton University Press, 1992).

Reinhard, K., "The Freudian Things: Construction and the Archaeological Metaphor", in S. Barker (ed.), *Excavations and their Objects: Freud's*

Collection of Antiquity (Albany, NY: State University of New York Press, 1996), pp. 57–79.

——. "The Jamesian Thing: *The Wings of the Dove* and the Ethics of Mourning", *Arizona Quarterly*, 53 (1997), pp. 115–46.

——. "Coming to America: Psychoanalytic Criticism in the Age of Žižek", *Paragraph* 24 (2001), pp. 156–64.

Rose, J., "Dora: Fragment of an Analysis", in *In Dora's Case: Freud – Hysteria – Feminism*, (eds) C. Bernheimer and C. Kahane (New York: Columbia University Press, 1985), pp. 128–148.

——. "Hamlet – the *Mona Lisa* of Literature", in *Futures for English*, (ed.) C. McCabe (Manchester: Manchester University Press, 1988), pp. 35–49.

Royle, N., *The Uncanny* (Manchester: Manchester University Press, 2003).

——. "The uncanny: an introduction", in N. Royle, *The Uncanny* (Manchester: Manchester University Press, 2003), pp. 1–38

——. "Supplement: 'The Sandman'", in N. Royle, *The Uncanny* (Manchester: Manchester University Press, 2003), pp. 39–50.

Rubin, B., "Freud and Hoffmann: 'The Sandman'", in *Introducing Psychoanalytic Theory*, (ed.) S.L. Gilman (New York: Brunner/Mazel, 1982), pp. 205–17.

Rudnytsky, P. and Spitz, E.H. (eds), *Freud and Forbidden Knowledge* (New York: New York University Press, 1994).

Scheie, T., "Body Trouble: Corporeal 'Presence' and Performative Identity in Cixous's and Mnouchkine's *L'Iniade ou L'Inde de leurs rêves*", *Theatre Journal*, 47 (1994), pp. 31–44.

Schleiner, L., "Latinized Greek drama in Shakespeare's Writing of *Hamlet*", *Shakespeare Quarterly*, 41 (1990), pp. 29–48.

Sellers, S. (ed.), *The Hélène Cixous Reader* (London: Routledge, 1994).

Shakespeare, W., *Hamlet* [Arden], (ed.) H. Jenkins (London: Methuen, 1982).

——. *Hamlet* [Oxford Shakespeare], (ed.) G.R. Hibbard (Oxford: Clarendon Press, 1987).

Shiach, M., *Hélène Cixous: A Politics of Writing* (London: Routledge, 1991).

Showalter, E., *The Female Malady: Women, Madness and English Culture 1830–1980* (London: Virago, 1987).

——. "On Hysterical Narrative", *Narrative*, 1 (1993), pp. 24–35.

Silverstein, M., "'Body-Presence': Cixous's Phenomenology of Theater", *Theatre Journal*, 43, (1991), pp. 507–16.

Sloterdijk, P., *Critique of Cynical Reason*, (trans.) M. Eldred (Minneapolis: University of Minnesota Press, 1987).

Sophocles, *Oedipus the King*, (trans.) B. Knox (New York: Pocket Books, 1972).

Stonebridge, L., *The Destructive Element: British Psychoanalysis and Modernism* (Basingstoke: Macmillan, 1998).

Trilling, L., "Freud and Literature" (1941), in D. Lodge (ed.), *20th Century Literary Criticism* (London: Longman, 1972), pp. 275–90.

Vice, S. (ed.), *Psychoanalytic Criticism: A Reader* (Cambridge: Polity Press, 1996).

Weber, S., "The Sideshow or: Remarks on a Canny Moment", *Modern Language Notes*, 88 (1973), pp. 1102–33.

——. *The Legend of Freud* (Minneapolis: Minnesota University Press, 1982).

Williams, L.R., *Critical Desire: Psychoanalysis and the Literary Subject* (London: Edward Arnold, 1995).

Willis, S., "Hélène Cixous's *Portrait of Dora*: The Unseen and the Unscene", in *Performing Feminisms: Feminist Critical Theory and Theater*, (ed.) S.-E. Case (Baltimore, MD, 1990), pp. 70–84.

Wright, E., "The Uncanny and Surrealism", in *Modernism and the European Unconscious*, (ed.) P. Collier and J. Davies (Cambridge: Polity Press, 1990), pp. 265–282.

——. *Psychoanalytic Criticism: A Reappraisal* (Cambridge: Polity Press, 1998).

——. *Speaking Desires can be Dangerous: The Poetics of the Unconscious* (Cambridge: Polity Press, 1999).

Žižek, S., *The Sublime Object of Ideology* (London: Verso, 1989).

——. *Enjoy Your Symptom! Jacques Lacan in Hollywood and Out* (New York and London: Routledge, 1992).

——. *Looking Awry: an Introduction to Jacques Lacan through Popular Culture* (Cambridge, Mass.: MIT Press, 1995).

Index

Abraham, Karl, 163, 168
Abraham, Nicolas, 22, 23
  "The Phantom of Hamlet",
    47–58
  "Notes on the Phantom", 58
  (with Maria Torok), *The
    Wolf Man's Magic Word*
    (1976), 4, 5, 58, 115, 117,
    118, 119, 120, 121,
    136–177
Adler, Alfred, 116
Agnon, Shmuel Yosef, 208
Appignanesi, Lisa, 218
Artaud, Antonin, 208

Bakhtin, Mikhaïl, 132, 135
Bauer, Ida ("Dora"), 180, 198,
  208, 210, 213, 215, 218
Benmussa, Simone, 208
Bernheimer, Charles, 219
Borges, Jorge Luis, 131
Botticelli, Sandro, 125
Bowers, Fredson Thayer, 35
Bowie, Malcolm, 46
Brecht, Bertolt, 167, 185, 197
Breuer, Josef, 193
  Studies on Hysteria (1895) (with
    Sigmund Freud), 1, 4, 5, 6,
    14, 126, 131, 135
Bronfen, Elisabeth, 12, 15, 183,
  184, 185, 211–219
Brooks, Peter, 2, 8, 9, 10, 11, 14,
  112, 116, 122–135, 184
Brown, Erella, 183, 185, 196–210
Brunswick, Ruth Mack, 115, 117,
  118, 119, 121, 123, 124, 136,

140, 141, 143–145, 146, 149,
  158, 168
Burd, Sarah, 208

Champollion, Jean-François, 145,
  167, 170
Chandler, Raymond, 26
Charnes, Linda, 20, 21, 25–35
Chase, Cynthia, 15
Cixous, Hélène, 11, 12, 62, 66,
  84–96, 110, 183, 184–185,
  186, 187–210
Clément, Catherine, 185, 187–195,
  197, 199
Conan Doyle, Arthur, 126, 128, 131
Conrad, Joseph, 131, 133
Copjec, Jan, 26
Crawford, Alice, 46
Crews, Frederick, 98
Culler, Jonathan, 116

Dali, Salvador, 63
Da Vinci, Leonardo, 125
Derrida, Jacques, 4, 24, 31, 66,
  120, 121, 135, 160–177
Dolar, Mladen, 60, 64
Dracula (Bram Stoker), 219

Eliot, T.S., 23, 186, 211
Ellmann, Maud, 1, 6, 7, 11, 15, 20
Engels, Friedrich, 190
Enlightenment, 117

Faulkner, William, 125
Felman, Shoshana, 1, 2, 3, 10, 15,
  24

Ferdinand, Archduke Franz, 124
Ferenczi, Sandor, 158, 163, 168
Fink, Bruce, 41
Fliess, Wilhelm, 5, 18, 19
Forrester, John, 218
Freud, Sigmund
  death instinct, 68
  deferred action
    (*nachträglichkeit*), 113, 114,
    115, 117, 129, 131, 134,
    176
  Hamlet as hysteric, 19, 51
  hysteria and feminism, 180–186
  Oedipus Complex, 5, 18, 19, 50,
    91, 182, 207
  "transference", 183–184
  Studies on Hysteria (1895) (with
    Josef Breuer), 1, 4, 5, 6, 14,
    126, 131, 135
  The Interpretation of Dreams
    (1900), 8, 12, 13, 18, 37,
    49
  "Dora" (1905), 3, 5, 9, 12, 115,
    180–219
  "Little Hans" (1909)
  *Leonardo Da Vinci and a
    Memory of His Childhood*
    (1910), 3
  *Introductory Lectures on
    Psychoanalysis* (1916–17),
    129
  "Mourning and Melancholia"
    (1917), 21, 22, 163
  The "Wolf Man" (1918), 3, 4, 5,
    11, 12, 83, 102, 112–177,
    184
  "The 'Uncanny'" (1919), 11,
    60–110
  Beyond the Pleasure Principle
    (1920), 68
  "On Fetishism" (1927),
    119–120, 158
  "Constructions in Analysis"
    (1937), 9
  "Analysis Terminable and
    Interminable" (1937), 9

Gallop, Jane, 185
Garber, Marjorie, 23

Gardiner, Muriel, 115, 117, 119,
  121, 126, 136, 140, 141, 144,
  156, 158
Green André, 10, 11, 15
Grosz, Elizabeth, 46

Hammett, Dashiell, 27
Hawkes, Terence, 35
Hermann, Imre, 168
Hertz, Neil, 110
Hitchcock, Alfred, 185
Hoffmann, E.T.A., 12
  "The Sandman", 11, 60–110
Huysmans, Joris-Karl, 125

Jacobus, Mary, 186
James, Henry, 132
Jensen, Wilhelm, 208
Jentsch, Ernst, 62, 69, 85, 86, 87,
  90, 95, 96
Johnson, Barbara, 121, 160
Jones, Ernest, 19, 49, 50, 58, 158
Joyce, James, 133
Jung, Carl, 116, 154
Juranville, Anne, 184, 212

Kahane, Claire, 211, 219
Kavja, Misha, 219
Kermode, Frank, 28
Kerrigan, John, 35
Klein, Melanie, 163, 168, 182
Kofman, Sarah, 11, 62, 66, 68–83,
  98, 110
Kristeva, Julia, 12, 61, 185, 186,
  195, 199, 208
Kyd, Thomas, 28

Lacan, Jacques, 1, 2, 4, 5, 7, 8, 11,
  12, 19, 20, 22, 26, 27, 29,
  36–46, 135, 183, 184, 197,
  204, 214, 216
  the phallus, 20, 38, 39, 40, 41,
    42, 43, 44, 46
  objet a, 39, 40, 41
  the Imaginary, 199, 208
  the Real, 199, 207, 208
  the Symbolic, 199, 208
Laplanche, Jean, 46, 113, 121
Lechte, John, 11

Levin, Hanoch, 208
Lupton, Julia Reinhard and
    Reinhard, Kenneth, 21, 22,
    36–46
Lynch, David, 43

Magritte, René, 63
Mann, Thomas, 125
Marcus, Steven, 5, 184
Mehlman, Jeffrey, 110
Meltzer, Françoise, 63, 110
Miller, Jacques-Alain, 46
Miller, J. Hillis, 23
Mitchell, Juliet, 211
Modernism, 116, 123, 125, 127,
    134, 184
Møller, Lis, 7, 11, 62, 67, 97–110,
    116

Nietzsche, Friedrich, 72

Obholzer, Karin, 117, 135

Parkin-Gounelas, Ruth, 3, 182
Petrarch, Francesco Petrarca, 43
Plath, Sylvia, 218
Poe, Edgar Allan, 167
Proust, Marcel, 125, 129

Rand, Nicholas, 4, 5, 22, 47–58,
    116, 158
Rashkin, Esther, 118,
Rembrandt, Harmenszoon van
    Rijn, 200
Romanticism, 117
Rose, Jacqueline, 186, 197
Rubin, Bernard, 110
Russian formalism, 127
Russian Revolution, 115, 123, 155

Schindler, Regula, 213
Schlegel, A.W., 47

Schleiner, Louise, 35
Sellers, Susan, 95, 195
Shakespeare, William
    Hamlet, 2, 10, 18–58, 108, 118,
        186
    Iago (Othello) 193
    Macbeth, 108
    Othello, 190
    The Merchant of Venice, 38
Shiach, Morag, 200
Showalter, Elaine, 184
Sloterdijk, Peter, 25
Sophocles
    Oedipus Rex, 8, 10, 15, 18, 19,
        37, 42, 49, 57, 204, 206,
        207
    Oedipus at Colonus, 8, 15
Surrealism, 63
Svane, Marie-Louise, 110

Torok, Maria, 57
    (with Nicolas Abraham), The
        Wolf Man's Magic Word
        (1976), 4, 5, 58, 115, 117,
        118, 119, 120, 121,
        136–177
Trilling, Lionel, 1

Villiers de l'Isle-Adam, Jean Marie
    Mathias Phillippe August,
    125

Weber, Samuel, 15, 110
Williams, Linda Ruth, 115
Willis, Sharon, 196
World War I, 115, 125
Wright, Elizabeth, 11, 14, 21–22,
    63, 110

Zeffirelli, Franco, 21, 32, 33
Zhirinovsky, Vladimir, 34
Žižek, Slavoj, 20, 21, 25–35, 46